One Woman Determined to Make a Difference:
The Life of Madeleine Zabriskie Doty

Madeleine Zabriskie Doty as editor of *Pax International*
(Courtesy of Sophia Smith Collection, Smith College)

One Woman Determined to Make a Difference

The Life of Madeleine Zabriskie Doty

Edited by
Alice Duffy Rinehart

With Research Assistance by
Anne Taylor Bronner

Lehigh
University
Press

Bethlehem: Lehigh University Press
London: Associated University Presses

Associated University Presses
440 Forsgate Drive
Cranbury, NJ 08512

Associated University Presses
16 Barter Street
London WC1A 2AH, England

Associated University Presses
P.O. Box 338, Port Credit
Mississauga, Ontario
Canada L5G 4L8

The paper used in this publication meets the requirements of the American National Standard for Permanence of Paper for Printed Library Materials Z39.48-1984.

Library of Congress Cataloging-in-Publication Data

Doty, Madeleine Z. (Madeleine Zabriskie), 1877-1963.
    One woman determined to make a difference : the life of Madeleine Zabriskie Doty / edited by Alice Duffy Rinehart ; with research assistance of Anne Taylor Bronner.
        p. cm.
    Includes bibliographical references and index.
    ISBN 0-934223-67-X (alk. paper)
    1. Doty, Madeleine Z. (Madeleine Zabriskie), 1877-1963. 2. Feminists–United States–Biography. 3. Women social reformers–United States–Biography. 4. Women journalists–United States–Biography. 5. Women lawyers–United States–Biography. 6. Women pacifists–United States–Biography. I. Rinehart, Alice Duffy. II. Title.
HQ1413.D69 A3 2001
305.42'092–dc21
[B]   00-069160

Set in Century Schoolbook at the Lehigh University Press.
Designed by Philip A. Metzger.

PRINTED IN THE UNITED STATES OF AMERICA

"The study of history can and should be used to nourish our sense of the past, to illumine our understanding of the present, to fortify us as we face the future."

— Max Lerner, *P.M. Journal*

"The world progresses, in the slow and halting manner in which it does progress, only in proportion to the moral energy exerted by the men and women living in it."

— Jane Addams, *Women at the Hague*

Contents

List of Illustrations   9

Preface   11

Acknowledgments   13

Notes on Editing   15

Biographical Introduction   17

Part I. FROM CHILDHOOD TO LAW SCHOOL

Introduction to Chapters 1 and 2   25

1. Growing Up, 1877–1896   29

2. College Days and an Innocent
   in Greenwich Village, 1896–1905   40

Part II. JUSTICE REFORM AND FALLING IN LOVE

Introduction to Chapter 3   53

3. The Women's Movement, Law, and Love, 1905–1911   58

Part III. REFORM LAWYER, COLUMNIST,
          PROGRESSIVE ACTIVIST

Introduction to Chapters 4–6   79

4. Court Work, Three Great Men, and a Love
   That Should Never Have Been, 1911–1913   82

5. Maggie Martin #933, 1913   93

6. Prison Reform from Within, 1913–1914   110

Part IV. ENLISTING FOR PEACE

Introduction to Chapters 7–10   127

7. Women of Peace in Wartime, 1915   132

8. "Snooping Madeleine," the *Tribune* Woman, 1916   136

9. Around the World to Revolutionary Russia in 1917: Japan, China, and Across Siberia   165

10. The Long Way Home, 1918   193

Part V. POST-WAR DEVASTATION. MARRIAGE

Introduction to Chapters 11 and 12   209

11. Love and Post-War Europe, 1918–1919   213

12. 50–50 Marriage, 1919–1925   232

Part VI. TO PROMOTE INTERNATIONAL COOPERATION

Editor's Afterword: The Geneva Years (1925–1963) and Her Enduring Legacy   249

Addendum. In Hindsight on the Marriage. A Husband's Reminiscences and Editor's Commentary   256

Notes   264

Bibliography   275

Index   282

Illustrations

Madeleine Zabriskie Doty as editor of *Pax
International*   frontispiece

Madeleine Z. Doty in her junior year at Smith College   46

David Graham Phillips   65

Madeleine Doty in a New York City suffrage parade, 1912   81

Madeleine Z. Doty, c. 1910–1914   87

Madeleine Doty as Maggie Martin, jailbird, in Auburn, N.Y.   98

Emmeline Pethick-Lawrence   134

From dust jacket of *Behind the Battle Line*   169

Roger Baldwin   216

Madeleine Doty and others at Peace Congress of the Women's
International League for Peace and Freedom   244

Preface

*T*HIS IS THE STORY of the life of one woman who, from her youth in the late 1800s until her death in 1963, was determined that her life should make a difference for others.

It is told through her uncompleted and heretofore unpublished autobiography, supplemented by my introductions to each of six Parts in order to clarify the roles of the then important persons and organizations she worked with on various activist causes for social change. In order to complete her story I have added Chapter 7, which is missing from her autobiography, and I have composed a brief Afterword to summarize her post–1925 years because her account of that is also lost.

When Doty's autobiography became available to me, I was amazed to learn of the many daring, radical, and leadership roles she had undertaken in various causes, for when I had lived in the same house with her during my junior year in Geneva just before World War II she was a gray-haired, sedate, yet still able and determined woman who did not talk much about her past accomplishments. Rather, she was intent on getting things done in the present to improve the future.

Despite humanity's slow progress and some backsliding, it is my hope that this volume will add recognition of how her contributions and example as an idealistic activist have made a difference.

Acknowledgments

OR PERMISSION TO EDIT and have published the unfinished auto-biography, letters, and other papers of Madeleine Zabriskie Doty, I am extremely grateful to Mrs. Katherine S. Strong, Madeleine Doty's friend and executrix, who inherited these papers and who has deposited them in the Sophia Smith Collection at Smith College.

I also wish to express my gratitude to the following: the Smith College Jill Ker Conway Fund for Research and Teaching on Women's Experience for a grant that has been of much help toward initial preparation costs of this biography; the Director of the Sophia Smith Collection for permission to publish the autobiography; and its staff for assistance with my research in the Madeleine Z. Doty Papers. Sincere thanks go to Carl N. Baldwin for permission to quote at length from Roger Baldwin's "Reminiscences" about Doty (located in the Doty Papers), and to numerous publishers for copyright permissions where necessary for works quoted.

Special appreciation and recognition go to Anne Taylor Bronner for having alerted me to the existence of the autobiographical chapters, for her great assistance in carefully examining and meticulously taking extensive notes on pertinent records in the Swarthmore College Peace Collection regarding Doty's work with the Women's International League for Peace and Freedom, and for distributing to and collecting questionnaires from all eleven surviving participants in the first Junior Year in Geneva, 1938–1939. Her daughter Margot B. Maroni helped greatly by adding the research on references to and articles by Doty in the New York *Evening Post* of 1915, located in the New York Public Library.

Thanks, too, go to the Swarthmore College Library for access to their Peace Collection, to the Princeton University Archives for use of much material from the Roger Baldwin papers, and to the staffs of the Lehigh University Libraries and the Lehigh University Press, and to the reference librarians of the Allentown (Pa.) Public Library for their ready assistance. I am indeed grateful to Richard Cowen, author and columnist for the Allentown (Pa.) *Morning Call*, and to the New York Public

Library, both of whom facilitated use of fascinating information about the American Fund for Public Service (Garland Fund). Cowen talked with me about his interview in 1979 of Baldwin, who had served on that fund's board. Thanks also go to Judith Watry, Comstock Scholar at Smith College, for her paper on Doty; to Susan von Salis, manuscript processor at the Radcliffe College Schlesinger Library on the History of Women; to Jane Mead von Salis, a graduate of Smith, who sent from Switzerland numerous old letters and recollections about her junior year in Geneva in 1946–1947; and to Dr. Patricia Hochschild Labalme, Bryn Mawr and Radcliffe Ph.D. graduate, for her very helpful interview about her recollections of her junior year in Geneva in 1946–1947. At the time of the interview Labalme was Assistant to the Director of the Princeton Institute for Advanced Studies.

Further information has been obtained through correspondence with several of Doty's friends in Switzerland, particularly the late Alice Goebel, former secretary at the Graduate Institute of International Studies in Geneva. Goebel donated letters, original copies of Doty's three books, and her own reminiscences.

Finally, I wish to express special appreciation to each of the participants in the 1938–1939 Junior Year in Geneva under the University of Delaware's sponsorship, and to fifty respondents from among the 105 former students who participated in it under Smith College during the first three years of that program immediately after World War II. Doty was founder and a director of both programs. Their letters and answers to questionnaires and their sharing of old documents and even a great scrapbook have provided written evidence of the enduring impact of Doty's last great accomplishment, which will be summarized in the Afterword, following her unfinished autobiography.

Dr. Philip A. Metzger, director of the Lehigh University Press, has been very helpful, and unlimited is my gratitude to him and to Mrs. Judith Mayer, assistant to Dr. Metzger, for hours of patient work on the final production of this book.

Notes on Editing

*P*UBLISHING A COMPLETE BIOGRAPHY from an incomplete auto-biography presents some major organizational problems. Furthermore, names of leaders well known fifty to ninety years ago have little meaning to today's reader, and so multiple notes and explanations must be added.

Chapters 1–12 (covering from birth in 1877 to 1925) contain the edited version of Madeleine Doty's unfinished and heretofore unpublished autobiography, except chapter 7 which, because it is missing from the available autobiography, I have summarized here from Part I of her book *Short Rations* (New York: Century, 1916). It is inserted in chronological order. Also I have composed two clearly identified supplementary sections in chapter 9 in the interest of condensation of her originals. And, because the last two chapters she had planned for her autobiography are not available, I have written an Afterword to cover briefly the story of the remaining thirty-eight years of her life (1925–1963).

The contents of my Introductions are based on her papers in the Sophia Smith Collection at Smith College including letters, clippings, Roger Baldwin's "Reminiscences" about Doty, and her three small diaries; on histories of the Women's International League for Peace and Freedom; on current letters from her few living friends; and on questionnaires and letters from 61 persons who participated in the early years of the Junior Year in Geneva, a program she started for American college students to interest them in international cooperation instead of the isolationist nationalism that still characterizes much of American thought.

Information for any additions and Notes has been gathered from the above sources and from histories, biographies, encyclopedias, newspapers of the time, and from letters she received from numerous well-known persons whose lives touched hers personally and/or professionally.

Throughout her writing it is evident that she was attracted from childhood to the spirituality and ethics of Christianity. But intensification and verbalization of this only came in later life. However, in editing the autobiographical chapters, the decision has been made to reduce, but not eliminate, the frequency and length of her references to God's "tap on the shoulder" which, in looking back to write her autobiography, she believed explained the twists and turns of her life. These changes seem justified in view of a recent letter from one of her close friends who had assisted her in revising the manuscript. This letter indicates that it was only after World War II that Doty added much of the religious emphasis to an earlier draft, after what Doty called "a great spiritual experience" in her late sixties.

Any editorial insertions within the quoted material will be found within brackets. Doty's spelling (e.g., "Gorki" rather than the Americanized "Gorky" and spelling often in the British style such as "labour" or "favour") has not been changed, nor have her references to others' race or religion, which today would not be "politically correct." It will be seen that she used these as means of identification, not prejudice. Today's reader should note that her frequent use of the adjective "gay" was with the meaning joyous, bright, lively.

A note about dates: to the consternation of historians and biographers, few of the nonprofessional letters to and from Doty left among her papers at Smith College were dated by their authors. Among her memorabilia even clippings from newspapers sometimes were not identified by publisher or date. As she began to organize her papers in order to edit her life story, she tried to date some of them, marking the margins in pencil. However, in recall she sometimes made errors of one to three years. These discrepancies have been corrected herein when cross-referencing justified such. Because of her preference to understate her age, her birthdate is incorrectly given in *Who's Who in America* (volumes 10–17), in *Woman's Who's Who in America* (1914–1915), and in *Who's Who in America* (vol. 6, 1976), and elsewhere, each making her one to two years younger than the fact. But, according to a transcript of her birth certificate, college application, some of her own numerous references to her age in her autobiography, applications for passports (obtained through the Freedom of Information Act), and obituaries, Doty was born August 24, 1877. All references to her age herein have been calculated from the 1877 date.

Biographical Introduction:
To Make a Difference

*T*HE STORY OF MADELEINE ZABRISKIE DOTY (1877–1963) is that of a progressive idealist and feminist who strove, through causes she believed in, to make a difference for others, as a lawyer, reformer, reporter, suffragist, and finally as dedicated worker for world peace. In the first two decades of the twentieth century she was well known as a New York columnist, but has been unheard of in the press since about 1932. In that part of her career as a reporter (approximately 1905–1924) not only did she have many articles printed in big-name newspapers, often on the front page, but the *Reader's Guide to Periodical Literature* (volumes covering 1908–1920) lists twenty-five articles by Doty published in nine different popular magazines.

By 1918 Doty's work was important enough to have her life included in *Who's Who in America* from 1918–1933 (in each of volumes 10–17) and cross-referenced through 1940–1941. She is also included in *Woman's Who's Who in America 1914–1915*, in *Who Was Who in America with World Notables* (edition of 1974–1976), and in *Who Was Who Among North American Authors* (1976). The rarity of a woman being listed in *Who's Who in America* in her day was pointed out in a 1924–1925 study reported in its volume 13. Authors of the article analyzed the contents of volume 11 covering 1920–1921 and found scarcely 6.8 percent of the entries were about women, 45.3 percent of whom gave "writer" as their occupation.

Slight of physical build, yet strong in will, determined and adventuresome, Madeleine Doty, a protected, innocent youth from a relatively well-to-do family and just out of Smith College, entered the Bohemian life of Greenwich Village in 1900 and was among the first females to attend New York University Law School, where at that time the men openly opposed having women as classmates. After law school she continued to live there for over 20 years in the thick of radical liberalism, circulating among the movers and shakers for reform, the avant-garde radicals who were advocating change in class relations, workers' rights, and in the position of and even the mores of women. Adjusting to these

17

liberal codes of behavior caused Doty considerable emotional stress at first, as she describes in chapter 2. But she soon developed into a champion for equality for women and justice for women and children, for rehabilitation and more humane treatment of prisoners, and then at the outbreak of World War I she plunged into work for world peace. For the remaining forty-eight years of her life (most of it spent in Geneva, Switzerland) she helped lead the cause for international cooperation, believing it to be the essential route to improvement of the human condition.

Doty was strong enough to be an individualistic participant following her own path of convictions, at times working on the edge as an activist reporter/columnist or as a secretary or as publicity agent, but at other times at the forefront by voluntarily entering into dangerous aspects of that life. She was a woman of tremendous social conscience and of Enlightenment faith in human reason, perfectability, universality. Driven all her life by a sense of commitment to idealistic causes, she fought for them with integrity and vigor, sometimes at great personal sacrifice. She did some demonstrating in the streets for women's suffrage, but never destructively, being opposed to civil disobedience and the use of violence.

This kind of life put her in close contact with many of the well-known men and women of her day — writers, politicians, and the vanguard of reformers. Among them were the muckraker novelist David Graham Phillips; the reformer of men's prisons Thomas Mott Osborne; the family of liberal Freda Kirchwey of *The Nation*; the pro-Communist journalist and author John Reed (*Ten Days That Shook the World*) and his liberal wife Louise Bryant; and the Russian moderate socialist, novelist, and playwright Maxim Gorki and his wife Marie Peshkoff. There were also the socialist feminist, writer, and worker for peace and labor's rights, Crystal Eastman; the well-known founder of Chicago's Hull House for the disadvantaged and major leader in the women's peace movement, Jane Addams; Theodore Roosevelt; Eleanor Roosevelt; Secretary of Labor Frances Perkins; and civil rights leader Roger Baldwin. Abroad she knew the Pankhursts and became a life-long friend of the Pethick-Lawrences, all of whom were adamant leaders in the British movement for women's rights; others were authors John Galsworthy and H. G. Wells and the Russian ambassador and radical feminist Aleksandra Kollantai, as well as other feminist leaders in Europe. Thus reading the story of her life is like dipping into a Who's Who Among Liberals of the years 1900–1945.

Her most adventuresome and often dangerous undertakings took place in her thirties and early forties as a reform reporter in New York and even abroad during World War I (see chapters 3–11). These experiences are all the more remarkable when one remembers that these were times when women were expected to stay in subordinate positions or in the home, when women wore long skirts almost to the ankle, high-necked bodices, always hats in public over unbobbed hair. In chapters 5–6 she writes of getting herself committed to a New York State prison for women, as if a veritable convict, in order to report on conditions. Would they let her out? Next she tells of traveling into Germany twice during World War I in order to report on the condition of civilians behind the battle lines in 1915 and 1916 and then around the world into Russia, unexpectedly arriving just three days after the start of the Bolshevik Revolution of 1917. Would she be shot at? Her running reports of these experiences appeared on the front pages of the *New York Tribune* and the *Evening Post*. *Good Housekeeping* and *Century* magazine serialized many of her articles. These she then expanded into three books: *Society's Misfits* (Century, 1916), *Short Rations* (Century, 1917), and *Behind the Battle Line* (Macmillan, 1918).

Doty sought a meaningful and independent career, and even her marriage to the long-time head of the American Civil Liberties Union (ACLU) was based on the ideal of equality and freedom.

Though she desired independence, she had a great need to love and be loved. Her striking features were her light, azure-colored eyes, a slender body, vigor, idealism, and a dogged determination. Modest yet daring, energetic, confident, concerned with public affairs, sometimes willful to the point of irritating those with whom she worked, Doty evidently was appealing to a variety of men, several of whose names are still known for their parts in the literary, political, or professional scene. And in her autobiography she tells of her three great love affairs with outstanding men. Each of these three relationships tore at her emotions, contributing, no doubt, to chronic stomach problems.

Immediate interest in her life can be seen in the similarities and differences between her world at the beginning and ours at the end of the twentieth century in its current upheaval in international, ethnic, tribal, and religious tensions and wars on almost every continent. In addition, in view of today's upsurge of feminist demands and achievements, her story also shows both similarities and differences in the women's movement then and now. For example, in August 1995 the United Nations Fourth World Conference of Women from 180 countries met in Beijing, China, the world's largest meeting of women in history. Just prior to it there was held near there a meeting of the women's Non-Governmental Organizations, at which the keynote address by Aung San Suu Kyi, a woman democracy activist in Burma, included a plea for women to aid the cause of peace and women's rights, very similar in theme to such pleas in the United States, England, and western Europe in the early decades of this century. Kyi's plea declared that because women have something special to offer, expanding women's power will bring greater peace and tolerance to the world. Yet differences in the times are also evident in the status of women today and, for example, in today's get-tough stance on crime, in contrast to Doty's public effort to reform harsh treatment of prisoners as a cause of recidivism.

"Plus ça change, plus c'est la même chose" — the more things change the more they stay the same — will come to mind at times as a frightening warning of how slow is human progress and how great the continuing need for dedicated idealists who believe we can and must find ways to make the world a more just and peaceful place.

Throughout the autobiographical chapters several themes recur, namely Doty's enduring enjoyment of nature, her determination and courage, the self-criticism (in hindsight), the intensity of her love affairs, and her dedication to justice and world peace.

Religion was always important to Doty but received different emphases at various stages in her life. In college Doty began to question dogma and the literal interpretation of the Bible. After that her professional life of almost fifty years became a remarkable demonstration of commitment to the practical application of the humanitarian and ethical side of Christianity, rather than the ecclesiastical. Yet in the last eighteen years of her life she turned to faith in the power of God's direct guidance for every act of the individual and sought with fervor to practice the ethical absolutes of the Moral Rearmament, or Oxford Group, movement. It was this faith that led her to title her autobiography *A Tap On The Shoulder* and to become so critical of her own imperfections.

Looking back, trying to find meaning in her life and drawing on the wisdom of her experience, she wrote this powerful metaphor in the proposed Introduction to her autobiography:

My life has stretched from Queen Victoria to the Space Man. Material changes have been fantastic. But behind these, God's world remains unchanged. We live in fear and uncertainty. We ask the meaning of life. . . .Through the dark ages the Church held mankind together in Europe. But then came separation, the breakup into rivalrous states, religious strife, the discovery of America. The discovery the earth is round, that we all dwell upon it. And with the first World War again came separations, nationalism, strife. Then a renewed attempt at unity in the League of Nations. Like waves on the seashore that come and go, we separate and unite. The waves draw back, bringing war, nationalism, and revolution, rise of dictatorships, the division of earth into groups, the Second World War. Then the oncoming waves, bit by bit each wave creeping higher until it is swept forward into the United Nations. Today we know the answer: it is unity or death.

Despite disappointment in herself and in the state of the world, Doty did not lose her supreme faith that individuals and nations will some day learn to work together, to unite for the sake of peace, of each other, and of self.

God has given freedom. With His guidance wars will end, tyrants cease to rule, cooperation grow, harmony spread. . . .

As I look back on my life, I see myself as a willful, proud, arrogant, persevering child. Now I see that despite these traits, God left me free to learn or not to learn, to do or not to do. . . .

Thus equipped I stepped forth into life. With eagerness and pride I set out to remake the world. I would study law, be a great woman lawyer, see justice done. I was the master of my soul.

Part I
From Childhood to Law School

Introduction to Chapters 1 and 2

M ADELEINE ZABRISKIE DOTY was born of a relatively well-to-do family on the beautiful, shoreside estate of her maternal grandmother at Bergen Point, Bayonne, New Jersey, in the year 1877.[1] Madeleine was the second of three children and was the only daughter of socialite Charlotte (Lottie) Zabriskie Doty and Samuel Doty, exporter of dairy products to Europe.

In chapters 1 and 2 of her autobiography Madeleine Doty tells of her home life and education. Her interest in public affairs and social issues during her prep school days foretold the kind of life she would choose. Although her father's income was to have its low periods, her mother came from wealth. The family traveled together to Europe with remarkable frequency. Her mother was a beautiful lady of leisure, who had inherited her parents' New Jersey estate, but Doty's mother's weaknesses were to cause consternation for the young teenage daughter and her older brother Douglas (who later became editor of Century publications 1914–1917 and of *Cosmopolitan* magazine 1917–1918).[2]

Madeleine entered Smith College in Northampton, Massachusetts, in 1896 and earned a Bachelor of Letters degree studying the following courses during the four years: chemistry (2 semesters), elocution (3), English literature (9), French (2), German (2), history (5), Latin (2), math (2), political economics (5), rhetoric (5), hygiene and physiology (1), logic (1), psychology (1) and zoology (1). Sophia Smith, when founding Smith College in 1871, advanced the belief that college education for women should be equal to that for men. Sophia was thus among the pioneers for women's higher education and feminist in her idealistic faith in the superior social conscience of women. She wrote that through thorough Christian education of women "their wages will be adjusted, their weight of influence in reforming evils in society will be greatly increased as teachers, as writers, as mothers, as members of society, their power for good will be incalculably enlarged."

When Doty graduated in 1900 a college degree was an unusual achievement for a woman; in that year only 2.8 percent of all women in the United States aged 18–21 were enrolled in college, and less than one-fourth of them completed the degree. Counting all men and women together in that age group only 4 percent went to college, of whom 36.8 percent were women. However, of the bachelor degrees achieved by both men and women an even smaller proportion went to women, less than 25 percent (5,237 women/22,173 men).[3]

In chapter 2 Doty wrote tantalizingly little about the academic side of her undergraduate education, which is surprising in view of her serious-mindedness as an adolescent. She makes no mention of the impact from the college courses and only superficial mention of her professors, except the one German professor with whom she had a deep attachment. Instead, she highlights the impact of peer pressure upon herself, one or two student escapades, and the college standards and rules for the behavior of proper young ladies in that day. However, social life is typically seen as important at the college age, and perhaps she needed this lighter side of development in her person. On the serious side she does say that her perspective on religion was broadened through discussion with some liberal classmates on such subjects as divinity and miracles. In view of her earlier interest in religion and social responsibility, it is surprising that her 1900 Class Book at Smith does not indicate that she joined the Smith College Association of Christian Women, the Christian Union, or the Missionary Society. After college she appears to have remained more of an ethical humanist until a spiritual intensification during and soon after World War II. The Smith College Year Book does list the following activities in which she participated: she was in the Novel Club, was one of three on the Junior Prom committee to sell tickets, was one of its twelve ushers, and in her senior year one of two in charge of class pins. She played a minor role in the campus production of *Twelfth Night*. As an indication of how different the standards for young women were at that time, it is amusing today to note that Smith's President Seelye had some concern about the appropriateness of this production. One classmate wrote for their 1900 class yearbook (pp. 97–99) that finally the President was convinced "we might manage [it] without its being roystering and bibulous" when it was decided that the "difficulty of the fighting might be obviated by having it done 'behind a genteel flower pot.'"

Ten years after graduation, *Delineator* magazine in its March 1910 issue published a long, caustic article by Doty titled "What a Woman's College Means to a Girl." In this article, reflecting her new feminist ideas, she attacked the superficialities of student preoccupations with dress, looks, friendships, and "making it" into the right circle, organization, or team. She also criticized the professors as "old maid" scholars and the courses as not essential, not related to what a girl needed to know in adult life, to what a girl will and can aspire to do after college, be that wise parenting or a career. She wrote that career ambitions are neglected; instead "we are to be simply women. Our fulfillment is to lie only in doing for others." She felt college women were not encouraged to think for themselves. A girl's "ideas concerning politics, economics and morality were fixed by conventional standards before she entered college" and remained so in college, unchallenged, tradition-bound. Women's colleges were producing only "an ornamental individual," whereas "we need to graduate men and women who think for themselves, who are capable, efficient, intellectually and morally free."

But for Doty graduation from college was only the beginning of both her formal and social education. Seeking a way to earn her living doing something that would make a difference, she chose to study law and to live in Greenwich Village near New York University. Its law school was only the fifth in the nation to admit women (1891), and at the time she entered, the men were protesting having female classmates. In Doty's 1902 graduating class of 173 law students there, she was one of only 18 women.

The Village at that time was the center of radical defiance of the status quo in personal relations, art, politics, and gender restrictions. It was a locus that attracted both men and women, mostly upper middle class and recent college graduates variously seeking more freedom, equality, and social reforms. She writes of her initial stress in adjusting to that avant-garde culture. Indeed, some of the press back then printed bitter criticisms of and warnings against the Greenwich Village lifestyle. She developed some concern that she herself may have had some lesbian desires toward former teachers; however, today in research by Barbara Solomon published in 1985 we are told that in the nineteenth century "crushes" between women were acceptable,[4] and Lillian Faderman in 1991 explained that "romantic friendship" without sexuality was frequent among college educated women in the early twentieth century — until Freudianism destroyed its plausibility in popular thought.

As for a woman becoming a practicing lawyer at that time, Doty was among the pioneers entering that forbidden, exclusively male-dominated profession. Another woman who became a lawyer wrote that so far as she knew she herself was one of only 108 women to have received a law degree in the United States from 1870–1901 and that most of them had had to appeal to courts and finally to the legislature for admission to the Bar (which generally excluded women until 1918). In 1902 another woman, writing to encourage women to believe they had as much ability as men in scholarship and creativity, nevertheless didactically warned that any woman entering any profession must pay the price, namely, give up the idea of marriage, because the dull monotony of household chores kills originality.[5] By 1920 only 20 percent of all women were employed in any career, and only between 1 and 3 percent of lawyers were women, by 1973 but 4 percent, whereas by 1995 their proportion had risen to about 25 percent of lawyers and 41 percent of law students.[6]

1
Growing Up, 1877–1896

*I*T WAS THE YEAR 1880. I couldn't have been much more than three. We were moving from New York City into the country to live. My father had rented a house in Montclair, New Jersey. It was night. I stood at the open window of the horse carriage as we drove from the station to the house. Suddenly the night was full of millions of tiny dancing lights. Fireflies, mother said.

Mother disliked the country and adored the city. It was only love of Sam that overcame her prejudice. Sam and Lottie — those were the precious beings who were my parents. They were as American as could be, yet each, of course, in the distant past had foreign ancestry. My father boasted of an Edward Doten who came over on the *Mayflower*, a lively young Englishman who fought the first duel ever fought in America. The name Doten was later changed to Doty. His family were strong abolitionists, living in Rome, New York, when he was growing up, in a fine old house. It had running water, he told me, a tin bath tub, and gas lights — great luxuries for those days. They also had a carriage and horses. In fact, they were a well-to-do family. Sam was the youngest, a quiet boy who liked to stay at home and read. But enormous changes were taking place as a result of the Civil War. In those changes the Doty's fortune declined, so in 1868 they moved to New York City to begin again. Sam was 19 at the time. He told me that when Abraham Lincoln had been assassinated three years before, his mother had wept bitterly, as did everyone.

My father often described his arrival in the big city, which in those days did not extend above 33rd Street. The puffing train with a coal stove to heat the car in which they came stopped at 40th Street. Here the engine was detached and six horses harnessed to the cars, which they then pulled to the station at Madison Ave. and 23rd Street. The station waiting room had a red carpet and a bright open fire. A horse cab took the Dotys to their boarding house, past the Fifth Avenue Hotel, a monstrous building of six stories on West 11th Street, with its brown stone front and wrought iron balconies.

Later when my father and I stood at 42nd Street and Broadway, by then the Great White Way with its dazzling lights and rushing traffic, he would often say, "When I first came here there was only a dirt road and a board walk and almost no houses."

My mother's ancestry was more mixed. Her father's name was Zabriskie. The Polish Zabriskies had emigrated in the seventeenth century, as had the La Tourettes about that time. A Polish Zabriskie married a French La Tourette and produced a big family. My mother was the youngest of the brood.

In 1871, at age 18, mother came to New York for the winter only, with her mother and eldest sister. Their home was across the bay at the mouth of the Hudson River in Bergen Point, New Jersey, eight miles from New York City; a big, square, ancestral house on the Kill Van Kull. Sam was by then 23, had lost his mother, and was very lonely. He had given up his studies at the College of the City of New York and gone into business with his father. They became exporters of butter and cheese. Then one night Lottie appeared at the boarding house dinner. She was a ravishing beauty, with great brown eyes, an olive skin, and a beautiful figure. She loved life. She loved pretty clothes. She loved to dance. My father fell for her at first sight. Sam had never seen anything so lovely, so gay, so dignified. She didn't chatter and she didn't giggle. Sam was enthralled.

He recalled that one of the topics of conversation at the dinner table that night was the Tweed Ring. Ulysses S. Grant was President and evil flourished unchecked. There was fraud in high places; Tweed had defrauded the City of millions. But Lottie wasn't interested in politics. Her world was a personal one. She loved people.

After dinner Sam was introduced. He knew then he had met the one woman in the world for him. His whole being became centered on Lottie. He discovered she adored the theatre so he got tickets to see [Edwin T.] Booth in "Hamlet" and invited Lottie and her sister. He sat between them and was dumb with delight. But alas, he had planned a trip abroad on $500 he had saved. His passage was booked. Because tourists to Europe were few in those days, he had boasted about his journey, so was ashamed not to go.

The day he sailed, Lottie and her sister saw him off. The ship was a tiny affair, three thousand tons, a flat deck, paddle wheels, and sails. But Sam had eyes only for "the most gorgeous of creatures." When she pinned a rose on his coat, he took courage and asked if he might write. "Oh, no," she said but added, "you can write to my sister and I'll read the letters."

So Sam set sail in March 1872. In high seas the waves dashed over the deck from end to end. He was horribly seasick, as was everyone else.

In London he was thrilled with the English Parliament. Queen Victoria and Prime Minister Disraeli were turning England into an Empire. In France he found a republic; Napoleon III had been overthrown. But the French people were bitter; they did not forget that the Germans under Bismarck had recently marched to Paris and had seized Alsace-Lorraine. In Venice Sam drifted on the canals and thought of Lottie. And suddenly he couldn't bear it any longer. He gave up a trip to Rome and dashed for home, Lottie's red rose pressed against his heart. Later, when Lottie knew, she said he was very foolish, but he grew in favor when he produced theatre tickets for the first night of "School for Scandal." For twelve long months Sam lay siege to his lady. He followed her to Bergen Point. He sat on the porch with her in the moonlight, with the sister near as chaperon. There were five other men in pursuit. Three had proposed. Still Sam did not give up. Flowers, candy, and theatre tickets continued. Finally there came "the night." They had been to see "The Rivals." They decided to walk to the boarding house. It was snowing and cold. Lottie wasn't wearing gloves. He slipped his hand into hers. She said, "Young man, you are losing your senses." He: "Young lady, I lost them a year ago when I met you. Oh, darling, I do love you so." She very quietly: "I've loved you for a long time, Sam, dear." They didn't seem to walk on earth after that. Somehow they reached the house. A fire burned brightly on the grate in the drawing room. No one was there. Long months he had waited for that first rapturous kiss. He felt he could never let her go.

So the marriage was arranged. It took place in 1873 in the old homestead at Bergen Point. The newspaper clipping said:

> The beautiful and spacious mansion of Mrs. Zabriskie is one of the loveliest spots within the environs of New York. The wide lawn slopes to the water's edge. At half past seven when the guests assembled, two brilliant calcium lights illumined the lawn and the silent water that stretches off to Staten Island. . . .After the wedding ceremony a large company gathered to attend the reception. The toilets of the ladies were remarkable for their richness and display. The bride wore a rich and costly white satin dress and long train with lace. Her simple elegance was noted by all. . . . The bridal party left for New York about eleven o'clock, intending to make a tour of the West.

Thus began the life together of Sam and Lottie. It lasted for 50 years, until her death in 1923. Out of this love union of two beings who had known no other love relation before their marriage, I was born. But I was not the first nor last child; my brother Douglas had arrived three years before me and Ralph was born after me. The family had moved to the City, which like the nation was growing by leaps and bounds. A railroad now stretched from the Atlantic to the Pacific. Vast fortunes were made; great trusts sprang up. Carnegie, Rockefeller, and Vanderbilt became multimillionaires. And along with wealth came poverty and the slums. Immigrants poured in, fifteen million between the Civil War and 1900.

But my father and mother paid little heed to these things. They were radiantly happy. My father's business prospered. After the birth of Douglas they went abroad. Paris was Mother's delight; perhaps it was the La Tourette blood coming out. Or maybe it was just the wonderful clothes. One day as they stood before the church of the Madeleine, my mother said, "If I have a little daughter she shall be called 'Madeleine.'" Soon that baby was on its way. Back to the old Zabriskie homestead went Sam and Lottie for the great event. It was August 1877. Father had gone to his office in the City. At three o'clock in the afternoon, as Sam bent over his desk, there came a knock at the door. A boy with a telegram stood there. The message read: "Lottie and Madeleine doing well." With a shout he grabbed his hat and ran. Wonder of wonders — a little daughter — all he wanted in the world. But his big sweetheart was not forgotten. He paused to buy her a camel's hair shawl as he rushed to the ferry.

Never was baby more welcome. A love baby, planned and arranged for. From the first I prospered, a laughing, happy child with blue eyes, confident that everyone loved me. Those first three years are a blank until that memorable night of stars and fireflies. It was then I awoke to the world around me. Bits of that year in the country still return to me — the memory of the country house and my room on the top floor and a man's face appearing in my window one night. I screamed. The nurse came and I was told it was only the painter. But fear was born. Another event stands out clearly: the birth of my younger brother Ralph, born a year and a half after my arrival. One day when he was three he grew very angry, flung his dinner plate on the floor, and ran from the room. I remember I listened breathlessly outside the bathroom door while punishment was inflicted. So, in those first few years three things had come into my awareness: a consciousness of the wonder of nature, fear, and a knowledge that wrong is punished.

Our stay in the country was short. We were always moving — to the country for father's and the children's sake, back to the city for mother's sake. This time we took a house at West 44th Street just off Broadway, then a residential district, and spent four happy years there. In 1882 Broadway had a horse car which ran to Central Park. On it we made almost daily excursions to the Park with our governess. We rode on the merry-go-round, and later had riding lessons at the Central Park Riding Academy. Somehow I taught myself to read and devoured the Dotty Dimple books and later the Elsie books. Fairy tales didn't interest me; it was tales of real life, the tragedies of childhood, that were enthralling. Grandmother Zabriskie came to stay with us for a year. I loved her dearly and often went to her room and sat by her side. She taught me to sew. Then one day she died. The funeral took place from our house. When no one was looking I crept into the drawing room where her coffin stood. There she lay in her black dress and white kerchief and a white cap on her head. Suddenly, as though she feared I might be frightened, she sat up and smiled at me. I told the grownups but of course no one believed me. Was it my imagination?

In summer we usually went to Saratoga Springs, which was the fashionable resort in New York State, where we had rooms in the United States Hotel. Father came only on weekends. Mother was the reigning beauty. He brought her clothes from Paris on his business trips, and he and I used to walk behind her just to hear what people would say. But I didn't like Saratoga. I had to sit long hours on the hotel porch by my mother's side sewing. She called me her "little lady girl." My brothers and I escaped whenever we could. Our joy was the Indian Encampment. Real Indians with feathers on their heads who sold enchanting treasures.

One evening when I was about seven I was irritable and behaved badly so my mother spanked me. It quite broke my heart, I who prided myself on my goodness. I cried most of the night and developed a sore throat and fever. My poor mother was frantic with contrition. There is no doubt I was a spoiled child. Gifts were showered upon me. My father once brought me from Europe a doll the size of a year-old baby. It came from Paris and had a gorgeous pink satin dress. When we went to the steamer to meet Dad, I was led to his cabin and there lay that doll. It was all I could do to carry it. As we left the steamer the captain stopped me. "Hi!" he said, "That passenger hasn't been paid for." After that when I was naughty the doll was punished. Once she was shut in a closet for hours, and I wept bitterly.

What magnificent Christmases we had! We three children were given everything our hearts could desire. Not only did I have dolls and doll houses, but heavy silk stockings and gold garter buckles. No little princess could have had more.

When I was eight I grew interested in God; I began to pray to Him regularly. I spent much time on my knees, for it seemed essential to pray for everyone I knew. My relatives would not have been pleased with my prayers, for I prayed for each in turn that they be "fat and healthy." In the case of my mother's family my prayers were only too well answered. When I was nine or ten we decided to go back to the country. The old homestead at Bergen Point was vacant and we took it. My brothers and I were wild with delight. We had a tennis court and rode a high bicycle, a big wheel in front and a tiny one behind. In the barn were a cow, a horse, and chickens. We built ourselves a wood toboggan slide, which we used even in summer by taking chunks of ice out of the ice box and sitting on them to ride down. One day we played a bad game behind the barn. A little half wit, a small girl of seven, was the victim. My younger brother seized her, put her head under his arm, and spanked the child unmercifully. I was horrified, but said nothing. Fortunately, such games were rare and soon forgotten.

When I was twelve my interest in religion became absorbing. Every Sunday we went to the City to hear Dr. Paxton, the pastor of the Presbyterian church on West 42nd Street opposite the great City Reservoir. Both church and reservoir have long since disappeared. Sunday was a great occasion for me. Mr. Paxton's sermons were excellent. I decided to join the church. I remember that occasion well. I wore a little white silk dress, and, as my older brother and I knelt before the altar, I thought how good and sweet I must look. Self-glorification had begun. Yet beneath it was a sincere belief in God.

My mother's desperate fear of lightning transferred itself to me. But my belief in God said this fear was wrong; I ought not to be afraid. So, with the courage of a little Spartan I sat on the front porch while the rain beat down, the thunder crashed, and the lightning flashed, until little by little my fear vanished. I had triumphed. I had shown God what *I* could do. About this time I joined the Temperance Society. The pictures printed by that organization convinced me that most of the evil in the world was caused by drink. I decided I would give myself to their cause.

Outwardly I was a plain, quiet little girl deeply interested in books. But inside flourished a passionate, self-willed little being ready to be a religious fanatic and die for a cause. How I wished I might be a Joan of Arc!

One memorable day I was allowed to go to school. Up to then we had had governesses. Close to our house facing the Kill Van Kull was the La Tourette House. It had been a first-class hotel. It still was a hotel but one wing had been given over to Professor Sloan's School for Young Ladies, which was both a boarding and day school. My delight in this school knew no bounds. There I experienced my first love. A Miss Clark, the associate of Professor Sloan, became my idol. I worshiped her and adored all the other girls in the school. One winter day of a great blizzard mother said I couldn't go to school. My anguish was so great that my Dad wrapped me in a blanket, hired a public hack, and literally carried me to school. These were very happy days. To go to school and then come home, curl up in a big arm chair, eat the apple my father peeled for me, and read a book left nothing to be desired.

Twice while living in Bergen Point we went abroad in the summer. On the second trip we were promised ponies if we learned to speak French. We spent a summer in Paris for mother's sake. We rented the apartment of a Countess, near the Arc de Triomphe. We children spent hours in the Bois de Boulogne with a French tutor. Soon my older brother and I were chatting gaily. But my younger brother couldn't or wouldn't learn.

We sailed for home on the S.S. *New York*, a newly built propellor ship of 12,000 tons on its maiden voyage. It swept the record for speed, so as we steamed up the New York harbor brooms were sticking out of all the portholes to announce the victory. At home two ponies were waiting for us. Poor little Ralph had no pony. He used ours but it wasn't the same. I believe that experience produced an inferiority complex, from which he never recovered.

I was nearing thirteen when my father's business began to decline. Butter and cheese from America were no longer in demand. Denmark was producing both and selling for far less. Up to this time we had been living in luxury. Father never saved anything; he spent it all on us. We had carriages and horses, and there was a colored coachman. I used to ride to the station to meet my Dad on his return from the City. I remember one occasion vividly: in a new dress and hat with a feather I felt very proud sitting in the open victoria. We passed some dirty and ragged urchins. They yelled at me and threw stones. I was deeply hurt. I did not realize what a little snob I was.

Dad's loss of money came at an opportune time, because mother needed a shock. Perhaps she had discovered the first gray hairs or a wrinkle, for she was now 40. Perhaps she realized she would not always be a great beauty. When we children were in school and father in the City, she had little to do. She never read. There were no radio, no television, no cinema, not even a telephone. One day she went to the City and had a glass of wine with her lunch where the waiter said he would put something in that would make her feel fine.

The mother who returned to Bergen Point was not the mother I knew. She shut herself in her room. I was wild with anxiety. Father must not see her like that. When he returned there was the sound of sharp words behind mother's closed door. I felt my heart would break. Never to be forgotten is one day when my father was returning from Europe. Mother had gone to town and the children were to follow later with the governess. We were all to be at the dock when the steamer came in. As we watched the great ship swing into place, mother still had not arrived. What would father think? As the steamer tied up to the dock we saw the passengers clearly and there was the beloved face searching for mother. I could not bear it. I pushed in front of the crowd and yelled, "Mother missed the train." It was terrible to have all eyes on me, but Daddy smiled back and soon he was coming down the gang plank. At that moment mother arrived. It was evident she had had her glass of wine.

Those last months at Bergen Point were sad, the breaking up of the old home, the loss of money. But there was one compensation — mother was temporarily her old self. She was going to live in the City! She bravely pawned her jewels to help Dad through his crisis. The Zabriskie mansion was sold for a song, alas, for a few years later it was bought by the Standard Oil Company and we might have been millionaires.

We moved to an apartment on 22nd Street just off Fifth Ave., then a residential area. I was 15 but still an innocent child; I didn't know how babies came into this world. Curiously enough, I never sought information on the subject. My thoughts were all on school and I was admitted to the Brearley, a private school in the City. Here the world of the intellect opened up. And what loving teachers I had; I lived in the warmth of their smiles. One teacher above all others stands out—Annie Ware Winsor of Boston. She was deeply interested in world problems. President Cleveland was serving his second term. The great Pullman Strike of 1894 occurred; the labor leader Debs was imprisoned though it was he who had appealed to the workers to refrain from violence.

Miss Winsor kept one afternoon a week for her students. I always went and sat at her feet while she read me articles on Labor. She belonged to a Social Reform Club, which met one night weekly to discuss the problems of capital and labor. I begged my Dad to take me, and we went often. There were many brilliant speakers.

The fact that school meant so much to me was fortunate, for again my mother began taking stimulants. We never knew what day she would shut herself in her room. I could never ask my friends to our house. From the age of 14 until I was 25 my mother's illness often made life tragic, though we had times of great happiness.

There was one gorgeous summer when I was 16 and we went to the Adirondacks. It was my first taste of life among mountains. My soul seemed to waken; it was joy untold. And in addition to the mountains there developed a wonderful friendship. Until that summer I had taken no interest in men. In fact I looked upon them as tyrants; my brothers could do so many things I could not. Among the people in the summer boarding house were Dr. and Mrs. Charles Levermore and their five children. Dr. Levermore was the President of Adelphi College in Brooklyn. He was 38, dark, with a small moustache, slender, and very hand-some. His wife was also attractive. I immediately adored them both. But my days were spent with him. He rode a bicycle and so did I. He played tennis and so did I. His wife took little exercise, so Uncle Karl (as I learned to call him) and I made long excursions. It was a revelation to be with a man of brilliant mind and a love of poetry. Many summers after that were spent with the Levermores, until my twenty-third year. Because of mother's illness, they became my second family. Most summers with them we spent in Sebago, Maine. There it was too hilly for bicycles but Uncle Karl and I roamed those hills. What a joy it was to stand on mountain peaks and feel the world at my feet. How close I felt to God. I wanted to shout for joy and in the deep pine woods to stand under the trees and worship and to read wonderful poetry. Uncle Karl and I gathered together all the poems we liked best. One of my favorites was, of course: "I am the master of my fate; I am the captain of my soul." Already the little self was rampant. I was making self the center of life. What suffering I might have saved myself had I changed my poem to "God is the captain of my soul." But that was a lesson still to be learned late in life. How good Uncle Karl was to me. At times we walked hand in hand, but there was nothing more. My love for him was like that for the teachers I adored. Of course there was passion, but I didn't understand that then. That struggle too was still to come. Naturally there was much gossip at the boarding house, but Aunt Nettie (Mrs. Levermore) knew my innocence and protected me.

The Dean of Columbia Law School, George Kirchwey, spent one summer with us. He was Uncle Karl's best friend. On that occasion we went on an all-day picnic at Hiram Falls, and after lunch the two men proposed to wade across the river. I took off my shoes and stockings and went with them. And that was shocking — for even to bathe in the sea one wore a skirt and stockings. The water grew deeper; my clothes had to be held to my knees. The boarding house ladies sitting on the river bank gasped with horror. . . . The body always seemed to me beautiful. It was the misuse that was wrong. Body and spirit should be one, the reverse side of the same coin. This was a philosophy I had from childhood. Spiritual beauty must have physical expression. But there is danger in this theory. . . . Still, those were halcyon days. After my graduation from college Uncle Karl wrote the following poem for my birthday about how he saw me:

M.Z.D.

A wayward, laughing, romping sprite,
Just eight years old! In wild delight

The dancing mischief hides and spies
Within the doorways of her eyes.
And willful, tricksome roguery slips
Around her teasing, pouting lips.
This elf we seem to see
When Madeleine is twenty-three.

A maiden shy, demure, and bright,
She shuns a crowd but loves a fight.
Yet vows as strongly as she can
She'll never love the tyrant man.
Should man or beast obstruct her path,
She'll do "em up" in righteous wrath.
Fifteen this girl appears to be
Though Madeleine is twenty-three.

A woman moves upon the hills
Or through the forests where the rills
Run laughing down the cool ravines.
No voice of nature in these scenes
Ever lacks its answer in her soul —
She lives in union with the Whole,
The nymph of brook or cliff or tree,
And Madeleine is twenty-three.

Now, is there need of one to tell
How three in one together dwell
In one creation of delight?
The valiant maid, the elfin sprite,
The radiant nymph on mountain height,
The secret is not far to see —
Fifteen and eight combined must be
To make our Madeleine twenty-three.

But this is getting ahead of my story. We moved three times while I attended the Brearley School, to a house when father had money, to an apartment when his fortune declined.

My mother's illness grew gradually worse. There were periods when she shut herself in her room for whole days and would talk to no one. She wasn't able to come to my Brearley graduation. She made my father unhappy and I resented it. I lay in bed and shivered and shook and

wept, and laid the foundation for indigestion which has tormented me
the rest of my life.

College Days and an Innocent in Greenwich Village, 1896–1905

J ENTERED SMITH COLLEGE in Northampton, Massachusetts, in 1896. What joy to be free to do as I pleased, wear the clothes I liked, have my window wide open at night. Those college years were happy ones. I lived in a small house at 1 Belmont Street the first year and in Wallace House on campus the next three.

The girls made fun of my highbrow interest in labor and politics, so I dropped it all, and instead went in for golf and tennis and gay parties. The two literary clubs did not invite me to be a member, though Margaret and Emily, my best friends, were. We three formed a triumvirate. One day we went on a picnic up the Connecticut River and ate our lunch sitting on the river bank. We were far from any houses, though the road was quite near. Presently a man drove by, saw us, and stopped. He jumped down from his wagon and came toward us. He began saying the most outrageous things. I didn't understand, but Margaret and Emily did. Suddenly we were all seized by the same impulse. We rose and faced the man. "How dare you," we shouted. The man was nonplussed. He evidently thought we would run and he could catch the last one. Our united front sent him scurrying back to his wagon. I was furious, particularly when my companions explained what he had said. That afternoon when we reached Northampton again, I bought a pistol. It had only blank cartridges. The next morning I hired a horse and buggy and set out to find the man. I meant to bring him in at the point of the pistol and have him locked up. I would see justice done. Of course I didn't find him. So I let off steam by firing off my blank cartridges on the back campus. The college hushed up the matter.

Those were the days of the protected woman, the Victorian era. President Seelye was most careful we should lead sheltered lives. Our dresses were long; they nearly swept the ground. We were chaperoned at parties. We never smoked. Once in the Wallace House when we detected tobacco smoke we traced it to the door of a student. With much self-righteousness we reported the matter. The poor girl was banished from college. In after years when I smoked freely, how my conscience troubled me about her.

Of course I had my special love in college; Uncle Karl was not enough. This time it was not a man. Though admittedly we trailed around the golf course after our history professor, Charles Hazen, and Dr. Ganis, that was only to admire them. My love was Harriet Seelye, the President's oldest daughter, who was my German professor. What fun the girls made of me and recited rhymes such as "She visits at the President's each day a little while." What tender love Harriet gave me! I must have been a big problem. One of her notes treasured for years read:

Herzens Kindchen, . . . I can't stop worrying about your cold, *Kindchen*. I'm afraid you may be ill in bed and I wish so much I might see you. . . .I wanted to all day and fought with myself (not just) for the girls' account but I feel so sure it would be a bad thing for you, and I want your friendship so much. . . . Please, mein *Herzchen*, send me a little note if your cold is bad, for it has worried me awfully. *Bitte, Kindchen*, do take care of yourself and don't come out at all and get well soon.

Life was full of love. My father wrote me constantly; his letters usually began "Little Sweetheart." In my junior year he decided I ought to have attractive clothes. He had seen one or two costumes worn by famous actresses and had them copied for me. And did I splurge! It quite changed my standing in college. I was now invited to usher at the Junior Prom. The small girl disappeared.

Senior year I tried for Senior Dramatics and got a small part in "Twelfth Night." During one vacation I met Maude Adams, the famous actress, famous for playing Peter Pan in Barrie's play, and I persuaded her to come to the College. That was a grand occasion. We decorated her dressing room, and she came for afternoon tea. And there was one last escapade in my senior year. Emily and I went for a last drive. We hired a horse and buggy and drove to Deerfield, some miles from Northampton. On the way back the harness broke. It took a long time to repair it, so we didn't reach the college till half past ten. In those days ten was the deadline — the house closed and all lights out. For a student to be out after ten meant expulsion. What to do? Emily and I had friends in town. When we got there their house was pitch black. We threw pebbles at the window. Finally the man of the house opened the door. His wife was sleeping. He gave us two night shirts and showed us the spare room. We had to laugh in spite of our panic. The next morning very early we crept into Wallace House unseen. No one apparently ever knew.

College brought many changes in my ideas about life. For one thing, we often discussed religion. Emily was a Unitarian. I was wholly unprepared to discuss such questions as the Virgin birth and the turning of water into wine. Gradually it seemed silly to believe such things. I came to believe Christ was the best man who ever lived but he was not divine. For a while I became a Unitarian. God remained a wonder and a glory, someone I worshiped on the mountain tops, who dwelt in Heaven but had little to do with my everyday life."I was the master of my fate".... God saw in me a creature full of pride and self-will, quick to condemn others, intolerant, self-righteous, emotionally uncontrolled; on the credit side a creature with a passionate desire for what was right, a willingness to give all, even life, for a person or a cause, without financial gain or personal profit, responsive to beauty particularly that of the outdoors, possessing a firm belief in a God.

1900–1905

The problem was what to do now that college was over. It was 1900. I wanted a career. Teaching did not seem important enough. Medicine was out of the question; I could not bear the sight of suffering or blood. Why not be a lawyer? One of my college friends said that was silly, women weren't lawyers and besides it was far too difficult. Her brother had failed in his exams three times. That settled it. "I was the master of my fate." I would show what a woman could do.

In 1900 there were few law schools that admitted women; neither Harvard nor Columbia did, but the New York University Law School had thrown open its doors in 1891.

The following are extracts from a diary I kept of my law school days:

Bound Brook, New Jersey, September 1900. I took the early morning train with father to the City and entered my name in the NEW YORK UNIVERSITY LAW SCHOOL. The school occupies the whole top floor of a large office building on Washington Square. The elevators, corridors, and library were crowded with young men. Among the students are two colored boys, a Chinaman, a policeman, a professional ball player, Russian and German Jews, such as one sees on the East Side of N.Y. There are a little over a dozen women among 200 men. One or two seem nice, but the others are dowdy and rather gay and older than I am. I guess they thought I was a kid, for it was raining and I put on my tam-o-shanter and a short golf skirt, which I had worn at college, and that made me look very young.

I bought several law books — big fat ones that weigh about a ton each and the contents look like Greek. Shall I ever understand about "administrators" and "probating a will?" I spoke to one or two of the professors; they were cordial and pleasant, particularly Dean Ashley. The school hours are from three to six in the afternoon, or evening classes from eight to ten. This is so the men students can earn their living while attending law school.

New York City, October 30, 1900

I have been at work studying nearly a month, and legal terms are beginning to run off my tongue quite glibly. The women sit in the front row at recitation. I wondered why at first but now I know. There is such a strong odor of garlic and dirt from the East Siders it would be unendurable anywhere else. We are allowed only a few cuts during the year, so all the seats are numbered, and instead of calling the roll, the faculty notes whether you are in your seat.

The women students seem to consist of three types. The flighty, illiterate stenographer, who comes to the law school to flirt, the hard working woman stenographer or bookkeeper who is trying to improve her position, and the woman who has a little money and some brains and doesn't know what to do with herself. I have already made friends with two women in my class. One is older than I, the other about my age. They both have money and social position. One is a Christian, Jessie Ashley, sister of the dean, the other a Jewess, Ida Rauh.

Yesterday brought an amusing event, which might have turned out disastrously. Some of the sporty-looking women invited me to lunch; I was flattered by their attention and accepted. We went to a first-class restaurant and my three women companions ordered cocktails and urged me to drink. Of course I refused, and they winked at each other. When luncheon was over two of the women pretended they saw an acquaintance and hurried into the street. The other woman an instant later slipped out also and spoke to the waiter as she passed. Before I could stir, the head waiter presented me with the bill for the entire lunch and drinks. Then I saw I had been tricked. Fortunately I possessed a ten dollar bill, so I was able to pay up. One of the women jollied me afterward and said, "You're all right, kid. You just need educating, and that's what we're trying to do for you."

I have acquired two nicknames. One is "Daughter" because of my father's frequent visits to the Law School; the other is "Dr. Parkhurst" [Rev. Charles H., religion columnist][1] because the women say I have a narrow, saintly, and collegiate view of life.

New York City, November, 1900

I spend much time with my classmates Jessie and Ida. We often study together. Jessie has quantities of money and is studying law because she wants to do something. Ida wears stunning clothes and has a fine, expressive face. All the men stare at her. She ignores them. It was with difficulty she got her family to consent to her studying law. They make a fuss when she is out after six without a maid, and she has to rush home from the Law School. She lives in a fine house near Central Park. Jessie, Ida, and I and several women in the senior class have started a sorority. It is very exclusive, for there are so few nice women. I black-balled one of the candidates; I am sure she is an inveterate smoker because her fingers are all yellow. The women here don't think smoking is wrong. I wonder if it is? Men smoke and that is all right. But when I see a cigarette between a woman's lips, it fills me with disgust.

I have little to do with the men students, but when I am sitting beside one in the library and we are working on the same case, I question him. The librarian says several men have asked to be introduced, but I don't care to know them.

February, 1901

The work is comparatively easy now. We read cases and then deduce the underlying principles. I like one or two of the subjects better than any work I had in college. I think the chief reason is that I have to do my own thinking. The girls are called on continually in class. The Dean makes me recite every day. I thought at first I should be afraid to recite before men, but I don't mind a bit, for they don't know any more law than I do.

Many of the men students dislike having women in the class, though they are so eager to meet us. They got up a petition asking the Dean to exclude women, but the Dean is partial to us, and he answered with the following story. He said, "I have a small daughter who runs races with the boys. She runs well. One day she outstripped one small lad many times, and when he came puffing and panting behind her at the finish, he cried out in his despair, 'It isn't fair for you to beat me; you are only a girl.' And so, gentlemen, that is my answer." This gives us a big responsibility to live up to. But one woman in the Law School has shown what women can do; she not only graduated at the head of her class, but did better work than has ever been done here by either a man or woman.

I can't get used to New York City. I forget I am not at college. The other night I nearly got into a scrape. One of the girls wanted me to go to the theatre. I had never been out in the evening with only another woman and I thought perhaps I ought not to go. We decided to take a walk instead, for it was early, only eight o'clock. We passed a parked hansom cab [two-wheeled carriage with driver's seat up behind], and the girl, who was from the South, suggested a drive. She told the driver to take us up and down Broadway, because she wanted to see the lights. He protested, but the girl insisted. It was exciting driving up dazzling Broadway with everybody in evening dress on their way to the theatre. When I told father about it he explained that it wasn't the thing to do, for we might have been spoken to. The girls at the Law School laughed a good deal over the hansom cab drive, and they sent me a Valentine addressed to —

"Daughter"

O, have you met our sport
 Our really truly one
Who hangs out at the Breevort
 With clerks and jolly fun,
Who rides alone on Broadway
 In hansom cabs at night,
Who lunches at the Hoffman
 And father thinks she's Right.

The desire for a taste of Bohemia made several of us go to the "Black Cat" in Bleeker Street for luncheon. They say it is a gay place. Ida had never been to a restaurant of the sort before and swore us to secrecy lest her family hear of such outrageous behaviour. They served claret with the table d'hote. We had some. At Jessie's they always serve wine with the dinner and she thinks nothing of it. I drank a little, but I don't care for it and still don't like to see women drinking in public restaurants.

Once recently I took a boy, one of the few gentlemen in the Law School, out home for Sunday. We were cramming up together for exams. The family liked him and I find him easy to entertain.

April, 1901

I have had a quarrel with some of the women — the same crowd who played the trick on me and left me to pay the bill. One of them possesses a weird, magnetic fascination. I feel her presence when she is near and it stirs me so intensely that I cannot recite — I just stammer and stut-

Madeleine Z. Doty in her junior year
at Smith College, 1899
(Courtesy Sophia Smith Collection, Smith College)

ter. I try to keep away, but I feel myself drawn toward her. I think I am beginning to understand more about physical attraction. They say knowledge is power, but this knowledge makes me sick and sorry. The other day she brought a cocktail to school and drank it to tease me. Then she tried to kiss me. I loathed the smell of her breath. I got very angry and cried out at her and all of them. I told them they were materialists and I hated them. It was one of my Dr. Parkhurst occasions, which make me disliked. My would-be teacher, the student, came to me afterward and said, "Don't be too hard on us, kid. The trouble is we are envious because we can't be what you are. You are not ignorant, but you are innocent." I like that girl in spite of her materialism. But she isn't always kind. Yesterday she told me I was still a little prig and it would take years to get my college education out of me.

New York City, June.

Three cheers — exams are over and I have passed. I actually had two "A's." Exams were nightmares of feverish striving. I clutched my head and wrote reams. Each exam lasts four or five hours and covers the year's work. Recitations are not marked, so the student's fate depends on the dreaded test papers.

To celebrate the conclusion of the winter's work we had a class dinner at the Hotel Manhattan. It was the first time that the women had been invited to join the merry-making. I sat next to a young Irishman. He is studying law, but his ambition is to write a history of Ireland. He wore a shabby, striped suit and a red and black tie. His collar and cuffs were not even clean. A good many of the men can't afford dress suits. The behaviour of the company, they say, was exceptional; hardly any of the men drank too much, which is unusual and to be accounted for by the presence of women.

Law School has been nicer than I expected. The work has been easier. It is not a world of dreams, like college, but a world where you see life as it really is. I am glad to be taking up a career. I feel in a bigger world, a man's world. That girl was right — I do need educating.

Senior Year, New York City, November 1901

The old story of last year over again. Lectures, lectures, lectures. The work grows harder and the Equity course threatens my destruction. My consolation is that the whole class is in despair.

I haven't any special friends among the men except the man who sits next to me, the one who spent the weekend at my home. I have had lunch several times with him, and the other night, an evening class keeping me at the University, we dined together. I shouldn't have thought that proper a year ago. We went to the "Black Cat"; the place seemed very Bohemian. After dinner we walked back through Washington Square, a wonderful spot at night. The electric lights sparkle and flash through the trees, the illuminated cross on the Hudson seems to float in the air, and the Washington Arch stands there big and imposing. It is a little area of beauty and peace, surrounded by a noisy city. F. took my arm and I could feel his hand tremble. I am afraid his feeling for me is beginning to be more than platonic, and I don't want any other kind of affection just yet. He smokes incessantly. He offered to give it up if that would please me, but I really don't care whether he does or not. He didn't like my attitude and wanted to know what he could do for me. I told him I'd rather have him get ahead of me in exams. Last year we crammed together, and I passed him by ten points. He didn't like that either.

Night before last marks an era in my life. Girlhood is slipping away and the woman demanding admittance. F. did have more than a platonic friendship for me. He came to call and — well, he said things. I saw he was intensely stirred and I realized the kindest thing was to send him away at once since I had no corresponding emotion. I got his hat and explained it was best he should go. He held my hand for a long time. He was very good; he did not try to kiss me, as he might easily have done for I was all alone. Later my brother came in to say good night. He is in the city this winter boarding in the same house as I do. I was standing on a chair taking down the sign over my door, a sign I made in college which reads, "Man delights not me." I told him a little about F. and that I thought the sign wasn't true any longer and ought to come down. For I *do* like men.

June 1902

Commencement has come and gone and I am a full-fledged attorney with an L.L.B. at the end of my name. It is hard to believe, for my legal education has not been strewn with the difficulties I had anticipated. In spite of several "A's" I just squeezed through Equity. On the whole I am convinced that a law degree is easier to get than one in medicine. But whatever the profession may be, I am sure a professional education is of value to a woman. There is more to learn than the mere subject. It trains the mind, develops the reason, and teaches the woman a lot of common sense, particularly in her relations with men. A law school is a better place than a ballroom for friendship. "My educator" has done her best for me and I think there are results. Two years ago I should have condemned her unheard, as a woman who drank cocktails, a materialist without a soul and would have held myself superior. Now I realize the temerity of judging. What would I be like had I been brought up in the same environment?

In order to have enough space, commencement exercises were held at the Metropolitan Opera House, for students from many departments of the University were graduating the same evening. The law students occupied the body of the orchestra, and the boxes and galleries were filled with proud relatives and enthusiastic friends. We all wore academic caps and gowns. I confess I felt excited and important. Twenty of us at a time filed up on the platform to receive our diplomas, and as each name was called it was greeted by universal applause from the friendly crowd, the women receiving a double share. Little thrills of pleasure flowed over me. I thought of my college friend who had said I could never pass my law exams, and I wished she were present. At length it was all over. I had won the right to practice law, provided the Bar exams were passed.

I had learned much as a law student, many things besides the law. Among others is the relation between men and women, the meaning of sex. I had learned about the misuse of sex and the impure relation that can exist between women. I was appalled and upset. During the spring term of my last year at the Law School I ran back to Smith College. I wanted to get back to college, to breathe again clean, fresh air. Harriet Seelye had married and was no longer there. But the woman in charge of the house where I had lived as an undergraduate was an exceptionally fine person. She gathered me up in her arms, revived my belief in the beauty of love. After my return to New York she wrote me: "I am hoping great things for the future if only you don't take it all too intensely, with that little steam engine in your cerebral region. . . . So much that you have told me comes back as I sit alone. I realize more than I did what all the new experiences this winter must have been to you and how awfully hard it was to keep your faith in human — and Divine — nature."

In the autumn of 1902 I entered the law firm of Hatch and Wicks at 100 Broadway, as an apprentice. Two years of law school, one year of practical work in an office were customary before taking the State Bar exams. All sorts of odd jobs drifted into my hands. Among others I was asked to put in order the papers of a prominent client who had died. I discovered he was paying two sets of bills, for his wife and some other woman. I remember the astonishment of Mr. Hatch when I brought this to his attention.

Because of a gastric attack I left the firm of Hatch and Wicks, expecting, however, to return. A letter from Mr. Hatch said, "We are pleased to learn you expect to return. Your hours can be shortened while you are working without compensation. Of course in due time we should expect to pay you and then we will expect you to observe office hours." I had made good; a career was open for me.

Meantime, my mother's illness had grown worse and worse. She began even to doubt my father. It was of course her disease. My father, unable to stand the strain, had left and gone to a hotel. My brother Douglas and I took control. He was then literary adviser and reader for *Century* magazine. Our doctor said mother was mentally unbalanced. We decided she must go to a sanatorium. One day our doctor and the doctor from the sanatorium met at the flat where my mother was living. The car was below to take her away. There would surely be a terrible scene. But the new doctor was a man of great skill; he talked quietly with my mother and examined her carefully. He had knowledge that few others had in those days. He promised complete recovery if mother would take his remedies. Then he told us that mother suffered from myxedemia, a drying up of the thyroid gland. My father was sent for and life between the two resumed. Mother faithfully began her treatment. In a few weeks she lost 40 pounds. Slowly she regained mental control. It took several years, but gradually she became the mother of early days. All her love for me returned, and mine for her.

An offer had come to me to teach in Boston. Since father's business suffered because of mother's illness, it was necessary for me to earn my living. For two years from 1903–1905 I taught Latin, algebra, and Bible in Mary Haskell's School in Boston. Life was peaceful but uneventful, except for a camping trip one summer in the High Sierras when for two months I lived out of doors. We had no tents but slept on the ground in sleeping bags. We went so high that sometimes we camped near a bank of snow. And on the mountain tops God as always was near.

Teaching for me was only a stopgap. I wanted to practice law. The tap on the shoulder was strong. To teach merely to earn money was wrong. Some day I would consider it the greatest profession in the world. But I had not reached there yet.

During the Easter vacation of my second year in Boston, I returned to New York and visited Ida Rauh. She too was restless. She wanted to get away from her conventional life and suggested we live together. And Jessie Ashley offered to take me into partnership if I passed my Bar exams. So, back in Boston I took a law course at Boston University and crammed for the New York Bar. To my surprise, I passed them and was admitted to the Bar in 1905.

Part II
Justice Reform and Falling in Love

Introduction to Chapter 3

$\mathcal{T}$HE WOMEN'S MOVEMENT, of which Doty writes in chapter 3, has strong roots among the Greenwich Village inhabitants, among whom she lived most of the time from 1900–1925. In *The Grounding of Modern Feminism* author Nancy Cott provides a strong definition of the feminists' objectives during the years just prior to World War I, saying that the feminists' real goal was "a complete social revolution: freedom for all forms of women's active expression, elimination of all structural and psychological handicaps to women's economic independence, an end to the double standard of sexual morality, release from constraining sexual stereotypes, and opportunity to shine in every civic and professional capacity."[1]

Despite Doty's struggle to accommodate to the new radical modes of female conduct, it was the serious, egalitarian, social feminist, and humanitarian ideologies of this environment that were to shape much of her adult value system and her career, provide her essential associates and models, inspire her determination to make a difference. Yet it was some of these same ideals, tempered by her own choices and by fate, that were later to cause her pain and loss in some of her private relationships with men.[2]

In coming chapters she will tell of living and/or working with many of the best-known leaders and writers advocating change, many of whom also lived in or near Greenwich Village (see many named in Judith Schwarz' on *Radical Feminists of Heterodoxy*). And eventually her role in reform would move to national and international positions.

Cott[3] describes the women's movement as drawing from three traditions: (1) Enlightenment, nineteenth-century rationalism, which argued that natural rights and liberties belong to all human beings; (2) some Protestant churches that stress equality (such as the Quakers); and (3) socialism, with its opposition to class conflict and inequality in the capitalist world.

Discontent has been said to be the mother of progress. In the first decades of the 1900s women's discontent was accompanied by a growing pride in the specialness of the female being, hastened by expansion of education for women, the growing sense of the injustice of inequality, and the general loosening of Victorian restrictions. In the years before World War I feminists were not prone to male-bashing nor seeking to be like men, though they obviously envied men's freedom and power. It was their *differences* from men that women emphasized and claimed gave them a responsibility to act differently from men, to contribute to society's betterment, "to redeem the world." These differences, they claimed, rose from their experience in nurturing and their special sensitivity to the woes of the underdog (women, children, laborers, prisoners, the poor) for which they felt men had less aptitude.[4] Indeed, even at the end of the twentieth century many women still believe that they have something special, something peculiarly female and humane to contribute because they *are* women. As recently as during the 1992 elections *Life* magazine (June, p. 35ff) reported on this claim of specialness in an article titled "If Women Ran America."

The organization of the women's movement in the United States had begun in the mid-1800s under such leaders as Lucretia Mott, Elizabeth Cady Stanton, Susan B. Anthony, and others. In the Industrial Revolution toward the end of that century as more women and children began to find work in the growing factories and mills, reformers saw the need for special legislation to protect women laborers against the miserable working conditions. Yet that need caused a contradiction to their demand for equality. In fact, in Doty's time some militant feminists consequently refused to support such special protective legislation.

And where does Doty fit into this women's movement? Various students of the movement differentiate several types of feminists. Friedman and Shade identify three types: (1) privatists (concentrating on their own identity), (2) reformers (who lead or join organized movements and groups for social reform), and (3) radicals (seeking to overthrow the economic and social system).[5] Doty clearly knew and worked among all three types, but she herself fits in the second classification. June Sochen, too, identifies three types of feminists: the General (e.g., editor Charlotte Perkins Gilman), the Pragmatic (who worked to solve specific problems), and the Radical.[6] Again, Doty fits the middle group.

Some of the radicals were socialists and some, for a time at least, became outspoken Marxists, supporting the Russian reforms of 1905 and the Bolshevik Revolution of 1917 (among them the ultra-liberal Lincoln Steffens and John Reed) because they felt capitalism and democracy had failed to produce equality and justice. Soon the movement was not limited to the Village. There were feminists across the country who burned with a sense of mission to use woman-power to effect societal change. By the time of the First World War national organizations for suffrage and for peace had overlapping membership, as these two causes became allied.

The Opposition

As would be expected, these highly idealistic, restless, even revolutionary women, some of whom here and in England and Germany used disruptive demonstrations and civil disobedience to call attention to their causes, were seen as a threat by the established society, particularly during and just after World War I.[7] Organizations formed to oppose them; some editorials in the press, including even the *Ladies Home Journal* of January 1910, attacked them vehemently. There was a National Association Opposed to Woman Suffrage in the United States which gave this warning at that time: "Pacifist, socialist, feminist, suffragist are all part of the same movement — a movement which weakens government, corrupts society and threatens the very existence of our great experiment in democracy." And in 1918 the Anti-Suffrage League in Missouri wrote "feminism advocates non-motherhood, free love, easy divorce, economic independence for all women, and other demoralizing and destructive theories."[8] Even as late as 1927 the DAR attacked Congresswoman Jeanette Rankin's Maternity Bill for pre-natal care (Sheppard-Towner Act, passed in 1921, which Doty had publicly supported); the DAR called it a Bolshevik device to destroy the family, and they joined other conservative groups in also opposing pacifists like Rankin. Today's reader will be aware that, in the face of considerable progress by women and liberalization of mores, such fears and attitudes are again surfacing. For example, a fundraising letter circulated by the evangelist Pat Robertson during the 1992 election, in appealing to the growing Christian right said in part, "The feminist agenda is not about equal rights for women. It is about a socialist, anti-family political movement that encourages women to leave their husbands, kill their children, practice witchcraft, destroy capitalism and become lesbians."

By 1910, despite opposition, the women's demand for the vote had gained considerable success here and abroad. The right to vote had been given to women in about a dozen U.S. states even before the United States ratified the 19th Amendment in 1920, and it had been won in Finland (1906), Norway (1907), Russia (1917), Great Britain (1918), and several others in 1919.

Among the growing number of women's clubs and organizations forming across the country between 1890 and the 1920s was the Women's Trade Union League, active from 1903–1906. Although Doty does not mention it in her chapter 3, her apartment mate, Ida Rauh,[9] was an active supporter of that League and Doty provided free legal counsel to women laborers.[10] And the Equality League for Self-Supporting Women was founded in 1907 by Harriet Stanton Blatch, daughter of Elizabeth Cady Stanton. "Among its self-supporting women were socialist intellectuals and Greenwich Village radicals passionately engaged in challenging the world around them, including lawyers and social investigators Madeleine Doty, Ida Rauh, and Jessie Ashley."[11]

Her First Great Love Affair

It was while living in Greenwich Village as a practicing lawyer and reporter that Doty had her first great, perhaps her greatest love affair — or at least the one about the romance of which she could write most freely. This was with one of the most widely read social critics of the time, David Graham Phillips. A journalist and novelist, he wrote for the *New York Sun* and the *World*, becoming editor of the latter under Pulitzer. As a freelance writer he was the author of some forty hard-hitting, investigative articles for *Cosmopolitan* and other magazines plus as many for the *Saturday Evening Post*.[12]

Phillips first made his name by press attacks on power both individual and corporate, on scandals in business and finance, and on corruption in government. It was his sensational series of articles in Hearst's *Cosmopolitan* titled "The Treason of the Senate" that made him the primary target at whom President Theodore Roosevelt in a speech on 14 April 1906, directed the pejorative epithet "muckraker," thus putting that word into common parlance. And on 23 May T.R. sent a letter directly to Phillips criticizing his negative *exposés*.

In addition to being a journalist, Phillips was a prodigious novelist, author of about 25 novels in nine years beginning in 1901, in which he decried the frivolity of leisure-class women and with new frankness expounded on women's grievances and the oppression of dependent women in marriage and in sex standards.

In Doty he must have seen the possibility of the opposite of what he abhorred in women of leisure and self-indulgence. Yet, whereas he, ten years her senior, was a disillusioned idealist who had become a driven, cynical realist disdaining the common man for his weaknesses (yet apparently hoping to change behavior by his writings), she was a young, hopeful idealist believing (at least until into her sixties) in the innate goodness of mankind and in the power of reason to improve people's behavior.

Phillips's letters to her hint at disagreement between them about how far they should go sexually. She did not want pregnancy without marriage; he wanted the loving but no resultant obligations. For him work and absolute freedom were primary. According to one of Phillips' biographers, "He abhorred the idea of anyone leaning upon him, because he regarded freedom as the very corner-stone of his scheme of life."[13]

Despite their obviously strong attraction for each other, his letters show a tantalizing mixture of support and constant criticism, no doubt to help her because he cared. He repeatedly and severely blamed her for her personal naivete and her lack of professional concentration on a single issue, while also expressing his encouragement and confidence in her ability in her career as a writer, and his desire to be with her.

Just as his biographers find autobiographical characters in his books, there can be seen in his last and most famous novel, *Susan Lenox*, considerable similarity between lectures to Susan on how to win in life and the contents of several of the 55 letters from him that Doty saved.[14] These letters were dated from 30 January 1907 to the end of 1910. For example, on 23 January 1908, Phillips wrote didactically to Doty, when she was ill from emotional tension, that she must develop strength, not just sweetness: "Be sure, my child, [that] persistent, unremitting, intelligently directed hard work is necessary, if we are not to be like the great mass of our fellows. . . . Shall I see you Saturday after dinner about nine o'clock?" And the following December he wrote, "I suppose you're blessed chasing some fabrication or other. . . . Someday you may discover that sober study, work in some one place at some one thing has its claim as a way of getting on."

A further similarity can be seen in his heroine Susan Lenox whom he has mature into the new woman who refuses marriage to those who would dominate her; it is evident he wanted Doty to be like Susan who gives herself in freedom to a man only out of love, not in exchange for protection. He is contemptuous of female passivity. Indeed, in their intense relationship Phillips apparently never forced her into submission, although the subject of more intimate relations becomes significant, as will be seen in her chapter 3, which follows. It is guardedly referred to as "it" in his January, 1907, letter and on 3 June 1907, ". . . when you won't do what we both want." By March of 1908 she has apparently been trying to "hide" from him, to use his word, in order to reduce her emotional strain, and she blames her own weaknesses for being unable to stay away from him.

The end of their affair is most startling. By quickly closing the chapter, Doty guards her privacy about the profound impact of that event upon her emotions.

3
The Women's Movement, Law, and Love, 1905–1911

*I*N SEPTEMBER 1905 I RETURNED to New York permanently and started cooperative living with Ida. My savings from teaching amounted to $250, which was my entire capital. Because it was cheap and because it was rather smart, we took a flat in a tenement on the Eastside. To reach it one had to go down crowded streets and pass push carts and screaming children and gutters littered with papers and decayed vegetables. The building was new, so our flat was clean and we had chosen the top floor. But to reach it we had to climb five flights of stairs, past other flats teeming with occupants and the smell of garlic and un-washed humanity.

The first room in the flat was the kitchen, which had a big coal stove. But the place was modern for those days, for there was a real bathroom. We quickly fixed up the place with gay chintz curtains and pictures, and it became quite the wonder of the neighborhood.

Meanwhile Jessie Ashley and another woman and I established law offices on Fifth Avenue in the Windsor Arcade, an address which today would cost a fortune. Our sign read:

Ashley, Pope and Doty
Attorneys and Counsellors at Law
569 Fifth Avenue

We hoped that a swell office uptown on Fifth Avenue would attract society women. But of course it didn't. In fact, we soon discovered that women are less ready than men to employ a woman lawyer. It was an expensive undertaking; the rent, telephone, and stenographer cost more than our joint business income. In order to live I had to earn other money. My old school, the Brearley, gave me some tutoring to do. Two afternoons a week I coached two young girls, who lived in a gorgeous mansion on Park Avenue. They each had their own bedroom, study, and bathroom, and the walls of the rooms were hung in silk brocade. The butler served us tea.

It made an interesting life hurrying from my law office on Fifth Avenue to the Park Avenue mansion and then to my tenement house on the Eastside. I soon discovered my greatest interest lay in the tenement life.

In those days many young people were engaged in social work; they wanted to remedy some of the evils that had come with industrial expansion. The Men's University Settlement was only a few blocks from our tenement. We often went there to dine. Among the men reformers was J. G. Phelps Stokes, the young millionaire who had married Rose Pastor, a Jewish girl from the Eastside earning her living in a cigarette factory. Then there were English Walling and Walter Wyle, both of whom later became well known writers. Such thrilling talks as we had there. Here I first heard about Karl Marx and socialism.

Tenement life brought me in contact with a side of life hitherto unknown. I discovered the suffering of the poor, their goodness to one another, the warmheartedness of tenement mothers who seemed ever ready with help. It was very different from the life on Fifth Ave. where richly dressed women in open victorias, each with a footman and coachman in livery, drove up and down. The contrast between wealth and poverty made me see many injustices in the law, that the law was frequently a game of shrewdness. A few unimportant cases came my way. When a Judge, whom I knew, made me a Receiver in Bankruptcy, the newspapers acclaimed me the *first woman receiver*. Whether this was true or not I do not know. It wasn't an important case; a small dressmaker just off Fifth Avenue had failed. It fell to me to settle up her affairs. As usual there was practically nothing left for the creditors. My only reward was a couple of dresses at bargain prices.

But now came a break in our happy tenement life. Ida came home one evening with a high fever. She was frightfully ill with pneumonia. Her family carried her home, and later much against her will she was whisked off to Europe.

Fortunately our flat was the kind one rented by the month, for an invitation had come to me to join a group of young literary folks for the summer in a house at 3 Fifth Avenue. They called themselves the "A Club."[1] Among them were Ernest Poole, who won fame as a novelist, Howard Brubaker, who later wrote a humorous column for the *New Yorker*, and Paul Wilson, who was to marry Frances Perkins, first woman Cabinet member.

It was also during that spring of 1906 that Maxim Gorki arrived from Europe. He came with his tragic story of the Czar's dictatorship and the abuse of the peasants. He told of the pogroms and the beatings and the people sent to Siberia. He came to appeal to America for aid. Alas, the day before he arrived the newspapers discovered that his marriage had not been legalized. Immediately outrageous headlines appeared: "Gorki Here With His Mistress," "Gorki And His Chorus Girl Refused Admittance To All Hotels."

The barbarity of this treatment was unbelievable when the truth is known. Marie Peshkoff, Gorki's wife, came from a noble family. At 15 her parents married her to a baron 30 years her senior. Marie never loved this man though she bore him two children. Finally unable to continue such a life, she went on the stage and became Russia's most famous actress. She acted in Gorki's plays. The inevitable happened; they fell in love. Gorki was a peasant by birth and she a baroness. She went to her husband and asked for release. He finally consented and let her have the two children. A legal divorce was impossible in Russia; the only ground was adultery and one must be seen in the act, which was unthinkable both to Marie and Gorki. So for sixteen years Gorki and Marie Peshkoff had lived together as husband and wife. She had given up everything for him, even her profession.

We who knew the story were horrified at the newspaper scandal. The Gorkis were invited to the A Club, where on the upper floor they were concealed from reporters. In a day or so the John Martins of Staten Island invited the Gorkis to be their guests; later they went with the Martins to the Adirondacks. During their stay in Staten Island we spent many Sundays with them on the beach. I have vivid memories of Gorki in his long black cape and soft black hat. He spoke only Russian, but Marie was his interpreter.

Nearly all my circle of friends in those days were the literary, artistic crowd. I had received a note in April 1906 from Gaylord Wiltshire, editor of *Wiltshire's Magazine*, inviting me to his house to meet Maxim Gorki and his wife. At the same reception I met H.G. Wells for the first time.[2] These people impressed me greatly. My intolerance began to drop from me. I had long since learned to smoke cigarettes and looked with amusement at my former attitude. I was living a far different life from the sheltered one of the Brearley School and Smith College. In my new freedom I was plunging into a turbulent world of good and bad to sink or swim. My companions now were mostly men. I forsook my feminine world.

But my mind was still intent on social problems. I naively believed that a change in the economic order was the answer, that economic security for everyone would transform the world. Admittedly, my own economic situation was far from good.

In September 1906 I learned that the *New York Times* was looking for a man to write book reviews. I asked to be given a three-week trial without pay, saying I would take a man's name and no one would know the difference. They reluctantly consented, and a weekly review about books and authors began to appear under the name of "Otis Notman," a name they accepted though it really meant "O 'tis not man."

Every week I interviewed three or four authors, wrote two or three thousand words, and received $20 a week. This covered living expenses. What I made from my law practice went back into the business. It was a hectic life. Most of the day spent around the courts, articles written Sundays and evenings, daily visits to my father and mother, and luncheons and dinners with an ever-increasing circle of friends. My articles brought me recognition. I interviewed all the leading authors of the day and wrote what these men and women had to say about their books. It proved most interesting and the best kind of advertising. A few excerpts illustrate this:

Maxim Gorki

> Maxim Gorki sailed for Europe Saturday [1906]. He has been spending the summer in a little cottage in the Adirondacks. He has been doing some hard work. He writes most of the day, from 9 to 5 p.m. . . . .

> When Gorki was not working he was to be seen on a hillside catching butterflies. . . . It was a rather unusual picture of him that one got — a big man in a white suit, with a tight fitting skull cap, and a butterfly net waving over his head.

> Gorki is a keenly disappointed man. His whole heart and mind are centered in the cause of Russian freedom. He came over so full of hope. He has been able to accomplish so little for his country here.

Theodore Dreiser

> "The mere living of your daily life," said Theodore Dreiser, "is drastic drama. Today there may be some disease lurking in your veins that will end your life tomorrow. You may or may not have a firm grasp on the opportunity that in a moment more may slip through your fingers. Life is a tragedy . . . because you can't use ability except under favourable conditions. The very power of which you speak, thwarted, may only serve to make man more miserable. . . . A man with something imperative to say and no time or strength for the saying of it is as unfortunate as he is unhappy. I look into my own life and realize that each human life is a similar tragedy. The infinite suffering and deprivation of

great masses of men and women appals me. My greatest desire is to devote every hour of my conscious existence to depicting phases of life as I see and understand them."

I held this job for two years. I had now moved into an apartment on Charles Street near Washington Square. Here Crystal Eastman joined me. She was just beginning her career as a leader in the movement.[3] Her brother Max was emerging as a poet; later he became editor of *The Masses* and leader of the young revolutionary intellectuals.[4] And when Ida came back from Europe in January of 1907 she joined us in the apartment. We made an unusual trio. Early that winter I left the firm of Ashley, Pope and Doty and set up my own office in a building at the corner of Nassau and Wall Streets. I had grown more and more socialistic. I wanted to reform the law and not conform to it. Jessie Ashley at that time was not with me in my radicalism. It is curious what life does to one; Jessie, who then accused me of being a socialist, later went far beyond me in leftist ideas. I carry in my mind a picture of her about a year or so before her death, parading down Fifth Avenue with the Communists and the unemployed. I stood on the sidewalk and watched; I had ceased to feel that was the way. But my whole heart went out to her. The courage of her, that frail, refined, slender gentlewoman tramping through the streets, shoulder to shoulder with the roughest kind of men, she whose father had been both the president of a railroad and of a bank, whose brother was Dean of the New York University Law School. She had caught a glimpse of what she thought was the truth. Her position, her name, nothing mattered. She gave most of her money to the workers and lived on a tiny income. When she died, a big memorial service was given her by her comrades.

By 1905 reform was in the air. Muckraking was very popular. Teddy Roosevelt was wielding his big stick and fighting the Trusts. One felt one had only to show up such evils and things would be put right.

Soon I was seeing much of Charles Edward Russell, a writer battling for a better world.[5] His articles exposed the big trusts. . . . But Russell was soon completely lost sight of after I met David Graham Phillips. I had met him casually at dinner. In 1906 as Otis Notman I interviewed him. He lived with his sister in a duplex apartment high up above the city. He was extraordinarily good looking, tall and slender, with beautiful hands. I sat on one end of the couch, he on the other. I felt very small and insignificant. As I left he said, "Aren't you going to invite me to come and see you?" It was wholly unexpected. I stammered in embarrassment. This man who must know all the loveliest women in New York, why should he bother with me? So began a relationship that changed my life. I was to learn through suffering and anguish the meaning of love between man and woman. I wrote of D.G.P. in my interview:

> If you see a man towering above the shoulders of other men, with a broad forehead, deep-set blue eyes, a high white collar, and a certain indefinable air of the thinker and writer, he is David Graham Phillips.

> He said of his recent articles entitled "The Treason of the Senate": "I dislike saying hard things about people yet one must give the facts. In fiction, which I prefer, you can show all sides of a man's life, especially the life within, where lie the springs and wheels of motive. To write a great novel a man must have a big philosophy of life, the ability to tell a good story and make his people real characters who justify his philosophy." "Do you feel," I asked, "that man today is unwilling to say what he really thinks?" — "Yes, I do," he said, "In every line of work there is a pose. A man is afraid of being his true self. Only the truly great man is at once unself-conscious and self-reliant. He is more concerned about truth than what people say of him personally."

This was the man who took me to dinner a day or two later, who thrilled me, who turned many of my ideas upside down, who made me face myself for the first time. He asked me what I had to give. I had eyes, nose, and lips. But so had every other woman. What else had I? How much character?

We met almost every week. We dined in restaurants all over New York. When spring came we went to Staten Island and while we walked to the ferry after dinner D. G. P. teased me and asked what I would do if we missed the last boat. Sometimes we dined in Central Park and afterwards walked back under the silent trees. Then we would go to the flat where I lived with Ida and Crystal. We would talk until midnight. There was so much to talk about.

But a great struggle was going on between us. This man wanted me, but he never spoke of marriage. He didn't believe in marriage for himself. "He travels fastest who travels alone." And he didn't realize how immature I was, how little I knew of love and sex. He thought a woman lawyer and writer must be sophisticated. His letters troubled me:[6]

January 1907

Your description of yourself was as wide off the mark as a Fra Angelico angel is of palpitating, electric, thrilling, feminine humanity. How nice it is to be young and to push away happiness with a heroic look in the eyes and a feeling of nobility in the heart. But alas, these pleasures are denied me. I dare indulge in them no longer. . . .

I want a certain peculiar distillation of delirium that is contained in only one fascinating vase [Doty] — a Gallic vase, wonderfully wrought, strong yet delicate. How long would the liquor last? How long could I have to drink it? How do I know? Not being a liar I do not pretend to know.

January 1907

Certainly "it" shall be as you say. You don't suppose I would want it otherwise, do you? That garden is not a prison into which one is thrust or dragged. And I don't wonder that you are not sure you want to go there. I am disposed to think you don't. I am also disposed to think that you are deceiving yourself about your state of mind in many ways. But that's the way it is with all of us. Now, wouldn't it be quaint if what you really wanted was to stop work and all the anxieties incident to a career and secure some man, nurse your children, and superintend servants?

February 21, 1907

It is a long time until next Sunday, but not as long as it was last Sunday.

March 1907

What a serious-minded young person you are. If God Almighty had had your solemn habits of thought he'd never have gone so far as executing his plan for a Universe. Also you've got some mighty poor advisers. Do change them, and stop reading the Ladies Home Journal and the Fairfax Wisdom for Maidens in Distress.

David Graham Phillips
(Courtesy of Sophia Smith Collection, Smith College)

April 1907

There wasn't a chance to call you up today, so I am writing instead. . . .I have tranquillized my nerves somewhat while away and am now working very hard and steadily. As soon as I am free I'll call up.

May 1907

You're so delightfully young, always imagining people were created for your purposes and disappointed to find them not to your taste. I am no more the sort you mean than you yourself are. Only I don't have to make believe, while for some reason you think you do.

June 3, 1907

Don't get cross at me because I won't do what you really don't want me to do. Be like me. See how philosophic I am in bearing with you when you won't do what we both want.

At the end of June D. G. P. left for his annual trip to Europe. He came to see me the night before he left. My whole being responded to him. Besides, I had begun to doubt my own philosophy. He took me in his arms and there were passionate kisses. Then he said something I have never forgotten: "I think one is nearer God at such a moment than any other. I know how my father must have felt when he held my mother." He left me a seething mass of emotion. My reason said that married or unmarried our love was justified. We were hurting no one! If man gave all, why shouldn't a woman? If there was real love nothing could separate us. As always I turned to my Dad. "David wants me to go to Europe with him." Dad didn't think I would be happy without marriage, but with his extraordinary faith in me, he made no opposition. His final word was, "I'm sure whatever you do, it will be right."

The first letter from D. G. P. written on the ship, had a new quality:

June 27, 1907

Having written and destroyed a letter that pleased me I will now write one that will please you. (He then gives a description of his trip and his plans but ends as follows): And you? Why, you are calm among your calm mountains (I had gone away for the summer) and have resumed the spiritual life which was so rudely interrupted. But at least you were splendidly human for a few minutes once. Even in the stupor that has fallen upon me at sea I remember and tremble and feel like running back to old New York. I can see the Hudson and the moon full and clear and the boat moving so swiftly and smoothly northward — and you — is it a delusion or a prophecy?

Believe me, old and experienced in reflection, we are never so near the immortal gods, never so intensely unearthly as when we are entirely human — alive to the fingertips.

And from Paris

I am delighted to have your letter and hear about the work you are doing — you will do it well. You are sure of a career.

As for me, I am not quite so miserable, thanks to the improved weather, though I still have a "catchy" breath-bereft feeling of one who has been led up the musical scale to within one foot of the top and then suddenly dropped back to the bottom — up in the balloon until the stars were singing in my ears, then bump, bang, ouch! Solid earth, hard and cold.

From Lucerne, Switzerland, August 9, 1907

You certainly write interesting letters. The one that came today, about your camp, was full of all sorts of suggestions. I shall write a novel about it if you don't.

Now, if you were here, I keep planning the walking trips we would take. I am sure you would love it. Well, there's next summer. The cost would be small and we'd just lounge along from village to town, always fine roads, always good cooking, or at least fair, always gorgeous views. And there would be times when we should see the land of which the rainbow is the gateway. Still, that land has been known to come into view in the twilight of a parlor. You should be glad, *mon amie*, that you are svelte and white and round and yet slim, and that you are young and a whole lot of things that I shall put straight out of my mind.

I am still working hard, perhaps not well but certainly hard. The best thing in the world is work, believe me, for it makes you almost independent of everyone and everything. And you can and will work well. You have intelligence, persistence, energy, and conscience, a fine instinct for what is just and right, and a very sweet sympathy that will be a great force for good, once you educate it out of credulity and sentimentality (not sentiment, but sentimentality). Yes, you can go far. Not because I say so or urge you, but because it is in you yourself.

That summer I had again made a camping trip in the High Sierras, hoping two months among my beloved mountains would help me solve my problem over our relationship. The trip started in at the Yosemite Valley and we climbed to an altitude of 10,000 feet. The scenery was superb. But I had none of the joy of my first trip, for my thoughts were elsewhere. On my way home I stopped at Carmel to interview the poet George Sterling for the *New York Times*. We had a blissful day on a point of land far out in the sea. He read me his poems. It was one of those days complete in itself without beginning or end. We never saw each other again but somehow there was no need. I wrote D. G. P. about it and he replied:

You were so slow about writing that I was about to assume you had met your real affinity — a first class tosser of star dust. And sure enough, you almost did. But I fancy it was just as well you didn't have a second go with the poet of the Pacific.

You are going to do splendid things. All that is necessary is that you get over that limiting self-consciousness that makes writing so difficult. When you are able to pour out that pure young soul of yours, why, no Swiss mountain torrent leaping and laughing in the sunshine from heights of snow to valley of sun will be in your class.

My life as a writer had really begun. *American Magazine* had commissioned me to write about Mormon women.[7] This took me to Salt Lake City that summer of 1907. D. G. P. had taught me many things, among others to look at life without pre-conceived prejudice. My study of the Mormon situation showed the women on the whole were happy. They were a finer lot than the men. Polygamy had taught them self-sacrifice. If the plural wives did not live together there was little jealousy. Each wife knew her husband must give her the same things he gave his other wives. If he took one to Europe, the others must have their turn. The man seemed to be running about from house to house, while the woman was mistress of her home and family. — All this was written to D. G. P. and he replied, "You have grown wonderfully this summer. . . .The girl I left in New York last June is not the girl I shall see when I get back." And later, "You will accomplish a great deal if you keep your health. [Editor's note: In each year of their correspondence he makes frequent references to her health, to her being ill, scolding about her diet and lifestyle.] Your articles in the *Times* which you enclosed certainly show a great improvement. . . .Have had the blues a good deal of late. The weather, probably."

With my return to New York from the West I was as unsettled as ever. There was the same conflict between body and spirit. I knew now that I loved D.G.P. so much that nothing else mattered. But my conscience said that if it was real love our relationship should be open. There must be no lies, no sense of shame. I must be ready to have an illegitimate child. But would D.G.P. be willing to live with me on such terms? Wouldn't his responsibility be as great as if we were married? Yet he wanted no ties. "He travels fastest who travels alone."

I went back to my law office and took up my work. But it was no use. Soon there was a bad gastric attack and a retreat to the country for convalescence.

My father's business had taken him abroad, and my mother, much improved in health, was with him. This left me alone. The peace and quiet of the out-of-doors calmed my nerves. In my walks I found an old, abandoned farm house on the edge of a lovely wood through which ran a small ravine and a rushing brook. It was a place of enchantment, and only five minutes walk from the main road which ran through the village of Sparta, New Jersey. When Dad returned, he came to see the place. That spring he bought the farm for a few thousand dollars. It became our summer home for 17 years and a source of endless delight, the last home we had together as a family.

Back in the city I found D.G.P. had returned and the same old struggle began. Nothing had altered. It was wonderful to feel his arms about me, and the realization soon came of my inability to hold out any longer. But he too had gone through a struggle. He had believed me a sophisticated and mature women. Instead he had found a girl of 28 who was intellectually mature but emotionally a child. He was far too fine to sweep me off my feet. He wanted me to agree that a secret relation without marriage was right. This I was never able to do. One little note from him on December 17 said, "I am afraid I wasn't very sympathetic the other evening. I appreciate more than you think what a struggle you are having and I admire, more than I will be able to say in words, the courage you show."

We nearly wrecked each other. One night when I was alone in my flat he remained until 3 A.M., without the ultimate union. Such a state

of affairs could not go on. We agreed not to see each other. His letter of
March 15, 1908, said in part:

> Thinking over what you said — I believe you're right. You take
> me and your charming self too seriously for such a practical,
> unimaginative, unromantic person as I. — So, I'm going to try to
> help you "hide" from me. . . . You haven't had the experience to
> realize that you really want what can be had. . . . I'm telling you
> that what you want is a husband and a flat and a family. And I'm
> a hard working, plain man with his life laid out for business —
> and with a horror of bonds and burdens . . . . Cheer up — the risk
> will tease you no more.

And on March 17

> Glad your digestion is better. You are a bad one! You tell me only
> weakness prevents you from hiding — and when I desire to help,
> you insinuate I'm not "playing fair." But, cheer up. Your longing
> for a family will be gratified, I've no doubt.

> Don't talk rubbish — of course you and Russell [Charles Edward]
> are going to dine here just as soon as it can be brought about.

Two important legal cases needed my attention. One was a large re-
ceivership. I found myself the Receiver of a large warehouse full of
men's garters and suspenders. The largest creditor was owed $10,000,
of which we won several thousand for my client, which was rare indeed
then. But when I suggested that he should let me handle his legal
business, he shook his head and said, "What would I look like employing
a woman lawyer." Yet this man was insistent on repeatedly urging me
to dine with him, but I would not, and finally he blurted out that he was
married.

The other case was against the American Ice Company. An employee
named Murphy, while working for the Company, had fallen from a
scaffold 40 feet in the air and been killed. He left his widow and nine
children, one a baby in arms. The family was destitute, for in these days
there was no Social Insurance. I took the case and brought an action
against the Ice Company for $20,000 for the death of Murphy. The case
was to be tried in the State Supreme Court and would tax my ability to
the utmost. The law is slow; the case had been on the calendar for nearly a year. Mrs. Murphy and her nine children had nearly starved. As she
had no money, I shouldered the expense of the trial. At the time I had
been reading John Galsworthy's play "Justice" and determined the case

should be tried on that basis. Unused to pleading, I asked a young man attorney to aid me. But he did not prove helpful; he was too cut and dried and believed in the law rather than justice.

Luckily the Judge had no prejudice against women lawyers. I felt if I could get my story to the jury the case would be won. But how get it that far? At any moment the case might be thrown out of court for irregular procedure. Never, I suppose, was there such an unconventional trial, which ignored the law and put the whole case on the human basis of what was right. The attorney for the Ice Company, a hard-boiled, efficient lawyer, was on his feet nearly every moment objecting to all I said and did. What was worse, my own assistant kept opposing me. But the judge saw my desperate efforts and he kept saying, "Let her alone. She is doing all right." I had the jury with me from the beginning and thanks to the Judge, who overruled every objection, it did not take them long to render a favourable verdict awarding Mrs. Murphy $10,000.

But the law, as I was learning, is in large part a clever game and often does not achieve what it is supposed to. The attorneys for the Ice Company were naturally versed in all the tricks of the trade. They appealed the case to a higher court. What could I do? I had no funds with which to carry the proceedings higher. A transcript of the record alone would have cost more than I earned at the law in six months. A few days later Mrs. Murphy came to me and said the Ice Company had offered to settle for $1,000. Regretfully I advised her to accept, as she desperately needed the money.

Each year my dissatisfaction with the law increased. Bankruptcy proceedings were riddled with corruption. Law began to seem a business instead of a fight for justice. My desire to practice law vanished.

Most of my weekends were spent now in Sparta, where we were re-building the farm house. One week I gathered a lot of spring flowers there and left them at D. G. P.'s door. Next day came a little note [dated 25 May 1908]: "Those beautiful flowers. I don't know when I've had such a thrill of pleasure. For in addition to their perfume there was the wonderful odor of the open air in the spring. Thank you — thank you." After that we began to meet again and dined together several times. But it was a terrific strain. And soon he was off on his annual trip to Europe.

Now sometimes whole weeks were spent in Sparta. I had a room with four windows opening on three sides. At night they were all open. The sound of the rushing brook and the great quietness of the night filled my room.

In the city I had moved to 68 Washington Square and Ida Rauh had joined me. She too was suffering from a love affair. Neither of us could settle down. My aching heart and my disgust with the law nearly brought despair. In October 1908 we decided to sail for Europe. D. G. P. returned a few days before our departure. He had had a slight operation and asked me to come to see him. Because he had suffered and I was leaving, those hours together were very lovely. There was less of passion and more of sympathy and understanding.

Though Ida and I were really running away, we had a wonderful trip. The days spent in Capri were especially interesting, though we had hardly arrived in Italy before another gastric attack seized me. We stayed at a hotel in Capri. Maxim Gorki and his wife had a house nearby, and when Marie Peshkoff heard of my illness she took matters into her own hands. Bundling me in a blanket, she had a man carry me to the Gorki villa. There I was nursed with the utmost tenderness. Goat's milk was prescribed. The doorway of my room opened onto a terrace, at which a boy arrived each morning with a goat, walked straight into my room, sat on the floor, and milked the goat.

There was always a crowd in their villa. People came from all over the world to see Gorki. Sometimes there would be people speaking different languages. Marie translated for Gorki; there was hardly a language she didn't know. One day at dinner Gorki and all his guests came trailing into my room and stood around my bed. They had been talking about America and wanted my opinion. Marie ran the Villa, presided at table, and typed all his articles. Also she had with her her half-grown children by her first marriage. In spite of this she often came and talked to me, or sat on my bed and did scenes from her greatest plays. It was like knowing Duse or Sarah Bernhardt.

D. G. P. was almost forgotten. Of course I told her about my love. Here was a woman who had given up all for the man she loved — her position in high society, her reputation, her work as an actress. Was she happy? For sixteen years she had lived with Gorki. Had the irregular relationship proved satisfactory? Then one night toward morning I heard running feet in the corridor. Something unusual was happening. Finally Zeni Peshkoff, Gorki's adopted son, came to my door. Yes, something very bad had occurred. Marie had nearly died. There had been a bottle of chloride she thought was her medicine and she had swallowed some of it. Only the doctor and a stomach pump had saved her. She was very weak, but would live. It was several days before I saw her. We would sit on the terrace in two chaise-longues. What had happened was treated as an accident. But was it? Or had Gorki become interested in another woman? This I never knew. However, years later at the end of the Russian Revolution I found them still living together in Moscow.

It was in February 1909 that I returned to America and had a great welcome from my father and mother. Their tender love never failed me.

My law office was reopened and there were a few small cases. Much of my time was spent in the Criminal Court. I discovered that the Judges were assigning to young lawyers the criminals who had no one to defend them. There was one case in particular which stirred me, that of a woman who had committed murder and was to be executed. While her baby was in her arms she had killed another woman with a hatchet. This seemed so unnatural that I wrote a letter to the *New York Times* protesting against the execution and pleading for the woman, saying:

Can you imagine a mother nursing a small baby deliberately taking an axe and hacking up a human being in cold blood unless she had a red twist in her brain? And because of this red twist we have decreed that Mrs. Farmer must die in the electric chair. As Carlyle would say: "Alas, was she not ... a hideous murderess fit to be the mother of hyenas?" But why? Because of those inherited ancestral twists and foiled potentialities.

I appeal to all the readers of the *New York Times* to act as my jury and decide whether the prisoner was guilty or not guilty. Mrs. Farmer murdered another woman in cold blood for her money. Still I say she was not guilty. She is not to blame for any insane twist.

This letter for some reason caused considerable controversy. There was editorial comment. In those days there were no psychopathic clinics; psychoanalysis had not come to the fore. Today undoubtedly she would be put in an insane asylum. Dr. Charles Parkhurst took the matter up editorially and also wrote me about his objections to my letter. He said, "I do not think we widely disagree. I recognize the great significance attaching both to heredity and environment, but I nevertheless believe that there remains a margin of autonomy which constitutes the ground of our personal and moral responsibility."

Toward the end of 1909 my courage deserted me entirely. Perpetual indigestion had become a torment. I knew I must straighten out my emotional conflict. My Dad offered me financial aid and I retired to a little rest house for Smith College girls in Northampton. I hadn't seen D. G. P. on his return from Europe that summer. It was no use.

My days in Northampton were spent reading Havelock Ellis' four volumes on sex and August Forel's *Sex and Psychology*. But the knowledge gained didn't help. I now understood my physical reactions, the kind of passionate nature I had, what lack of control meant. But my indigestion still went on. I might read that colitis came from emotional disturbance, but that did not cure it. It seemed that God in his great wisdom was teaching me the lesson that true love was selfless and meant control of self. Without that control love was only sex. Also my first lesson in humility was being learned: I was not "master of my fate." I could not change D.G.P. Nor could I change the law. My dream of being a great woman lawyer, a Portia, seemed a silly dream. I was afraid. Afraid I would never be able to earn my living. Afraid of my love for D.G.P.

It was while in Northampton that someone told me about Dr. Richard Cabot of Boston, who had established a social service at Massachusetts General Hospital.[8] He believed it was no use curing bodily ills unless a man's heart and mind were made well. A patient with no money, worried to death about his family, though his physical wound had healed, was still ill. Every human being needed work, play, love, and worship.

I got up out of bed and went to Boston. After my first interview with Dr. Cabot my health improved. He put me to work in the Massachusetts Hospital. I soon saw that forgetting myself and working for others wrought peace. With Dr. Cabot's assistance my balance and courage were restored. With returning health my one desire was to find the right kind of work. In three months I was back in New York.

One day, some months later I met D.G.P. in the street. He seemed very glad to see me. I found I could meet him now on a wholly new basis. I had learned it was possible to live without him. I was free and able to stand on my own feet. He sensed the change at once, and his attitude changed. He had feared my utter dependence on him; now he no longer did. He was as eager as ever for my success and now ready to meet my friends. No other man save my father ever has had such intense interest in my personal achievement. He really cared *about me*, not merely what he could get from me. His ideal for women was always high. He wanted them to be free, not subservient. To have to ask your husband for money to buy a hat was humiliating.

In March 1910 a real opportunity opened for valuable work: a Child's Welfare Exhibit was being planned. One portion of the exhibit was to deal with children's courts and delinquent children. That section was turned over to me. A comparative study showed that New York City was behind other cities in its care of delinquents. I made a trip to the West to gather facts.

I went to Niagara Falls, Buffalo, Indianapolis, Chicago, St. Louis, and Denver, everywhere studying what was being done for delinquent children. In Chicago I stayed at Hull House and was enormously impressed by Jane Addams' simplicity and goodness and what she had achieved for social betterment.[9] Chicago had far surpassed New York in its social work. It had a special children's court, a staff of probation officers, and was making an intensive study of mental defectives. New York City had achieved none of these things. In St. Louis the work was also excellent. Roger N. Baldwin was chief probation officer there. As I talked with him I little thought that this very attractive young man would one day become my husband. In Denver I met Judge Ben Lindsey of the Children's Court and made a new friend.[10]

In the Exhibit I prepared, New York was shown far down the list. Cases of juvenile delinquency were still heard in dingy, dirty magistrate's courts. When the Exhibit, held in a U.S. Armory, opened in New York, I was on hand from early morning to late at night to furnish information.

Because the Russell Sage Foundation became deeply interested in my exhibit, I asked them to form a Juvenile Court Committee to reform conditions in New York. They agreed, and a committee of four judges was set up, consisting of George Kirchwey, still Dean of Columbia University Law School, and several other prominent men, with me as executive secretary.

But one day [it was January 23, 1911] before D.G.P. had come to see the exhibit as he had promised, I noticed my Dad hurrying to me across the Armory floor. He held a paper in his hand. When he reached me he said, "Dear, there has been a terrible accident. Phillips has been badly hurt."

"Not dead?" I pleaded. "No, not dead, but there is little hope that he will live." Then he spread the paper out before me and there in glaring black letters running all across the page were the words: "DAVID GRAHAM PHILLIPS, THE WELL KNOWN WRITER, SHOT BY A CRAZY MAN. Attacked When Leaving the Princeton Club."

It just didn't seem possible that this was the end of a love story that had had no ending. I couldn't believe he had gone. I remember he once said to me, "You can do something about everything except death, and about that you can do nothing." He lingered only a day in Bellevue Hospital. His sister told me he was conscious to the end. His last words were, "Do something quick. I'm going. . ."

There was nothing I could do about his death. After the funeral I went to Sparta for the weekend, and one night I had a lovely dream. Or was it a dream? Anyway, I saw D. G. P. plainly, the clothes he wore, a brown suit, one I had never seen, and a soft hat. He smiled at me and said, "I'll be waiting for you," and then he vanished. That was all, but it was a great comfort.

Part III
Reform Lawyer, Columnist, Progressive Activist

Introduction to Chapters 4–6

*I*N CHAPTERS 4–6, which cover the years 1911–1914, Doty continues to combine the story of both her professional and personal life.

In these years she made a major professional contribution in the effort to reform the court system of New York State by exposing in the press conditions in the prisons and the need to consider the sociological and familial causes of juvenile delinquency and adult criminality and of recidivism. As early as July 1911 a long article by her about how to reform the system of handling juvenile delinquents appeared in a publication of the *Proceedings of the Academy of Political Science* (694–704). In the popular press numerous articles by others about her work, as well as supportive letters sent to her, indicate that her reports and service at this time were making a considerable difference. Chapter 4 includes her brief explanation of her role in establishing New York City's first juvenile court system, separate from adult criminal courts.

In chapters 5–6 Doty describes her dramatic and daring experience in the women's Auburn, N.Y., state prison in early November 1913. Her experience received much publicity, which was needed if she was to make a difference. Because her entire purpose was not for self-showmanship but was to expose the truth about conditions and provoke reform of treatment of adult prisoners, she wrote many, many articles on her findings for magazines and newspapers after her discharge, to the dismay of the state authorities. There followed some immediate improvement inside that prison, albeit temporary. Yet even at the beginning of the twenty-first century, debate still goes on, with considerable support for more money for more prisons, longer terms, death sentences, tough treatment, rather than on preventive intervention or work training or rehabilitation. Doty's experiences and study convinced her that harsh treatment only increases the prisoner's rage and sends him back into revengeful crime after release.

The publicity began immediately. On 15 November 1913, the New York *Sunday Post* featured her long article of some 40 column-inches starting on the front page. It ran under their headline "Cultured Women Voluntary Prisoners." By 26 November news of the event had reached England; her friend John Galsworthy asked her to send him and his wife more details, because of his same concerns.

As noted in her autobiography, *Century Magazine* in October 1914, carried her article "Maggie Martin 933," with introduction by state prison superintendent Riley, and the following April its sequel "Maggie Martin's Friends." Further attention was drawn to her reform work when the well-known feminist, social commentator Charlotte Perkins Gilman, wrote a "Comment and Review" about it in the *Forerunner* of November 1914.[1]

In each issue from March through August 1916, *Good Housekeeping* carried six articles by Doty about prisoners' lives, prison conditions, and needed reforms. And in that same year her full-length book, *Society's Misfits,* was published by the Century Company incorporating much of what had appeared in the papers and journals. The book opens with her own prison experience, much as related here in her autobiography, and concludes with a major section based on 1700 written case records which she had studied and 200 stories from her interviews with male prisoners in Auburn and Sing Sing in which she sought to learn from them about the familial and social factors in their childhood and in reformatories which could have led to their later criminal behavior. She wrote that she undertook these interviews and the study so that in her reporting and in Children's Court work she could know what to recommend.[2]

Thomas Mott Osborne, formerly warden of Sing Sing prison, wrote the Introduction to her book; in it he said that he could verify the male prisoners' stories therein "since I know most if not all the men whose stories Miss Doty has recorded." But by this date (August 1916) Osborne was disillusioned by the failure of the Prisoners' League at the Women's Prison and the fate of the reforms Doty had started. He called the curtailment of those reforms "a depressing tale," explaining it in these forthright words:

[It] is the story of a noble effort — the struggle of the women prisoners at Auburn . . . to participate in the wonderful movement which was transforming the men's prison from a hopeless sink of human failure to a great school of genuine reform. It is also the story of the failure of that effort, because of the hopeless, crass stupidity of the matrons in control at the prison, who had the chance of a lifetime to make themselves a power for good and were too indifferent and too ignorant to take advantage of it. . . . Without an intelligent head no prison can be run intelligently (viii).

But juvenile courts and prison reform are not all that preoccupied Doty in the years just prior to the First World War. She took up the cause of the vote for women. Among her papers is a newspaper photo of her as a leader carrying a banner in a New York City suffrage parade in 1912, marching with women lawyers. And when the war broke out in Europe she became deeply involved in the peace movement, joined the Woman's Peace Party of New York — founded in November 1914 by Crystal Eastman — and the next year became a part of the international peace movement, as described in chapter 7. Thereafter she devoted her career to the cause of peace.

Madeleine Doty (front row, far right) marching with lawyers in a
New York City suffrage parade, 1912
(Courtesy of Sophia Smith Collection, Smith College)

4

Court Work, Three Great Men, and a Love That Should
Never Have Been, 1911–1913

FTER D.G.P.'S DEATH I threw myself into the work of the Children's Court Committee of the Russell Sage Foundation. The prominent men who made up my committee, particularly Dean George Kirchwey of Columbia University Law School, were absorbed in the work, as I was. He and I lunched together day after day. He was a wonderful antidote to the wound in my heart. He was full of tenderness and admiration. Everything I did was perfect. I was the best comrade a man ever had; I was sweetness and light. Hungrily I lapped it up. I adopted as my own the whole Kirchwey family, a wife, two daughters, and a son.[1] I went with them to Lake Placid in the summer. I was utterly selfish in this relationship because I ignored the hurt I was inflicting on his wife Dora, though she knew I would not run off with her husband. He was twice my age. But the hours he might have spent with her he gave to me. I excused it on the basis of our work. Another man on the Committee, Judge Franklin C. Hoyt, also became a great friend. He had tried children's cases in the Municipal Court and was eager to become a special children's judge.

My days were now spent in the Municipal and Magistrate's courts, following the cases of delinquent children and tracing these cases back to the homes. This led to astonishing revelations.

Johnny had been arrested for throwing stones and breaking a window. The judge devoted three minutes to the case. His opinion was, "Boys will be boys." He gave Johnny a good scolding and dismissed him. This seemed a wise decision, but my investigation showed that Johnny's mother had been arrested three times for drunkenness, his brother had been arrested six times for truancy, petty larceny, and attempted burglary. Johnny himself, who was 15, had previous records against him. His home and his gang were a breeding center of crime. He was costing the city a lot of money. The three minutes allotted to his case were a farce.

82

Then there was the case of Jimmy. He stole a bucket of coal because his mother and baby sister were freezing. He was hauled into court. The Judge knew only that he was a thief and that was a serious offense. Jimmy was sent to reform school. His baby sister died and his mother went to the poor house. The reform school didn't reform Jimmy. It made him a menace; his heart was turned to stone.

The Municipal Court judges had no way of knowing the background from which the children came. Yet case after case showed how important this knowledge was. Fifty percent of the cases studied revealed that the child came from a broken home. The broken home, no place to play but the street, getting in with a gang, truancy, these were the causes of juvenile delinquency.

My reports to the Committee were printed in the newspapers and aroused the public. The city fathers began to be worried over the publicity. The Mayor's representatives came to the Russell Sage Foundation ready to make amends. They offered a large appropriation to buy a piece of land on East 23rd Street, condemn and tear down the old buildings, and build a children's court. Five judges were to be assigned to deal with delinquent children. Franklin Hoyt was appointed the Chief Justice. Nor was this all: the appropriation was large enough to pay the salaries of 60 probation officers, who were to investigate all cases and report these findings. It was astonishing how much we had accomplished in the space of three years — largely because the officials were ashamed of the disclosures.

But having made amends, they now demanded that there should be no more damaging evidence, that further researches and reports stop. Consequently, the Director in charge of the Children's Court Committee came to me and said I had earned my salary and could sit and twirl my thumbs for the next six months. Indignantly I refused. Children's reformatories badly needed investigation. I meant to go on with the work with or without the Russell Sage Foundation. With a heroic gesture I gave up a well paid job. It was a silly way to end interesting work but I had a strong belief that it was the work not money that counted. This conviction remained with me to the end of life; as long as there was enough for necessities, money was never a temptation.

Three Great Men

It was during the three-year period with the Russell Sage Foundation that three great men came into my life. One was a well known novelist, another a surgeon, and the third a famous ex-president. The novelist was John Galsworthy. When he came to the U.S. in the spring of 1912, I sent him a little note saying his play "Justice" had inspired me to try the case of Murphy against the American Ice Company on the basis of justice. Back came a note inviting me to lunch with him and his wife. He was a fascinating person, very handsome and very friendly. They were eager to hear all about the new courts. One evening we visited the Night Court, where women prostitutes were tried, and on another occasion a Magistrate's Court. The Galsworthys hadn't been married long and they were very much in love. As we drove to the Woman's Night Court they confided to me their story. She had been the wife of a brute and drunkard who made her life intolerable but refused her a divorce. Galsworthy persuaded her that she must run away with him; only then could she get a divorce. This she had done and now they were married. Many of Galsworthy's books deal with the theme of the ill-treated wife. While the Galsworthys were in the city there was a big suffragette parade. I marched with the women lawyers who proudly bore a banner which read, "Law is for man — not man for the Law." The Galsworthys stood on the sidewalk and waved. [Editor's note: The Galsworthys and she remained close friends. She was frequently a guest at their home in Devon or their seaside place in Sussex during her various trips to Europe, according to the many letters she saved from each of them dating from 1912–1918.]

The famous ex-president whom I came to know was Theodore Roosevelt. He had returned to the U.S. after hunting lions in South Africa. William Taft was then President. Because Teddy Roosevelt was thoroughly dissatisfied with the Taft administration, he entered the 1912 campaign and tried to capture the Republican nomination, but failed. So his advisers persuaded him to run on an independent ticket. The Bull Moose or Progressive Party was formed, splitting the Republican party. One of Roosevelt's promises, if he were elected, was to stand for woman's suffrage. This won a big group of women to his side, me among them. Because of my work for delinquent children and the campaign for a Children's Court I was invited to be on the Roosevelt Campaign Committee. I was to be responsible for the planks in the platform dealing with women and children. This brought me in personal contact with Roosevelt. [Among her papers are three letters from T.R. in the month of January 1912 asking for information to use in his campaign. In one, dated 16 January addressed to Doty at the Charity Organization Society, 105 East 22nd Street, and sent from his office at the *Outlook*, where he was a contributing editor, he tells Doty, "I am now using the material you sent me." And on the 23rd, he wrote asking her for more facts about the Children's Courts. On 6 December 1912, a letter from his secretary said T.R. wanted Doty to come to lunch.]

One day, during this campaign, there was an attempt on his life. The bullet fired passed in at his neck and upward. But it touched no vital organ. He was in the hospital for some days. I too was in another hospital after an operation for appendicitis. With all the arrogance of youth I wrote him a letter advising him to have the bullet removed. His reply sounds as though we had been mixed up in the shooting affair together. In part it read:

November 27th, 1912

Miss Madeleine Z. Doty
N.E. Baptist Hospital
Boston, Mass.

My dear Miss Doty:

I will send your letter to Dr. Alexander Lambert, but it does not seem to me wise to take out the bullet if the physician thinks it unnecessary. . . . Of course I knew that you were to take charge of the Legislative Bureau for Women and Children. . . . I am very sorry that you are in the hospital. Just as soon as you come out, will you let me know and I will get you to come to lunch somewhere.

Faithfully yours,
Theodore Roosevelt

Soon afterward we did have lunch together, in fact several times. I have never met anyone with such vitality. You couldn't help liking him, though you might disagree violently. He was wholly inconsistent. He had been converted to woman suffrage, but that hadn't changed his ideas about women. The place for woman was in the home.

One day the Campaign Committee journeyed with him to Newport. He was to speak at a big meeting there. We traveled by boat and I was sitting on the top deck with him. He began scolding me, saying I ought to get married and have a dozen children. He knew just the man for me: Gifford Pinchot.[2] Poor Gifford! He was on the boat that day and little knew Roosevelt's plans for his future.

My third great man, the surgeon, I met also in 1912. My work at the Russell Sage Foundation had been broken into for three weeks by an operation for appendicitis. Richard Cabot had come to New York to see me and advised it. The operation was undertaken by a well known surgeon in Boston whom he recommended. I didn't like the idea of taking an anesthetic and being made unconscious. I wanted to be sure nothing but the appendix was taken out. So Richard Cabot held my hand while the surgeon operated. I was still a spoiled child, demanding attention even of a Cabot of whom it is said, "The Lodges talk only to the Cabots, and the Cabots talk only to God."

The night before the operation was spent reading the "Life and Death of Socrates." If Socrates could die calmly drinking a cup of poison, surely I could face with equal calm an operation. My surgeon was much amused. But alas for my pride, it seems that as I came out from under the ether I was declaring, "I don't want to be a free, economic independent agent. I want to be loved."

Of course my surgeon was intrigued, and that was the beginning of something that should never have been. He was soon making long daily visits to the hospital. He had never met anyone like me, for his patients were the upper society set. My ideas as a suffragette, a woman lawyer, and a wild young radical were wholly new to him. We had endless discussions.

After my recovery I went back to my work for the Children's Court Committee. But every month or so my new friend came to see me. It was the attraction of opposites. No one could have been more unlike D. G. P. This man was essentially a *he* man. He believed in the protection of women. He wanted to dominate and care for those he loved. And I discovered that, like many women, there was within me a secret desire for domination. I was now a mature woman and knew what was happening; D. G. P. had freed me from my Victorian notions. I justified myself with the belief that all real love is pure, that body and spirit are one, that if I asked nothing for myself I had a right to love whom I chose.

And it was fascinating to see this man change as our friendship grew. He ceased to be just a surgeon and began to speak and work for causes. He took up the fight for a woman's right to her own person, testifying on behalf of a patient of his whose husband had forced her to live with him; she had bolted her door, and the husband had taken the case to court. One day we went on a long drive into the country to see her.

I didn't see much of this surgeon because he couldn't get away from his work. But inevitably the affair came to a climax. He was as strong for honesty as I was. We agreed his wife must be told of our love. I suggested he invite me to his house for a visit. And it was arranged. Of course it was absurd and ridiculous. The first evening after dinner the wife came to me weeping: "He is giving you all the things he never gave me. He tells you everything. I'm nothing but a housekeeper and mistress." It was useless to tell her I didn't want to take him from her and the children, I only wanted a little of his love. It was foolish to expect her to share him with me. We got nowhere during my ten-day visit.

Doty ca. 1910–1914
(Courtesy of Sophia Smith Collection, Smith College)

When I left I asked his wife to return to New York with me, where I found her a volunteer job in a settlement house. I tried to make her see that if she became self-reliant and interesting he would respond.

But nothing was accomplished. On her return home she wept bitterly. She began to talk to her neighbors. This would never do. His whole career would be ruined. The only solution was separation. His letters to me were very beautiful; most have since been destroyed. In them he put me on a pedestal. I was "pure gold." He said he had never known a woman before who, if she loved, was willing to give everything and ask nothing in return. Unlike D. G. P., he felt the woman gave more than the man. He blamed himself for our attachment. But I was quite as much to blame as he was, if not more, for I had let my feeling run away with me. It was now more than two years since D. G. P.'s death. I had lost him and I didn't want to lose this love also.

But we both soon saw our love was impossible. Deceit and scandal would be the outcome. In a final little note which I kept, he wrote, "Without what you have given me I should not be what I am today, without what you can give me I shall achieve less than I might — yet the relation has reached a point highly dangerous to the integrity of both of us. I have done you more harm than good. The thing has been beautiful and uplifting; how can we keep it so? God bless you."

Naturally there were weeks of deep anguish for me. But thanks to Richard Cabot I had learned to stand on my own feet and I knew work for others was a sovereign remedy. I only saw that other surgeon once after that, three or four years later.

I put aside all personal life and plunged into the task of investigating reformatories and prisons. One of the first was Sing Sing.

[Excerpts from] The Story of Happy Jack

"Happy Jack" was the man who awakened my interest in prison reform. As an attorney I had free access to all prisons. It was a warm spring day when I made the first visit to Sing Sing. As I entered the doorway of the gray, grim building a prisoner passed me between two sturdy guards . . . . One of the guards spoke to him, and he smiled, a radiant, Irish smile that made the blue eyes sparkle and had won for him the name of Happy Jack. In that first glance I felt that the man, whatever he had done, was worth saving.

He disappeared into the Warden's Office and I immediately made inquiries about him. He was behind bars on a charge of murder. His execution was to have taken place a few days earlier, but at the last moment he had obtained a reprieve on the ground of newly discovered evidence. . . .

The only evidence against him was a signed confession, wrung from him after three sleepless days and nights when he had been bullied and badgered under a glaring electric light and under the influence, so he claimed, of drugs. . . .He had, however a bad prison record. He had been in and out of reformatories most of his 31 years. There had been a stay of execution because Jack claimed he had an alibi. . . .

The retrial was being held in the Warden's office and I secured permission to attend the proceedings. The District Attorney and a criminal court judge had come up from New York City to rehear the case. They were the same men who had heard the original case, and they wanted their judgement of "guilt" vindicated.

At a long table sat Happy Jack and beside him an officer with a thick, wooden club watching his every movement. . . .

The judge leaned across to me to whisper: "The man is a typical criminal. I want you to watch him."

Suddenly the significance of the scene burst upon me. Here was a human being fighting for his life, appealing to a legal-minded, noncomprehending body of men who, without compassion, analyzed and judged him. The prosecuting attorney did his work, coldly and cleverly twisting and weighing every word the prisoner uttered. The perspiration stood out on Happy Jack's brow. . . . "Why didn't you tell that story to your attorney at the first trial?" inquired the judge. "Because," replied the prisoner, smiling brightly, "I didn't trust him. I was sore. A pal of mine said you had given me my attorney to frame me, that you thought me guilty". . . . Such honesty under such handicap was astounding. . . .

For several days the trial dragged on. From the first it was almost a foregone conclusion that Jack would be reconvicted. The prosecuting attorney was relentless. Only twice in his career had he lost a case and he did not mean to lose this one.

So this perfectly sound, legal proceeding continued to pile up fact upon fact until the verdict was "guilty." The execution was set for three weeks hence. As the prisoner was led back to his cell I asked to speak to him: "Would you like me as an attorney to see if there isn't still something to be done?" Thus I became Jack's lawyer for the three memorable weeks that followed. My whole time was given to Happy Jack's case.

His cell was in the death house — a long corridor-like room with cells on either side and at the end of the corridor a small door that led to the death chamber. I secured a court order to visit Jack, and the guard would place a chair in front of his cell so I could talk to him through the bars. He sat on the edge of his cot, grasping the iron bars and gazing at me.

But little by little he told me his story. A child of the slums, living from hand to mouth, getting a kick or a punch from all sides, and hating everyone. Often he went hungry to bed; often he had no shoes. His parents were too poor to bother with him. . . . When he was ten years old, Jack stole a pigeon. He stayed away from school to take care of it. He was convicted as a truant and thief and sent to a reformatory. From then on it was a series of crimes, reformatories, and prisons. Each time he was locked up he learned more and more of evil. . . .

I told Jack why I had come to Sing Sing that first day he saw me. It was because of my distress at conditions in reformatories. I thought perhaps the convicts who had been through children's institutions could help me with their stories, and we could campaign for better conditions. This interested Jack greatly. He wanted to help in this work. His chief advice was, "Don't put innocent kids with the bad ones for it's like putting good apples in a barrel of rotten ones."

Meanwhile, I did everything in my power to get Jack's sentence changed from death to life imprisonment. I went to the Governor of the state, but all in vain. . . . Then I tried the newspapers. Perhaps public opinion could be roused. But I was told politely that my story was not news. The day Jack was executed they would print anything I cared to write. Never had I felt so helpless. A human life was at stake and I couldn't make a ripple on the placid surface of affairs.

Finally came the day for my last visit to Jack. He said I mustn't be unhappy. He knew I'd done my best. He promised to write down all he had told me about his life. I promised to write a letter to the papers, which would be printed with the story of his execution, telling of my belief in him, that he was not a coward and could not have committed a cowardly murder. The last time I saw him he was pressed against the bars of the cell. We talked for several hours and it was time to leave. "Goodbye," he said, and his hand shot out between the cold bars and grasped mine. I held his hand a minute as I whispered, "Courage — die bravely and we'll prove the judge was wrong". . . . Again he smiled as I turned and left the death house with sinking heart.

The next day I left the state. I couldn't bear to remain there. But before leaving I sent to all the leading newspapers a copy of the letter I had written to be printed with the story of Jack's execution.

On Monday, May 19th, within an hour after he had finished writing me a letter, the end came. In the New York *Evening Journal* appeared the following headline: "HAPPY JACK DIES IN CHAIR WITH A SMILE – WOMAN DEFENDS HIM. May 19. Happy Jack convicted of the murder of Pady B., a saloon-keeper, went cheerily to death in the electric chair today. . . . He began his last, short trip down the hall just eleven minutes before six o'clock. . . . At 5:50 he was strapped in the chair. The current was switched on at 5:50 and left for one minute. . . . Even then Jack was wearing a smile. He had come into the room smiling and his last words as he sat in the death-chair were: 'Tell them I'm not afraid.'"

A few days later a letter was sent me. It was the letter Jack Mulraney had written the night before his execution. A few extracts from the letter follow:

Dear Friend,

Only a few hours more and they come for me. Dying isn't hard — it's the waitin' — waitin' and thinkin'. . . . For 15 months I've been locked in this cell waitin and thinkin. It nearly drives a man crazy. There's 15 of us in the death house. . . . If you or someone like you had gotten me when I was a kid I wouldn't be here now. I didn't believe there was a good man in the world but now I'd make any sacrifice for you. You are doing God's work and my only regret is I can't help. . . .

As for a man's who's a convict getting justice it ain't possible. It is easy to believe the judge didn't like me when the first remark he passed was: 'You've a bad face. You look like a criminal. The world would be better off without you.' That made me hot under the collar and I wouldn't talk at my first trial. . . .

Again I thank you for what you done. Good-by and may God bless you always.

Yours in gratitude
(signed) Jack.

It is good to think that Happy Jack Mulraney's life was not lived in vain. His story stirred the public and particularly all the members of my Children's Court Committee, especially my friend George Kirchwey. He wrote me: "It has been a good as well as a brave fight. Don't let yourself believe for a moment that it wasn't worthwhile. . . . It is only the first skirmish in a campaign. We will go on . . . and fight until we have wiped out the whole atrocious system." And later he wrote: "It certainly looks as though we will accomplish something. The plan will be put up to Governor Sulzer tomorrow by Mr. Morgenthau and Thomas Mott Osborne, the two men who have the most influence with him." The plan that was proposed was a New York Prison Reform Commission consisting of 12 members, 10 men and 2 women, to be appointed by the Governor of N.Y. State. (Osborne was named chairman.)

So it was that (as of July 7, 1913) I suddenly found myself a N.Y. State Prison commissioner, without a salary but with full liberty to investigate all prisons and reformatories. God had been good to me and I didn't have to sit and twirl my thumbs for six months.

Within two years a change has taken place in the prison — a change beyond belief. Jack's life was not lived in vain. . . . The work that Mr. Osborne has since done, his appointment as warden of Sing Sing, the establishment of the Mutual Welfare League and self-government within the prison are a tale famous from coast to coast. And through Osborne it was possible for me to get from the men in Sing Sing and Auburn prisons the stories of their boyhood in reformatories, stories that have stirred women's hearts and brought ready help from every state in the Union.

5
Maggie Martin #933, 1913

$\mathcal{S}$ HORTLY AFTER THE ORGANIZATION of the New York Prison Reform Commission in 1913, Mr. Osborne, its chairman, spent a week in Auburn Prison to get at the heart of the problem. He believed this the most effective way to make an investigation. He was dressed like a convict, lived like a convict, but everyone knew he was Tom Osborne.

It seemed to me that even this was not enough. To really know the prisoners' needs and thoughts it was necessary to go behind the bars as a real convict. I asked to be allowed to make the experiment. It was arranged by the N.Y. State Superintendent of Prisons that I and a friend of mine, Elizabeth Watson, be sent to the State Prison for Women in Auburn as convicts caught in the act of forging a check. No one was to know of our identity; we were to be Maggie Martin and Lizzie Watson, forgers.[1]

Those days in jail throbbed with big moments. Never have I felt so bound to any group of women. They taught me things I could never have learned in any other way. Cut off from life, made an outcast, one feels one's common identity with all the other prisoners. In everyday life we hesitate to relinquish even a small comfort for a friend, but in prison often no sacrifice is too great. Even punishment in the "cooler" (solitary confinement) was gladly accepted as the price to be paid for a chance to do a kind deed. I found this spirit in so-called hardened offenders extraordinary.

In what follows I have described prison life as I found it in the year 1913. I hoped by my experience to shed light on our whole system of punishment. Today prison conditions have been vastly improved, but I fear the main object is still punishment rather than reform.

On Monday, November 3, 1913, I awoke with beating heart. This was the day. I knew the prison superintendent and the members of the Commission questioned my strength. They said some of the convicts were colored women of hard and vicious character, occasionally violent, and I must be careful. It was the hardened criminals who were sent to the state prison at Auburn. I was glad Elizabeth was to share my fate.

We spent the last night in the home of Thomas Mott Osborne, enjoying every luxury before appearing at the station near the prison.

We had arranged to enter prison early the following evening. A policeman was to be at the station when the New York train arrived, conduct us to the prison gate, and hand us in as convicts just up from the City. In this way we would hide our identity. With care we had concocted a criminal past for Lizzie and Maggie, forgers, caught in the same deal and sent up for from one to two years.

After a gay little dinner party that evening, we drove to the Auburn station. Soon the sound of the whistle announced the train, and we stepped out bravely across the platform to the waiting policeman. As we passed out of the station and up the street, suddenly fear descended upon me. I was glad it was dark and that few people passed. There was a feeling of disgrace in this walk by a policeman's side past the high, forbidding, gray wall. I wondered if Elizabeth also was beginning to wish she had never come. Then we reached the iron gate, and it opened and clanked behind us. In that instant the big outer world had vanished.

Pride said I must go on, but I was afraid. What lay inside that silent building? Up the path with reluctant steps I went. Why had I been such a fool? Surely my knowledge of prisons did not need this experiment to convince me of the evil of the system. But my sensations belied the thought, for no written word had ever made me realize how great may be the dread of what lies behind those gray stones and barred windows.

But we had reached the front door, it was opened, and we were thrust inside. I longed to clutch Elizabeth, but two matrons in blue uniform and white aprons stood guard. These women gave no greeting and made no inquiry. We might have been four-legged animals or express packages for ought their expression showed. Without comment we were led through twisting passages and doors. Then began that persistent sound of prison — the locking and unlocking of doors, the jangling keys, which forever break the silence and beat in on one: "You're locked in, you can't get out."

We passed down a long corridor along which were the barred doorways of twenty cells. There was light in the corridor, but none in the cells, and I wondered how many breathing, restless creatures were gazing out. At the end of the corridor in a small room was a bath tub. Here our procession halted. Then more jangling of keys, and a little colored convict was released to help with the task ahead.

In utter silence the ceremony proceeded. A sheet was spread for each of us, and on it we stood, taking off our garments one by one. The solemnity was as great as an initiation into some fraternity. I had an insane desire to giggle, but the curious and hard eyes of the matron were upon me. I had forgotten before entering to remove my watch and gold cuff-links, and my long brown ulster had just come from London. Surely these things would be noticed. Only a few hours before I had bathed and put on fresh underwear. But this also roused no comment. Evidently convicts on entering must often be clean and well-dressed.

Then came the bath, taken in public, with the aid of the little colored convict. Under direction, she scrubbed and scrubbed. We were told to keep hands off. A convict means dirt, physical, mental, and moral, and is treated accordingly. That this may not be true matters not. Every convict is supposed to be covered with vermin. I saw Elizabeth's head being ducked into the same water in which she was bathed. With shrinking, I begged to be let off, pleading a headache. To my surprise, the request was granted. But the next instant I was told to bend my head, and the contents of a dark green bottle were poured on my hair and rubbed in. The penetrating and biting odor of kerosene pervaded everything. Two days before my hair had been washed and waved, and was soft and sweet smelling. But I was a convict and all convicts were dirty.

Only one small towel the size of a table napkin was given to dry both head and body. A coarse, white cotton nightgown, clean but old, bearing the name of the last wearer, was handed out. Clad in this and barefooted, I was led to a cell and locked in. A few minutes later I heard the reassuring sound of the door in the next cell being closed and locked, and I knew that for the night at least Elizabeth was my neighbor. I rapped on the wall to make sure, and immediately there came a satisfying answer. I examined my bed. The mattress was covered with stains, but the sheets were clean, though coarse. I crawled into them. At first I did not notice the steely hardness of the bed. I was too occupied with my straw pillow. But the mattress rested on iron slats, and as the night advanced I began to trace the exact location of each.

My light had been switched off, but through the bars the light from the corridor filtered in. Whenever I opened my eyes that barred door obtruded itself. It glared down upon me, it seemed to run up against me, it haunted me, it forever reiterated the fact, "You are shut in a cage." The little iron bed, the wooden stand in the corner, with its basin and cup of water, the three-legged stool, the yellow walls, the painted window — all were lost sight of in the presence of the barred door. That barred door and that only, together with the endless jangling of keys, became the center of my existence. Drawn by a weird fascination, I crept out of bed and to the door, and, grasping the cold iron, shook it. But all was secure. Then I pressed my face against the bars and listened breathlessly. I could hear the breathing of other prisoners and occasionally a moan. What were they feeling? Already I knew the worst feature of the prison system — the brutal officialdom and indifference that treated human beings as though they were cogs in a machine. Then I heard footsteps, more jangling of keys. The night matron was making her hourly rounds, and I scurried back to bed. Down the corridor she came, pausing at doors to shake them and jangle those keys.

All night I tossed and turned on my pillow. The kerosene from my hair had made it sticky and vile. I choked with the odor and, seizing my towel, vainly tried to rub it off, but it permeated everything.

Morning came at last. A dirty, yellow light struggled through the painted window. The little girl who had assisted the night before was moving busily about, helping the matron. Food had arrived and she was distributing it. Slices of bread were left between the bars to be plucked off by the inmates. Then later the cell door was unlocked and a mug of coffee and a bowl of stew were handed in, all in absolute silence. The coffee was only dishwater, the stew chiefly a thick, flour paste. I remembered yesterday's breakfast and contented myself with the bread. After feeding time the dishes were collected, and the little convict took them to the sink at the end of the corridor. I envied her her task, as I am sure every inmate did, just to be out beyond the barred door doing something, anything.

The minutes dragged on. I had no clothes so I lay still. After what seemed hours, the matron returned, this time accompanied by a convict laden with clothes. I was ordered to take off my nightgown and stand naked. Underwear many sizes too large was given to me, a heavy coarse petticoat of bedticking, also much too large, and finally the thick, white canvas dress, frayed and gray from washing. The dress was all in one piece, buttoning tightly down the front. The sleeves were much too short, the collar too loose. Anything more unbecoming and degrading would be hard to imagine. Across the front of the dress was sewn a number, and on the sleeve one or more colored stripes to indicate the number of prison terms served. One had ceased to be a human being. A pair of speckled, knit stockings and heavy, round-toed shoes completed my outfit. I knew there was no good protesting, but I wanted to speak out. Prison has a curious way of dragging to the surface all the profanity one has ever heard. Nothing else seems to express one's hate and indignation.

I could hear Elizabeth in the adjoining cell getting dressed. I heard the matron's voice say, "Eh, there, git spry, git spry. Where do you think you are?" We were both unmercifully hurried, for we were wanted in the office. As we left our cells I glanced at Elizabeth. There had been no mirror to view myself, so I was not prepared for the transformation. With hair slicked back, prison shoes sticking out from a dress much too short, she was a ludicrous object, and I snickered. Laughter in prison is a sin.

The matron turned on me fiercely. "Be still! Don't you know where you are? If ye hain't ever been in prison before, you're in one now." I pulled myself together. The gloom and horror of the night vanished in the light of the enormous comedy being enacted. But I did not wish to be sent to the punishment cell, so with supreme effort controlled myself.

We waited a long time in a hallway before being called. We sat patiently side by side. We didn't dare to whisper, for our matron stood guard like a dragon, and when Elizabeth's eyes once sought the floor to gaze at a cat, she stormed, "Stop looking at that cat! Look at the wall!"

Did the system of nagging never end? Was the prison system planned with the view of filling the heart with rage and hate?

In the office our names, addresses, names of relatives, criminal career, etc., were taken down in businesslike manner. Then we were returned to our cells. In my ten-by-six-foot room I found dinner piled on my stool, though it was only shortly after eleven A.M., for today was election day and a holiday for the matrons. Holidays are days of torture for prisoners. On these occasions and on Sundays the convict is locked in his cell all day as well as all night. Who would be elected mayor seemed unimportant to me — only one thing mattered, those gray prison walls.

The dinner provided was a mass of coarse cabbage. Hidden under it was a piece of corned beef. It was too revolting to touch. The boiled potato was soggy and cold. In a bowl was a quantity of apple butter, but this was sour. Bread was again my meal. When the dinner things were being removed, we were told to keep a supply of bread, because no supper would be served.

We had no plates, so I placed my three slices of bread on my stool and sat on my bed or paced my floor again. There was not even a Bible to read. There was nothing to see. Often I pressed my face against the bars of my cell and listened intently. Two or three times there was the sound of a baby cooing. The mother occupied a cell down the corridor; I had seen her feeding her child as we passed. Born in prison! What a fate for a struggling little human soul!

Once there were groans, then a voice: "I've got the devil in me. I can't stand this. If they don't let me out soon, I'll smash things." Another voice urged courage and said tomorrow we would be let out to get the air and walk in the yard. A third voice asked, "Did you see the new girls?" One of the previous voices replied, "Yes, I seen them when they came. They had good clothes." At this moment our dragon came tiptoeing in and the whisperers were caught. Lucky I hadn't entered into the conversation, for later I learned the penalty inflicted was three days of close confinement in the cooler on a diet of one slice of bread and one gill of water three times a day, in addition a fine of fifty cents for each day

Identification card of Maggie Martin

Madeleine Doty as Maggie Martin, jailbird in Auburn, N.Y.
(Courtesy of Sophia Smith Collection, Smith College)

of punishment, and days added to the term of imprisonment. After this excitement there was no sound. The minutes dragged on. There was no way of knowing whether it was two or six. All sense of time was lost. I had been told prisoners were violent and used obscene language. Thus far they seemed creatures but half alive, enclosed in a living tomb.

Occasionally I rapped on the wall, but the response was feeble, and this bothered me. Presently there was the sound of someone violently sick. It was horrible to be unable to give assistance. No one could give any help. No one stirred, and no one dared speak. Later, when the matron made her rounds, she paid no heed to the sufferer. It was Elizabeth who had been ill. She went uncared for. Her slop jar was not emptied until the following morning. Jars used as toilets were emptied only once a day, and the small hand-basin was filled with fresh water only once in twenty-four hours. I had already washed twice in my basin, and the water was sticky with kerosene. I did not make another attempt; I no longer cared whether I was clean or not. At supper time basin and cup were filled with water, that precious cup of water received but once a day. Half must go for supper and half for the night; my teeth must go unbrushed.

When twilight came at last, I undressed and went to bed. The heavy blankets were made of shoddy, and gave little warmth. I shivered with cold. Once when the night matron made her rounds I asked for another cover. She met my request with annoyance, "You should have asked the day matron." Through this incident I learned the lesson all convicts soon learn: it is wisest to suffer in silence, for only suicide and severe illness compel attention.

So I lay and shivered, horribly uncomfortable, dirty, hungry, and thirsty, and my bed grew hourly harder. The day had been bad enough, but the night was worse. All the evil in me rose to the surface. I wanted to grasp my bars and shake them and yell. It came to me that it would be easy to join in a smashing orgy. Rebellious thoughts surged in my mind. What right had man to abuse his fellow man even though he had sinned? What right to degrade him, to step on him, to ignore him? What right to nag and browbeat until he can no longer keep silent, till self-respect flares up?

What wonder if prisoners are occasionally violent! It would be unnatural if they did not grow to hate all mankind and come out of bondage bent on revenge. My heart ached with pity. One thing at least had been accomplished: I had become a convict. I was one with them in spirit.

At last daylight came. The end of the week seemed years off. Could I stick it out? Just as I was about to get up, the matron appeared. I had no idea of the hour. "Why ain't ye up?" she demanded. "Ye should be dressed when I come. And what business had ye to ask for a blanket? I'll teach ye. Now hurry, make your bed, sweep your floor, and be ready to empty your jar when I git back." Cowed and obedient, I hastily obeyed. Active rebellion is rare among convicts. There is one consuming desire — to make good and get out. The hunger for freedom, the torture of bars, and the dread of punishment are so great that only the bravest souls refrain from lying, hypocrisy, the betrayal of others, and the surrender of self-respect in order to win favor and shorten the term of imprisonment.

My tasks despatched, I stood humbly at my door. When the matron arrived, she merely said to come. No instructions were given. Bucket in hand, I followed, meekly emptying my jar under her watchful eye. It was evident she awaited some blunder in order to reprimand me. Like a real prisoner, fear entered my soul. Patiently I listened to a flood of abuse, finished my task, and returned to my cell.

But this day was to prove eventful, for we were to be Bertilloned and then examined by the doctor, processes all newcomers go through. To be Bertilloned is to have your photograph taken, your hands, arms, and feet measured, examined for marks for identification, and a general description of your personal appearance made. This is then inserted in a volume for the rogue's gallery, and you have become a known criminal, easily identified by the police. We sat in a row of convicts, one in front of the other, back to face, that we might not look at or speak to each other. But when the matron took one of our number to the adjoining room, I faced about and made mental notes. Elizabeth was back of me, and near her a dark haired girl whom I shall never forget. Her face was tragic, her chin quivered, great tears rolled down her cheeks. Her manner was gentle, yet she was vitally alive. But there was no opportunity for conversation.

We were ordered to take down our hair and take off our shoes and stockings. I noticed the dark haired girl's delicate foot. It became startlingly clear that there is no criminal type, no criminal manner. However, the man who made the Bertillon records was not of this opinion, for, as Elizabeth told me afterward, when he finished with her and looked her all over, he remarked in a low voice to his companion, "All the stigmata of criminality."

The difference between the criminal and the average man, if there is one, is often only that of an unusual type, namely, someone possessing greater originality than the average, gone wrong through misdirected power.

From the Bertillon room we went back to our cells to await dinner. That over, we put on our Sunday dress preparatory to a visit to the doctor. This costume consisted of a shirt-waist and skirt of khaki-colored, cotton drill fabric. So arrayed, my head went up. Again we had an interminable wait. Presently a young matron, trim, pleasing, and efficient, approached. She and the dragon exchanged tribulations, and the story of my audacious demand for another blanket was related. As the tale progressed, the pleasing qualities of the young matron vanished. She became a hard, cold, vindictive bully. She turned upon me with fury and denounced me in angry tones, warning me to remember I was a prisoner and entitled to no *luxuries*.

I wondered whether the doctor knew who I was. I hoped so; otherwise it might be embarrassing. But immediately I saw he knew nothing. I was merely a convict. After examining my heart and lungs he turned to my history. He was kindly, the only official who had treated the make-believe Maggie Martin as a human being. It was difficult for me to make up a past on the spur of the moment. I stuck to the literal truth where I could.

It was now the middle of the afternoon, and instead of returning to our cells we were led to chapel. Once a week, as a great privilege, singing is permitted for an hour. My hopes rose that now I could see my fellow prisoners. But we were placed in the last row, and only the backs of the hundred and twenty women were visible.

I turned to observe my companions in the chapel. I did not dare let my eyes wander far, for already I had had a warning look from an officer. But I saw with some surprise that many of the prisoners were good-looking, intelligent-looking women. Then my eye strayed to the song book, where Elizabeth's finger pointed to the words we were singing: "Columbia, the gem of ocean. The home of the brave and the *free*."

At the close of the exercises we were told we were to move to another ward. Our cells had been in the reception ward, where the sole object in this prison was apparently to break and subdue the new prisoners by isolation and no work to do. After my forty hours of such confinement I shuddered to think of the days, weeks, and sometimes months endured by the average prisoner. Such treatment in the case of a nervous, hysterical woman, eating her heart out with anxiety over some family problem, easily causes temporary insanity. Our early release from isolation had been *arranged* in order that we might have the experience of another ward and the workshop. I was the type who ordinarily would have been kept long in isolation: I held my head too high, and my smiles showed a freedom of spirit not to be tolerated. Elizabeth, with her tears and sadness, was being less rudely handled.

I was quickly transferred to another part of the building through a broad corridor off which opened the cells and at the end of which were great windows that, though partially painted, let in a flood of light. In the recess below them were two, long wood tables. This space served as a dining room for the twenty-seven women in the ward. At the extreme end of the ward, leading off on the right and left, were two ells. Down the one to the left I was led. Five cells opened onto a narrow hallway, and into one of them I was thrust.

My new quarters were precisely like the old. But I soon discovered that the new cell was more depressing, for the outlook from my door was cut off by a gray plaster wall just across the three-foot hall space. Moreover, at the entrance to this ell was a large wood door many inches thick, which, when closed, shut off this wing from the main corridor. I fervently prayed it never would be.

I had been brought here without Elizabeth; I hoped against hope she would follow soon. Standing at my door, I heard sounds in a nearby cell. Pressed close against the bars, I whispered hello. In a moment back came a whispered answer: "I don't dast talk; I'm just up from punishment." But my curiosity was great and my loneliness greater, so I persisted: "What were you punished for?" There was a little chuckle, a negro's chuckle. Then came the reply: "Well, child, I sassed the matron. I was all right until I was bad. I don't know why I done it. I just couldn't help it, and I up and called the matron a _____."

My new friend's statement filled me with joy. All lady-like instincts had left me. Presently I ventured again: "How were you punished?" Softly came the answer: "Put in the cooler." "But what is the cooler?" "A dark cell in the basement where you only gits bread and water. I was there five days." But soon my neighbor was taken out and put elsewhere. Vainly I waited for Elizabeth.

Supper was served, or rather, tea was passed. Bread had already been left in our rooms. To my joy a small can of milk was given me by the doctor's order. I had told him I could not eat. It was well he had come to my rescue, for I was finding a diet of bread and water wholly inadequate. The nightly supply of water was passed from cell to cell by a colored woman who was at least six feet tall. I soon discovered her cell was the one next to mine. She and I were the sole occupants of what might be called the servants' quarters of the main yard. I tried to reconcile myself to Elizabeth's absence. The one redeeming feature was the new matron. She was a good looking, middle-aged woman, vastly more human than our old dragon. She treated us like a bunch of children and laid down the law with a mighty hand. But her voice, though dictatorial, was not harsh. She stopped at my door long enough to give directions, and said if I behaved and did not talk there would be no trouble. Then she departed and, to my despair, closed the massive door of the ell. My colored friend and I were alone in our fortress.

There was still light outside; it could not have been more than five
P.M. What should I do until morning? The fourteen long hours till breakfast seemed monumental. But I could not sleep. But I was cold in the
unheated cell, so I went to bed. I had just gotten under the covers when,
hearing a whisper, I hurried to the cell door. "Say, what's your name?"
came the voice. "Maggie Martin. What's yours?" Her answer, "Minerva.
I don't dast to talk now, but when the night watch is on, I will." "Before
you stop," I pleaded, "tell me where my friend Lizzie is." "The other new
girl? She is on the other side of the ward." Here conversation ceased. I
crept back to bed. I turned on my light until all were automatically
switched off at nine. It was wholly inadequate for reading, but then I
had nothing to read. I lay staring at the electric bulb and pondered.
Suppose there were a fire, or Minerva were taken sick or attempted
suicide, what could I do? No sound would penetrate the wooden door
that shut us off. I imagined the scurrying for keys, the time needed to
unlock the ward door, then our wood portal, and last the barred door of
the cell. In a sudden fire there would be no hope.

I tossed on my bed. Would morning never come? Thank goodness for
Minerva; her companionship was the one ray of comfort. In the middle
of the night the hall door was flung open, and the gray-haired matron,
with jangling of keys, came trudging down past our cell. Having assured
herself that we were alive, she hastened on. To my joy she left the ell
door open. I learned from Minerva she did this to save trips our way,
and that it was safer to talk with the door open because the sound of
footsteps warned of danger.

Minerva, true to her word, now undertook to comfort me. We exchanged ages and crimes and dwelt on the horror of prison. Then Minerva, desiring more intimate knowledge, began a series of questions:
"I'm a sportin' lady, are you?" Meekly I said, "No." "Single?" "Yes." "Do
you write to your mother?" "Yes." All right, kid, don't you worry." So
concluded the catechism. I tried to draw Minerva out further about
herself, but failed. When she found I was not on the streets, but an
innocent thing from home, I was not to be polluted by bad stories;
rather I was to be protected. Conversation languished. All night I heard
Minerva sighing and groaning. She had confessed to a morphine habit.
Later I learned that on the outside she ran an opium den.

Prison had begun to grow in on me. I could no longer take things
lightly. The hopelessness, the dreariness, the ugliness of the life preyed
upon me. But if I could not sleep, neither could many of the others.
Faintly from the ward came coughs and groans all night long. Only
when the jangling of keys and the hourly rounds began did the sounds
cease.

At the first peep of dawn I was stirring. I ached with fatigue from nights of unrest on the hard, uneven bed. It was a cold November day; there was no heat in the big stone building. Yet I longed for fresh air; so, climbing to the window ledge and pulling myself to the small, open space at the top, I sought to see the morning freshness. I yearned for sight of the blue sky and tried to scratch the paint from the window. But it was useless; the paint was on the outside of the glass. Then I searched for a peep hole, and, finding a spot the size of a glove-button, I placed my eye to this. My reward was a glimpse of the yard and high stone wall. Discouraged, I jumped down.

Presently we were ordered out into the ward's corridor to form in line. My eye caught Elizabeth's, but gave no sign of recognition. We had already learned one of the unwritten rules, which is that any form of greeting between inmates is considered immoral, evidence of "lady love," and promptly punished. In grim silence we filed to the table. I noticed with interest that Elizabeth was seated between two powerful colored women. Elizabeth comes from the South and has race prejudices. Will these survive or will she lose all race consciousness, as I have with Minerva, and feel only a sense of companionship, the kinship of common suffering? Breakfast was literally shoveled down. It was the same unpalatable stew and coffee. As I stole glances at my companions, I noticed the neat hair and the clean hands, even when those hands were worn with toil, and I was aware that the lack of table manners was chiefly due to pressing hunger and want of time. When we were back in our cells and the matron had gone, Minerva whispered: "Say, Maggie, if you don't eat, give it to me." I eagerly promised.

Again we were left in our cells with nothing to do. About an hour later we were released and again formed in line, always in the same grim silence. Minerva was the tallest and led us. Next to her came my friend "Lizzie." Slowly we marched down stairs and into the workshop, where, with hands folded, we sat at long tables for five or ten minutes, abject and patient. Then a bell rang and we were told to put on rubbers and capes. Now we filed out into the prison yard, clad in our little black capes, which came scarcely below the waists of our clumsy white wrappers. Upon our heads we wore a knitted, woolen head-piece, called by some strange freak of absurdity a "fascinator." We resembled a group of dejected little orphans suddenly grown old, as round and round we marched.

But what a joy it was to feel the fresh morning air in my face and see the blue sky overhead. I quickened my step, and I noticed that Minerva, with head erect, was striding forward with the power and freedom of some Greek goddess. I saw Elizabeth's arms begin to swing with her body, but only for a moment, for an ever-watchful matron's eye was upon her and she was directed to fold arms, walk in the middle of the path, and stop jerking. Under this dreary regime the joy of exercise vanished, as round and round we went in rigid order and forlorn silence. On three sides rose the red brick wall of the building, while on the fourth was the stone wall shutting out the world. The path led round a struggling grass plot over which hung clothes lines. It was all sordid and ugly. By the time the fourteenth round was reached, one would give a kingdom to turn about face and walk in the opposite direction.

At last the half hour was up and we were ordered back to the shop. I attempted to sit next to Lizzie but that was not permitted. Part of prison discipline is to separate friends, and I was placed at the extreme other end of the work table. Our task was to hem heavy, red blankets. At another long table women were picking cotton. The dust from this rose and filled the room, causing great discomfort and coughing. A few women were making mattresses. The extent of the industrial equipment was some hand sewing-machines and three old foot-looms. There were fifty of us in the workroom with three matrons keeping guard. They sat at high desks, glaring at us, ready to scold or punish if hand flagged or eye wandered. Then, no less momentous an event than the weekly bath interrupted our work. A morning sacrificed to this task, though prison abounded in idle hours! Locked in our cells, we were brought forth one at a time and scrubbed by the same "trusty" in the presence of the matron. Each individual bath took only a few minutes, and then came the dreary hours till dinnertime.

The whole prison system seemed based on stupidity and ignorance. With a little common sense the physical if not the spiritual aspect could be transformed in a day. As it is, hundreds of working people are given into the State's care and are taught nothing, produce nothing, are ill-housed and ill-fed. Their time and that of the guards or keepers is wasted. The result is an organization which manufactures criminals, and is maintained at great cost to the State. I begged off from a bath on the score that I had had one the day before. The rapid immersion of one person after another in the same tub was not hygienic. Once a week, along with the bath orgy, clean underwear is furnished, and from these the newcomer must rip off the name of the last wearer, replacing it with her own.

I had finished labelling my garments with "Maggie 933" when I heard the matron ask Lizzie to sew labels on the dirty floor rugs of the cells, that they might be sent to the laundry. But Lizzie was still busy with her clothes, and I darted forward to claim the privilege. For it was a privilege to sit in the open ward with something to do, even though it meant handling nasty, dirty rugs. There was rivalry even for the privilege of scrubbing the floor.

After a lunch of the same pastey stew, came an hour in the cells followed by another dismal half-hour march in the yard. At 1:30 we sat silently over our tasks. I made various experiments: first I sewed fast and then slow; sometimes I hemmed well and then poorly. But all brought no comment, as long as one's fingers were busy and eyes down. To work faithfully for a State that ill-treats and ignores one is no satisfaction. And the cent and a half a day that one rarely receives is no incentive. The total of this large wage is five dollars in a year, but, as a fine of fifty cents a day for each day of punishment is imposed, it is seldom that a prisoner has any funds upon release, even after a long term. Carfare and the ten dollars furnished by the State are usually the capital with which the ex-convict must face the world, with small chance of securing employment.

So we stitch, stitch, stitch, and sigh, sigh, and do as little as we can, and move our feet restlessly but silently. Some visitors came, and we stole glances from under half-closed lids wanting to see these well-dressed and happy human beings. The bent head and the downcast eye are due not to shame but to fear — fear that a smile or a glance will be punished. The average convict is as completely cut off from mankind as though he were buried six feet underground. His one letter a month to the outer world is inspected, so he dares make no complaint. His one visitor a month must be seen in the presence of a guard or keeper, and he dares not tell of the prison miseries. The few brave souls who have spoken have frequently suffered torture for it. It is a cruel thing to give one human being unlimited power over another whom we have rendered helpless.

But at last it was 4:30, and the one event of the day was at hand. For ten minutes the barrier of silence was broken and conversation permitted, but with an alert matron listening. I longed to know how Elizabeth felt. Her face was white and drawn. Did she want to leave? If I could not inquire, I had at least bested the authorities by sending a secret message through Minerva, who sat next to her. She was to inquire whether Lizzie thought we would be sent for as witnesses on Friday or Saturday. The fiction that we were to return to the city as witnesses in a case had been decided on as the best away to avert suspicion when we made a sudden departure. I saw Minerva and Lizzie in earnest conversation, and I knew I should have my answer that night.

That evening I could not even eat my bread; it seemed to have acquired a prison odor. However, it was not wasted, because all bread was gathered up and passed out for the next meal, a splendid method of transmitting disease. The horror of prison life was overwhelming me. My endurance was at an end. I decided not to wait for further word from

Elizabeth, but seek relief at once. So I asked the matron for permission to write the warden. To my consternation, my request was refused, and I was told that notes could be written only in the workshop in the morning. Then indeed I was a true prisoner; no power I could exert would release me. If I told the matron I was a prison commissioner, she would merely think me crazy and clap me forthwith into the cooler. It required all the will I possessed not to make some desperate move for liberty. I tried to calm myself. I trudged up and down my cell. I began to have the horrible sensation I had been trapped, that my prison adventure was a scheme to lock me up for life. I imagined the prison authorities accepting no explanations. I should merely be considered "dippy" or "bughouse," as the prisoners call it when they lose mental control.

I realized that I was on the verge of a breakdown. If ordinary prison life could have this effect, it was lucky I had not sought the experience of punishment in the cooler. The tales of its horror came to me! The dark, windowless cell in the basement, which contained nothing but a bag of straw. Into this dungeon the despairing human being is thrust, and if she grows hysterical a canvas strait jacket is strapped about her and she is left to lie on the floor. Then in the dark of night mice and rats issue from their hiding to play about the prostrate body. The girls in the ward above the punishment cells said they frequently heard cries from below.

I no longer cared whether I made a success of my prison investigation or not. I had one consuming desire — to get out. The next morning I had hardly reached the workroom before I made my request. This time it was not refused, and with a prayer of thankfulness I saw the sealed note sent on its way. My heart grew lighter now, and while some visitors were at the door I daringly turned my head for a glimpse of them. They had scarcely departed when the officer who acted as industrial instructor turned on me and in the presence of the fifty women upbraided me for boldness and indecency. Her strident tones fell like blows. I shrank from her fierce anger, yet I saw in the attitude of my companions their indignant protest and a longing to rush to my rescue. But nothing mattered now, for as I looked from the window I saw coming down the yard the warden's secretary. My heart leaped in wild joy. At last my deliverance was at hand.

A few minutes later Lizzie and I were sent for. The eyes of all were upon us as we went eagerly forth. The fiction that we were needed as witnesses had been carried out, and we were told to hurry so that we might catch the noon train for the City. In the clothes room our possessions were returned. We found some of our things had been badly damaged as a result of fumigation and several articles missing, including

Elizabeth's stockings. But such trifles were insignificant. Somewhere outside were the blue sky and great open spaces and fresh air. We flung our clothes on in any way and pieced out with the prison supply. The two matrons who presided at our departure to make sure we carried out no concealed notes had become almost human. As we walked down the long hall leading to the entrance, my arm slipped through Elizabeth's and I gave it an ecstatic squeeze. But though release was at hand, this unseemly behavior was not to be tolerated. "Girls, girls, that won't do!" came the warning. "Let go of each other!" But only for a moment was our ardor damped, for just beyond the iron gate was the great, green, fresh world.

With thumping hearts we emerged into the street. Silently and timidly we moved toward the station, because a matron was with us and our hour for speech had not come. In perplexity we pondered how to make our escape. Would this woman insist upon seeing us on the train? This would be embarrassing because we had planned to seek refuge in the home of our former host. Fortunately the train was late; so, having safely landed us on a bench in the station, the matron made her departure. With furtive glances, like true ex-convicts, we watched her go, and as she left by one door we made for another with stealthy caution and hailed a taxi. Safely within the cab, the floodgates burst open, and the pent-up speech of days poured forth. We were two pallid and wobbly-looking objects as we climbed up our host's doorsteps.

A few days later, before the news of our voluntary imprisonment had been made public, Elizabeth and I went back to the prison. We felt it our duty to tell the prisoners why we had made the experiment and not to be led to believe we had been spying. As we journeyed back through the long corridors to Ward VII, it was queer how the old prison feeling returned. The matrons were aghast at the disclosure of our identity. The old dragon slunk off, not daring to face us. We stood at the end of the ward while the girls formed in line, and then hand in hand Elizabeth and I stepped forward. At first there was no sign of recognition, but I smiled and waved to Minerva and said, "It's Maggie and Lizzie come back to you. Don't you know us?" There were exclamations of astonishment and wonder. Then I told the women who we were and assured them that our whole object in becoming prisoners was to help them, that I hoped we might succeed, that our hearts were with them and always would be, and they could rest assured that anything said in confidence would be guarded as sacred. All this time I watched Minerva's face. At first it was grave, but at my last sentence it became wreathed in smiles. Then we all shook hands and began to talk. But the women hardly knew how to be friendly; it was too sudden a breakdown of the relentless prison barriers. As we left, one woman grasped our hands, uttering with passionate fervor, "You're brave women."

6
Prison Reform from Within, 1913 – 1914

*O*N MY RETURN TO NEW YORK after my prison experience I began to wonder what my experiment had achieved. My report to the Commission, together with pictures of Elizabeth and me in prison dress, had been printed extensively in all the leading New York papers along with articles describing what we found. These had stirred the public. There was instant demand for prison reform. Elizabeth and I had become temporarily famous. But what did it amount to? Had it had any effect on Auburn Prison? Had it made changes there?

Almost immediately came an answer to these questions in the form of letters from the convicts. In the first one I opened my eye fell on this sentence: "The paint has been taken off the windows and we can talk in the shop." This brought me a glad rush of happiness. With eagerness I opened the other letters. Every word bore evidence of a new and humane prison system. But woven in with the glad tidings was disturbing information: the matrons and keepers, guardians of the old order, were rebelling at the change. "We are talking now and the paint is off the windows, but we pay dearly for this. The head matron says she thinks it ridiculous. We are accused of using language that is of the lowest. We are promised talking will soon stop." Or this: "One of the girls asked for paper to write you and said you were a friend to her and the rest of us. The matron said. 'How dare you!' And then they put her on bread and water in her room. She is a long-timer. The matrons are mad because we can talk, and they pick on us all the time."

Evidently the new freedom was not to be won without suffering. The advocates of the old system were fighting desperately against any change. It was hard for me to be patient during the next few weeks.

As my correspondence grew, the women I had met casually in prison came to be distinct personalities. There was Mary, the young colored girl who had scrubbed me so vigorously. She proved to be a jolly, light-hearted, irresponsible young person, a child of nature, with no power of control; she was always in trouble. But she was everybody's friend, the defender of the downtrodden, for whose sins she was punished. Her first letter was pitiful:

I was locked in my room and only leave it to empty my bucket and for a few minutes' walk in the morning. Two women and I were sewing on a mattress in the shop. One was kidding me. I don't know what was said, but someone laughed. The officer reported us. We were put on bread and water and locked in our rooms.

I asked five matrons if they knew what I was punished for. No one knew. The Head Matron would not come to see me nor send any word. My temper got the best of me and I destroyed my table, chair, and window. I guess I was crazy for the time. You see, I had just talked to the warden, and my time was nearly up, and he had promised to get me out if I was good.

Once I was locked in a cell for five months. There was no light at night, and there was a wire screen over the window so it could not be opened to get air, and I was not allowed with the other women.

It seems as though being put in a strait jacket and kept on bread and water for seven days ought to be punishment enough. But the first time I was locked in for seven months, the second four months, and the last time over five months.

This made sixteen months in the seven years of Mary's imprisonment that she had spent in solitary confinement. Small wonder if occasionally her temper got the better of her. Her crime against society was the theft of two dollars. Not ordinary theft. One night Mary and two other girls were out for a lark. As they left a saloon they met two men and stopped to chat. Presently one of the men was missing two dollars. Then arose an outcry. Mary's companions ran but she was caught. No money was found on her, but she was convicted. The sentence was from seven to nine years for two dollars. For if a woman steals money from a man at night, when he has sought her for illegal purposes, it is grand larceny, whereas for plain pickpocketing the punishment would have been trivial.

In contrast to Mary's wild gaiety was the patient meekness of little Christine. She was twenty-three and had been sent to prison for murder when nineteen. Later I spoke to her of her little child born in prison. In an instant she was a new person. When she showed me her one treasure, a picture of a radiant, laughing child, her small face was transfigured with love. But only for an instant. Then came a look of patient hopelessness. It was six months since she had seen her baby. He had been taken from her shortly after his birth in prison. For three years he had been in a children's asylum. Since she spoke only broken English, I asked her to write out her story in her own language, and I had it translated. For two years she had been having an affair with a man where she worked; he had insisted she give him the $100 she had worked so hard to save, telling her there was but one pocket for their expenses. When he had refused to marry her she was so overwhelmed from grief and shame that she murdered him with his own pistol. She had meant to kill herself too but was prevented by people who rushed to the room. For this she was imprisoned for ten to fifteen years.

Prison is as full of diverse personalities as is the outside world. It is populated by the meek, the gay, the talented, the ignorant, the defective, and the vicious. No special shape of head or hand marks the convict. There was the case of generous, passionate Harriet. She was the Russian Jewess who on the day I was Bertilloned had attracted my attention by her bitter grief at the shame of being catalogued as a criminal. She had lived intensely. Eager to satisfy her mind, she learned several languages, became a student of law and a reader of Shakespeare and Dante. Equally eager to satisfy her body, she wanted fine clothes, gay little suppers, and the luxury of taxis. Added to this was a generous nature which never refused aid to others. The result spelled ruin. For several years she worked as a private secretary and drew a good salary. But the cost of books and clothes and untold loans to friends left her bankrupt. Soon her debts could not be met and she forged a check. This was Harriet's second offense, and she was sent to prison for four years.

Another woman whose story haunted me was Rose. Her whole life was dedicated to her man and her two little boys. At seventeen, with the sure conviction that she had found her mate, Rose fled to him. For ten years, through sickness and poverty and the birth of two children, they had struggled on together, with an ever increasing love. But Rose was an outcast, for this man had not married her — he could not; he was already married. This is what she wrote me:

> I met him and loved him, but three years before, one night while drinking, he got married. He never saw the girl but that once. I made my mistake when I went with him, but I thought we could save money together for a divorce. But when we had $70 saved, I fainted at my work, and then was told I would be a mother in three months. I didn't know before.

Ed only earned $12 a week. I worked in the YMCA; then I worked in a bakery taking crackers off hot pans until my fingers were burnt to the bone, but it was $5 a week. After my second boy came I got in trouble. I did sewing at home for a few I knew, and when I was offered things instead of money in pay for my work I took them, though I suspected how they were got. I wanted to sell them and get money. . . . But I was arrested for receiving stolen goods. Someone wrote to the court that I wasn't married, and they showed me no mercy. I was bad for living with the man. I love my darling so much I would give my life for him. Do you think I am bad for saying this?

Immediately I wrote to Ed. He came at once in response, a fine, up-standing young man, well dressed, well mannered, and attractive. Behind him tagged two small boys, shy and clean and even wearing kid gloves, the father's supreme effort to bring them up as gentlemen. This would-be husband and father was still deeply in love. It was true his faith had been shaken. He had thought Rose a divinity, and he found her human. Besides, since Rose's imprisonment there had been no letter. He did not know that a prisoner without a marriage certificate is not allowed to write to her man. Rose had not been permitted to send out or receive a letter in all her weeks of imprisonment. When I explained this to Ed, all the man's love returned.

After seeing the husband I went to the lawyer who had handled Rose's case. He was sure she was all right, that she had taken the stolen goods to make the house attractive and to hold the man upon whom she had no legal claim. Rose's people and the family clergyman were all confident of Rose's innate goodness. It was very puzzling. Here was the law ruthlessly tearing a man and woman apart, leaving two children homeless and illegitimate. It could not go on. Rose would go insane. She was sobbing her heart out in the prison hospital.

I appealed to the administrator with the kindly heart who had let in a flood of sunshine through unpainted windows. Some days later there came an official letter from the Warden's office enclosing a note Rose had written him, which explains itself:

Dear Sir, I want to thank you for the first night's sleep and the happiest day I have had since I came to prison. When I received my husband's two letters I forgot I was behind prison bars. Accept my thanks and my sincerest wishes for a Happy New Year.

Little by little the convicts grew to be real persons in my mind. I longed to go to them. Then one morning came the news that the head matron had been dismissed and, pending the arrival of the new head, I was invited to take charge of the prison for two weeks. This was staggering news. I was only thirty-six.

Within twenty-four hours I stood at the prison gate, bag in hand. With beating heart I rang the bell. The gatekeeper with his great key ceremoniously unlocked the clanking gate. A wicked delight possessed me at my power to open and close that barred door at will, where before I had been helpless. As I stepped into the big, barren hall, a group of convicts filed past. So deep was my prison experience that I almost turned to fall into line. Even the matron at my elbow felt the pull, for she addressed me as "Miss Maggie." Then I saw this was not the prison of a few weeks before. Instead of sullen, expressionless faces, there were smiles, waving hands, and turning heads as the convicts flashed their welcome.

We had a happy reunion, meeting in the chapel without keepers or guards, to discuss prison problems. This seemed to me the first step, for the more I studied the whole prison system the more it seemed designed for punishment and not for regeneration. Though the paint was off the windows, there were few other changes. Day after day the women hemmed blankets or made mattresses, while the men convicts at Sing Sing made women's kimonos. The food boiled in vats was still uneatable. Yet the prison circular announced that the inmates were learning to sew and cook! True, the punishment cells stood empty now. But something more was needed if prison was not to be a place to mark time, futile and wasteful.

As I made note of the various activities going on I discovered that one woman's entire five-year term had been spent scrubbing floors. What would she do when released? Continue to scrub or in disgust return to crime? Another woman, an expert stenographer, was washing clothes in the laundry.

Brooding upon these things, I seized pad and pencil and worked out a wonderful social and industrial program, all in accord with the best ideas on the subject. Then I had the convicts meet me in the chapel. A hush fell on the 114 convicts as they sat there quietly without keeper or guard. All the rigidity of bearing that comes from iron discipline had vanished. Here a hand was carelessly resting on the back of a bench or a shoulder drooped or a body was bent forward in eager attentiveness. Simplicity and humanness were visible in the eager faces. The mask of sullenness had been torn aside.

Suddenly, as I faced this awakened audience, my own plans crumbled. What godlike qualities did I possess that would enable me with wisdom to map out in smallest detail the lives of these women? Before me flashed my own life with all its weaknesses, dishonesties, and unkindness. Like accusing fingers on the white paper before me appeared my elaborately worked out prison schedule, with its hours for sewing, its hours for cooking, its hours for recreation. I saw myself as a prisoner again, with the crushing need to insist on being treated as a human being. That was the keynote — the need for being treated as a human being, not merely a contemptible number.

Throwing aside my position as prison commissioner and becoming again Maggie Martin #933, I jumped down from the platform. In halting sentences I said I came not as a commissioner, but as one of them, to work out with them a prison program. As I proceeded, joy and self-respect crept into many faces. The response was tremendous. From all parts of the room rose the buzz and hum of discussion. Bodies straightened, shoulder squared as the women faced this new and wonderful thing demanded of them. With disconcerting intelligence that put my machine-like plans to shame; they went straight for the vital issue, leaving for later the minor details. The first matter discussed was "Shall all be treated alike?"

On one side of the chapel, occupying the first few rows of benches, sat the "old-timers," the second and third time offenders. On their sleeves were branded the marks of shame. The system herded them together as incorrigible. All that was hardest in prison life fell to them. They lived in the cold, damp cells in the basement, where sunshine never came; by day they worked in the moist, steaming laundry. They were the victims of rheumatism. This patient, dejected little group was now all alive to know the verdict of their companions on the other side of the chapel, the "trustees." These official favorites had the better and easier tasks and occupied a sunlit ward, where there were plants in the unpainted windows, had pillow shams on their beds and tablecloths on the tables. For they lived in the show ward.

I waited. The crushing shame of iron bars binds prisoners together in a sisterhood. "One ain't better than another" was the general verdict. "The world didn't give you a chance, you had to go back to crime or live on the streets." So they reasoned. The vote was unanimous. Every prisoner, regardless of creed, color, or previous prison record ought to be given the same treatment. As I listened, it seemed imperative that the women have the opportunity to live up to this ideal. Temporarily I had the power. Probably what I did was against all prison rules, and at any moment a higher authority might intervene, but this was the time for deeds, not fears. Waving my hand at the two groups, I said, "If you are in earnest, why not change places? For months the old-timers have had the worst of prison and the trusties the best." It was a daring suggestion. A hush fell on the chapel, but only for a second; then swiftly came tumultuous applause. With one accord every woman rose to the occasion, swept on and up by the ideal demanded.

Such enthusiasm demanded action. I called the two groups to come forward. I suggested they pack their belongings and effect a transfer of cells at once. Gaily they departed, some forty or fifty women in all, without keeper or guard. Quietly they went their way to pack up their few odd treasures. One by one they came back, some almost sorrowful that they were to gain by the transfer and others serenely content with the opportunity for sacrifice. It was good to be trusted and to prove worthy of that trust.

In a few minutes each had chosen her new cell and returned to chapel. Thirty minutes was the time consumed to make the transfer. Ordinarily such a readjustment would have been a day's work, each prisoner solemnly escorted by a keeper or guard. Thus is the State's money wasted on unnecessary guards, and the convict deprived of all freedom of action and responsibility that alone builds character. A little deed — this changing of wards — yet by the spirit in which it was done I felt we had been lifted out of ourselves into a true democracy and a real unselfishness.

As I left the chapel it was difficult to walk sedately. I wanted to run and shout and tell the whole world of the innate goodness in human beings. But at the foot of the stairs I met a group of guards. Their glum, scowling faces hit me like a blow in the face. They had been kept a half hour overtime. I tried to explain our meeting and the wonder of it. To them it was nonsense; they were not interested. Their task was to see that prisoners did not escape; they were not paid to reform convicts.... I knew then what I was up against.

But in spite of the scowls and opposition, having been put in charge of the prison for two weeks I determined to give the prisoners a chance at self-government. We worked out a democratic system in which convicts in each of the five wards were to choose their representative by secret ballot. The persons who had been so elected were to be members of a committee of five and to elect one of their group of five as president. They were to meet with me regularly and discuss plans. Only if a prisoner abused her privilege was she to be suspended from the organization, but even then a period of good behavior made reinstatement possible. Rose and Harriet were each respectively made representatives of their wards and, still more wonderful, Mary released from months of solitary confinement was to prove the best representative of all. Under her guidance her ward, which held the most difficult cases, became a model.

It was a serious and earnest group that met in chapel to take the oath of allegiance. Gravely we signed the document that was to us the charter of enfranchisement. For the first time in the history of this prison, reform was to come from within.

It struck me anew what a melting pot prison is, as we shook hands. Christian and Jew, coloured and white, prostitutes and mothers, women of many races and backgrounds bound together by a common misery, now joyfully working together for a common cause. Solemnly each woman filed back to her cell. And a deep hush of peace fell upon the place.

Naturally, in the ensuing two weeks all was not a bed of roses. There were ups and downs. There were defectives or those with uncontrolled passions to be dealt with.

The first department we attempted to transform was the kitchen. I really did nothing; I only secured for the women the opportunity to talk, to play, and to work. But now all was bustle and activity. Seven convict teacher-cooks with seven convict pupils were chosen. Long and eager were their debates and untiring efforts. When dinner was served that first day, a little sign of contentment ran around the tables as each prisoner gazed at her plate. Instead of a tasteless mass of boiled codfish and potatoes, there were slices of fried fish and a baked potato, the regular Friday food transformed by a labor of love. It is curious what a small thing it takes to awaken a feeling of good fellowship; this deed of the convict cooks stirred in all the desire to contribute some service.

The small administrative committee of five, however, was having many problems to solve. One of the hardest perhaps was the passing of dirty notes. If there is a common characteristic of women convicts it is that most of them have lived intense sexual lives. Most of their crimes are in relation with some man. Prison suppresses the urge for physical satisfaction, and the one outlet is found in perverted love for one another and sensual notes passed clandestinely. The governing committee wanted to stop this. They proposed separating from each other those who claimed to be "lady lovers," putting them in different wards. Personally I doubted if separation would effect a cure but felt the governing group must learn from experience, so we separated the known cases. Within twelve hours the committee was seeking my help because a white girl and a colored girl who formerly had had cells side by side and were writing love notes to each other were assigned to different wards. Soon the white girl, who was extremely well educated and intelligent, was apparently having an epileptic fit or at least a very good imitation of one. It took some time to bring her around, and hardly had this been accomplished when word came that the colored girl had attempted suicide. She had tied the bed sheet around her neck and was trying to strangle herself.

The committee members were in great consternation. What was to be done? I asked if they wanted me to try an experiment. They agreed. I sent for the two women. We had a long talk on the difference between love and sensuality. Real love meant caring more for the other person than for one's self. I pointed out that one with her ability and brains was the person to edit the prison paper and that the other girl, who was an excellent cook, ought to help with the meals, but that this inevitably meant separation. Were they willing, since they professed real caring for each other, not to seek their own gratification, but to help each other to do what was right?

Then I left them in my office for half an hour to talk the matter over. When I returned it was to find two sober young women ready to do what was asked of them. For the rest of my stay there was no trouble with them. But this was no guarantee, of course, that good behaviour would continue.

Another reform achieved was the release from cells on Sunday. The interminable solitary hours from Saturday night to Monday morning were one of the greatest hardships. Now on Sunday afternoons the women were to be allowed to mingle together freely and talk for an hour. They behaved exceptionally well and even drew favorable comments from officers.

But my two weeks were soon up. A new head matron had arrived, a jolly Irish woman, someone who undoubtedly would be kind but had no understanding of what self-government meant. It was with sinking heart I left the prison. The majority of the matrons were already in active rebellion. They could no longer exert their authority, move prisoners about from place to place, and lock and unlock them at given hours. They were just waiting for their opportunity. Then one day a convict became violent. She was gradually going insane. She pulled an iron slat from her bed and threatened to kill anyone who approached. Panic spread among the officers. As if the whole prison had gone mad, they seemed to imagine the only safe course was to lock everyone up. A few days later the insane woman was sent to Mattawan Insane Asylum, and the panic subsided. But it was the beginning of the end. Soon readjustments were made to suit the matrons, and favors conferred on certain convicts. The program of equality, hard work, and fair treatment was undermined. Self-government was receiving its death-blow. For example, when the committee had suspended a girl for unworthy conduct and had put her on probation, instantly that girl was befriended by the keepers, and the self-government league was ridiculed. This put a premium on flouting the Committee. Not many days later I learned that the head matron had made herself the league's president and that the representatives had been directed to report misbehaviours to her. Such

self-government was an absurdity. My friends must not be left in such
a predicament, so I returned to the prison to disband the league. The
head matron immediately withdrew from the presidency, but it was
futile for the league to proceed when there was neither comprehension
nor backing from those in charge.

It was a grief-stricken group that met me in the chapel. I feared a
riot. The league had grown dear to every heart, but the vote to disband
was unanimous. An organization whose representatives must report to
officers made them stool-pigeons and tattlers. That was intolerable. I
determined there should be no secrecy about why the league was broken
up. As I made my brief statement, I saw the joy go out of 114 faces. The
women sat in huddled, discouraged groups muttering together. Two
matrons angered at being held largely responsible for the league's
failure rose to do battle. In shrill voices they denounced the inmates as
traitors and called upon certain prisoners to testify to their loyalty and
kindness. It was a queer scene, those in official position seeking vindi-
cation from the convicts whom they held to be the scum of the earth. As
I looked into those prisoners' faces, flushed with struggling emotion, I
wondered if any one of them would have the courage publicly to face the
official world and state the truth. One word against an officer, and that
prisoner is likely to be harried and worried for the rest of her term. Yet
I waited, hoping against hope, for that courage which defies the world.

Then half way down the chapel I saw Harriet slowly rising, white to
the lips but steady. Respectfully her words came: "You really haven't
been good to us," she said to the matrons. "You didn't like the league
and made fun of it." She got no further, for her mates, thrilled by such
courage, burst into applause. And now from the other side of the room
another girl had risen. But for their sake I dared not let matters go on.
My position as commissioner placed me falsely on the side of the officials; I was obliged to adjourn the meeting. Self-government under the
given conditions was impossible. Perhaps I had expected too much;
perhaps I ought to have been content that Rose could write to Ed and
her boys and that Christine could see her small son twice a month.

Except for material changes and the closing of the worst punishment
cells, the prison would now go on as before, the convicts marking time
until the day of release. In no department was real training given.

Upon release, many of the women came to me in the city. My door bell
began to ring as early as 6:00 A.M. The pitiful helplessness of most was
only too apparent. One woman begged me to meet her at the Grand
Central Depot. The noise and glare of New York after the long years of
banishment from the world terrified her. She clung to me like a frightened child. When she passed a policeman she quivered and shrank in

fear. I got her a room in a boarding house until she could get employment. When I handed her the latch key she was paralyzed; the strain
of locking and unlocking a door was nerve-racking for her who had been
locked in for many years. So she stayed in her room to avoid it. Her
landlady soon came to me to ask questions and reported that her
boarder walked back and forth six feet one way then six the other as
though she were shut up in a cell. Had she been in prison? It was days
before the woman was able to take a job and before her awkward fingers
readjusted themselves to pots and pans and kitchen utensils, her former
implements of trade.

Among others who came to see me were some of the so-called
hardened criminals. There was a woman who had been in prison for
running a house of ill fame. She had decided to lead a different life. She
was about 60. Her peroxided hair had returned to its former state; she
weighed 200 pounds and had epileptic fits. She had lost her false teeth.
It seemed hopeless to find her a job. When I asked if she had ever done
anything else besides conducting a fast house, she said, "Oh, yes. Once
I was a snake charmer in the circus." What possible job was there for
her? The only thing I could find was that of a dishwasher. She stuck to
that job for six weeks and then disappeared. Two years later on my way
to a movie one evening I was stopped by a woman with dyed yellow hair,
resplendently dressed and covered with imitation jewels. Clinging to
either arm were two coloured girls. It was the snake charmer, and it
was plain she had returned to her old trade. She greeted me with
enthusiasm, while I secretly prayed that no policeman would observe
the company I was keeping.

Then there was Christine. Within a year I had secured a pardon for
her from the Governor of New York. She and her child came to me for
a short while. Soon she had a good job in a factory and became a
respected member of the community. She begged me never to let her
child know of his birth in prison and the crime of his mother.

And finally there was Minerva, the one who had the cell next to mine
and formerly ran an opium den. I made a special effort for her and
through a charitable organization found her a position as a domestic
servant in a doctor's family. The doctor's wife agreed to take her in spite
of her prison record. I went with Minerva to her new post and was
rather disturbed to have the door opened by a scantily dressed young
woman who said she was the doctor's wife. But there seemed nothing to
do but leave Minerva with the lady who had been vouched for by the
organizations which found placements for released convicts. After a
week came a note from Minerva: "Miss Doty, I don't think the lady is
the doctor's wife." Another week: "Miss Doty, the goings on up here is
something awful."

Before I could get to Minerva came the third and final note: "Miss Doty, come and get me quick. Me morals is being corrupted." I rushed to the rescue but alas too late. Minerva and her lady employer had fallen into the hands of the police. Minerva was sent to Blackwell's Island for six months on a charge of immoral behavior. It was wisest to let her serve her term there, because had I gone to the rescue and her former prison term become known, it would have meant two years of imprisonment. This time on Minerva's release I asked her to come to see me. She proved a good cook but was quite unfamiliar with the niceties of life, such as the small dumb-waiter which carried up packages and took down garbage. Seeing a small door in the kitchen wall, she promptly opened it and dumped down a pail of garbage. Unfortunately the tenant on the floor below at that moment had her head in the shaft. It took a good deal of explaining to soften that lady's wrath. But Minerva was happy. She had no longings for her opium den.

One day a prisoner from Sing Sing turned up. Bill was a burglar but had decided to go straight, despite seven prison records. He came to me seeking a job. I called up several social agencies. All declared it was impossible to find work for a man imprisoned seven times. I suggested I could write the newspapers pointing out the problem and the failure of social agencies to meet it. This produced results; one of the agencies said to send him along. In two hours he was back, washed and shaved and a clean handkerchief tied around his neck. He had been given the job of driving a garbage wagon. Work was to begin next day. When I asked if he had eaten he said no, that he had no money. A pressing engagement obliged me to leave my flat, so I asked Minerva to give Bill a good meal and then send him away. Then I left my flat in possession of the "sportin' lady" and the burglar.

On my return Minerva was singing happily. She informed me she knew now what she wanted to do with her life. She wished to become a probation officer and look after criminals and see that they went straight.

Now I was learning not only that prisons needed reform but that provision for released convicts was a crying necessity. Not only was it difficult to find them jobs, but there was no respectable place where penniless convicts could congregate socially. In desperation I organized a Burglars' Smoker. Every Sunday afternoon about twelve burglars who were trying to make good came to smoke and to chat. One day, finding there had been a burglary in the neighborhood, these men kindly put burglar-proof locks on my door.

But my task soon seemed hopeless. It was like trying to fill a bucket full of holes with water. Society was not ready to give the convict a chance. And the convict could break from former habits only with difficulty.

The place to begin was with the children, for it was evident children's reformatories did not reform. They probably were scarcely better than prisons. How could one find out what went on behind reformatory walls? Some of the gray, grim, barred reformatories had recently been replaced by farm cottages with a mother and father in charge, but even here in the majority of cases I could not get the children to talk freely. How was I to get to the bottom of the problem? How find out what was wrong? Why was it that so many naughty children sent to reform school were worse on release than before? Then it came to me. Why not consult the convicts who as children had been in reformatories, men who, like Happy Jack, might be willing to tell me their stories!

Through the kindness of Thomas Mott Osborne, who had become warden of Sing Sing, that prison and the Auburn State Prison were thrown open to me. I was allowed to interview hundreds of prisoners in each place. My first visit was to Auburn. It was Sunday morning and I was asked to address the men in chapel. They filed in 1500 in number, without keeper or guard under the new system of self-government inaugurated by Mr. Osborne. As I looked at these faces before me, scarred and torn with conflicts, I read in them a new hope, a desire for a better life. Suddenly I knew what to say: "Let us fight to save the children of the future from a life of crime. Will you help in the fight? Tell me what is wrong with reformatories. What has crushed and broken your lives? What must we do to save children from your fate?"

The appeal went straight to their hearts. As I left they rose and stood in hushed silence. There was not a sound, not a hand clap, but, as I walked out from the chapel between long lines of men, plainly on many faces was written the promise to help save children. In Sing Sing I had a similar opportunity to reach the men. In this case not in chapel, but in a big dining hall with its long wood tables and benches. I stood on a table with the convicts all about me. I made the same plea and had the same response.

That is why I'm sure the stories they later told me of reformatory life are true. Yet the world will doubt the truth of these inmates' stories. For these doubters I verified many records. With unfailing trust, the prisoners gave me not only the facts of their imprisonment but even revealed crimes unknown to the police. A convict serving a short term as a first offender would tell of four or five previous arrests under an alias, which, if known, would have imprisoned him for many years.

From the material collected, about 1700 records, I chose fifty cases for verification. Under his different aliases I looked up a man's record in the numerous reformatories and prisons in which he had been confined. In each instance the statements made were correct. As study of these records disclosed, the fact is that two-thirds of all the men confined in prison had as children been in some sort of juvenile institution, which had failed to reform them.

In addition to the records, two hundred convicts wrote out the stories of their lives. These pitiful tales told of physical, mental, and moral abuse and neglect as children. There were stories of sadistic beatings and perversions. In no juvenile institution apparently was there some-one whose business it was to love and understand the child. There were stupid rules, such as the one that a child could only write to his mother once a month and only on good behavior.

How could such evils be eradicated? At heart people are fundamentally good. Even the so-called hardened criminals had responded to appeals. Surely the public would demand changes if conditions in reformatories were known. Two articles of my own prison experience were appearing in the *Century Magazine,* of which my older brother Douglas was the editor. I sought out the editor of *Good Housekeeping* magazine and asked him to take six articles on Children's Reformatories, which he did.

Since leaving the Russell Sage Foundation I had been earning nothing and my savings had been exhausted. But now the magazines were ready to pay me $250 for an article. That was real wealth. Moreover, I was frequently asked to speak on my prison experiences. But the pay for lectures was small in those days, only $10 to $25.

Many of my weekends and other days as well were spent at my beloved Sparta with the rushing brook and great silence. Here I wrote my articles, surrounded by the love of my father and mother. When in New York the days were devoted to the never ending stream of convicts who wanted to go straight.

Then, suddenly in this absorbing life, like a bomb from the sky, came the news that war in Europe had broken out. On August 4, 1914, when all America was peacefully vacationing, we heard that England had joined France and Russia in declaring war on Germany. It just didn't seem possible. We were too civilized to fight. Europe had had no war involving the entire continent since the Congress of Vienna in 1815. America since its independence had had no European conflict. It was fifty years since our Civil War.

But there it was. It was staggering. I shall never forget the day I crept into a movie theatre to see on the silent screen the European armies marching out to battle. My heart turned sick. All my dreams for a better world came tumbling down like castles in the air. The optimism of my youth of 1900 vanished. Our plans for reform seemed futile. Of course, America was not at war. Woodrow Wilson was declaring we never would go to war. We had friendly neighbors on the North and South and an ocean on both sides of us. There were no radio, no submarines, and few airplanes. All news came through by telegrams. America seemed perfectly safe. But what was the good of working for prison reform when the world was on fire? God was again tapping me on the shoulder and showing me a wholly new vision — not prison conditions but world conditions must be changed and war forever ended.

Part IV
Enlisting for Peace

Introduction to Chapters 7–10

Editor's note: This introduction to four chapters highlights some of Doty's significant actions which she does not mention and indicates the tremendous amount of recognition of her reports in the press.

CHAPTER 7 DESCRIBES how World War I caused a major change in Doty's career, prompting her to attend the international conference of women for peace at the Hague in 1915, and includes what she reported on her first trip into warring Germany.

Not included is the fact that the *Smith College Alumnae Quarterly* reported that on 21 February 1916, Doty made a "very able address at a suffrage meeting in Northampton [Massachusetts]."

In chapter 8 she recounts her extraordinary experiences during her second wartime trip to Europe, from 15 July to mid-October 1916. The *New York Tribune* had commissioned her to go again inside Germany to report on wartime conditions there. By that time, almost a year before the United States was to enter the war, the Austro-German military successes against the Allies on the Western Front were massive. Having pretty much driven Russia out of Poland, East Prussia, Lithuania, and Serbia, Germany was now able to turn more power against the West. When Doty entered Germany, the long, costly battle in France for Verdun and environs was still raging (February to November), where each side lost over 300,000 men.

By going behind the German lines Doty was among the few able to expose the fact that German military strength was being obtained at tremendous cost to its civilians back home, where, in addition to lost lives, severe rationing was causing starvation, especially among the poor, so widespread that she felt there could be a revolt to overthrow the Kaiser's government.

Her press reports of this 1916 trip into Germany and home via England and France she composed from notes after her return. This explains why the publication dates postdate her trip. In an account worthy of a spy story she tells how she secreted these notes out from Germany. Her articles appeared in and won favorable reviews in a large number of newspapers and journals. The *New York Tribune* ran a series of ten articles on the front page every Sunday (except 31 December) from 12 November 1916 to 14 January 1917, under her own prominent byline and large headlines. Soon the contents of these *Tribune* articles, supplemented by considerably more detail, became Part II of her book *Short Rations*.

Articles by Doty or reviews of her reports ran in a number of other publications across this country, among which were the *Chicago Tribune, Outlook* magazine 3 and 5 December 1916, and the *Atlantic Monthly* of June 1917. And, of course, she received personal letters of appreciation, including two from Jane Addams and one — that must have been especially gratifying — from Charles D. Hazen, her former history professor at Smith College, by then (22 April 1917) professor of political science at Columbia University, and author of *Europe Since 1815* (Henry Holt and Co., 1910). In the letter he expressed "admiration for your ability as an observer and your power of simple and graphic narration. . . .The war has revealed many kinds of courage . . . , and not the least was the kind you have shown."

Besides in the newspapers, the *Reader's Guide to Periodical Litera- ture* cites 20 articles by Doty published by six magazines between 1916 and 1918, articles based in this trip and her next one.

In her Preface to *Short Rations* she said she hoped through these re- ports to affect eventual peace terms by helping America extend to the Germans not punishment but understanding and rehabilitation. Here one can see a reflection of her earlier conclusions about treatment of prisoners. Indeed, many historians today do feel that the harshness of the Versailles peace terms may have led to World War II. Of this book the *New York Post* said it was "one of the most concrete revelations of conditions within the German Empire . . . a graphic account of an ever growing tragedy," while a long review in the *New York Evening Globe* on 11 March 1918 said

> Miss Doty seems to believe absolutely in the social revolution in Germany. . . . She does not want the German people punished for what the German militarists have done.

> We may not sympathize altogether with Miss Doty's point of view. . . . But we must be impressed by her sincerity and honesty. Her one desire has been to tell the truth. She does this in admir- able simplicity and clarity. Her style is a model.

Yet there was opposition to Doty's point of view among many in America (including Theodore Roosevelt) who feared what the suffragists and women in the peace movement stood for. This criticism grew as patriotic fervor increased once we had declared war.

And, significantly, the *Cologne Gazette* in Germany reacted with anger to what she had reported to America, as she tells toward the end of chapter 8.

Besides her writings between her return from Germany in the late fall of 1916 until departure the next fall on another wartime trip, Doty had an article on a different topic printed in the *New York Tribune*, 4 April 1917, expressing her enthusiasm over the election of the first woman to the U.S. Congress, Jeanette Rankin. In it she urged Rankin to stick to Rankin's belief that the issue of peace must be put before pressures for the vote for women. And, in fact, Rankin voted against America's declaration of war.

Yet, on 24 April, just two days after the United States' declaration of war, Doty delivered a speech before a Senate Committee on the need for women to have the right to vote. This speech was printed in full in *The Suffragist*, 5 May 1917.

Chapter 9 tells of her next dangerous adventure — into turbulent Russia at the age of 40. *Good Housekeeping* magazine expressed pride in having obtained her as a special feature writer, running two conspicuous 5-by-8-inch ads about it under headings in half-inch letters. In obvious appeal to its female readers they said "She is a kind of far-seeing, universal sister — bringing together . . . the tremendous qualities that make women the apotheosis of love and service and unending sacrifice."

Doty's reports came out in six issues of *Good Housekeeping* the following March to October 1918. Again these and special items published in other magazines (including four articles by her in the British *The Nation*) brought praise.

Doty returned to the States in April 1918. Late that year Macmillan published her more complete story of the trip in a hard-cover volume titled *Behind the Battle Line: Around the World in 1918*. Despite this title, her trip and her book include also the last three months of 1917. This volume elicited favorable reviews across the country from the *Boston Herald* to the New York *Morning Telegram*, the *Duluth Herald*, and the *San Francisco Bulletin*. The book appeared with a unique and fascinating dust cover showing a reproduction of many of her visas with dates, as stamped on her passport.

Little could *Good Housekeeping* or Doty know that she would reach Petrograd just three days after Lenin and his Bolshevik followers had seized power. She stayed in Russia well over two months, as she describes in chapter 9.

In chapter 10 of her autobiography the indefatigable Doty tells how she completed that six-month-long trip around the world, describing her departure across Scandinavia, her wait in Norway to cross the submarine-infested Channel, three weeks in embattled England, and on to France.

Selections from a letter she wrote to her family from Bergen, Norway, on 22 January 1918, give a worthwhile summary of her trip, as not written in her autobiography:

> Russia has now reached the stage of the last phase of the French Revolution and much that happens is tragic. Personally I had no fear for my own safety but human life is not valued very highly. The Revolution in Russia has become economic. The workman has set out to get what the rich man has and he doesn't trouble much how he gets it, whether at the point of a bayonet or with a bullet. The Germans had begun to arrive in Petrograd before I left — 60 representatives of their Peace Delegation, so I thought it was about time I got out. My experiences these last few months have certainly been varied. From Japan, where to be a member of the YWCA was to be a revolutionist, to Russia where Maxim Gorky [a moderate Socialist] was considered a counter-revolutionist and in danger of being put in prison as a conservative, to Sweden where I saw the king sitting on his ermine-covered throne, I . . . don't quite know whether I'm living in the fifteenth or the twenty-first century. . . . I spent a week in Sweden, for I went down into the country to see Ellen Key. . . . I had a wonderful day with her. . . .

It is perplexing that in this chapter of her autobiography she omitted telling of her visit to and inspiration from Ellen Key,[1] pacifist, early proponent of the *Mutterschutz* movement, and internationally known advocate of radical changes such as equal rights, reform of marriage and divorce laws, and support for unwed mothers and illegitimate children. Margaret Sanger is said to have been strongly influenced by Key's advocacy of birth control. In Doty's book, *Behind the Battle Line*, she does devote several pages to her meeting with Key, and *Good Housekeeping* carried Doty's five-page article about Key in its August 1918 issue (33ff.). However, the feminist radicalism of Key was to add to suspicions of Doty, as seen in a 10 May 1921 report from a State Department official in New York when her passport application was being held up. He pointed out that Doty had contributed a chapter to a book published in Swedish on the anniversary of Key's birthday. This fact had been noted by Justice Brandeis also.[2]

7

Women of Peace in Wartime, 1915

As previously noted, this important chapter is missing from the available copy of Doty's autobiography, so regretfully it can only be summarized here from her account in Part I of her book Short Rations *published one year after the trip described herein.*

*D*OTY HAD AT ONCE JOINED the American Union Against Militarism when it was organized in 1914 by her former roommate Crystal Eastman, along with Lillian Wald, Rabbi Stephen Wise, Oswald Garrison Villard, and Jane Addams. Early the next year she and Ida Rauh supported Crystal Eastman in organizing the Woman's Peace Party. The outbreak of World War I caused a momentous new direction for her career, as seen in the remaining chapters of this volume.

Early in 1915, she began stimulating public opinion about and helping organize the following undertaking by concerned women. At almost 37 years of age, with the courage of her commitment, Doty sailed with some 50 other women across submarine-infested waters in order to reach the Hague in the Netherlands to attend the first international Conference of Women for Peace. The delegation included such well-known leaders as Jane Addams, Emily Greene Balch, Mary Heaton Vorse, and the British feminist leader Emmeline Pethick-Lawrence.[1] Despite the war, the conference was attended by some 1500 women (figures differ) from 12 nations, both belligerent and neutral. She went as a delegate, representing the Women's Lawyers Association, and as a reporter for *Century Magazine* and as Special Correspondent for the New York *Evening Post*. Both the *Post* (often on page one) and *Century* were soon publishing her articles. From this conference, chaired by Jane Addams, there grew the Women's International League for Peace and Freedom, which is still alive today. For its cause Doty was to work for the rest of her life.

On the day that the ship *Noordam* sailed with the delegates from New York to the Hague, 13 April 1915, the New York *Evening Post* ran a long article of admiration by Charles Johnson Post, in which he said that the departure of the delegates that day

> formally initiated a movement unique in the history of great crises and one whose full significance can only be realized by the historian of the future. . . . For many hours (their ship's) path is through the area prohibited by Germany to all vessels under penalty of submarines . . . through the mine fields, with her great special peace flag flying from the fore.[2]

The *New Republic* on 17 April carried a glowing editorial about the significant purpose of the Hague Conference. What was the impact of that conference on U.S. policy? Since the war various sources have stated that the resolutions at the Hague Conference influenced President Wilson's Fourteen Points.[3]

Doty's detailed account of this trip filled 62 pages in her book *Short Rations*. She wrote that at the conference there were several moving moments, for example when refugees made it through from German-occupied Belgium or when women from countries that were enemies in the war embraced each other.

It was at this conference that she met two strong, leading feminists from Germany, Dr. Anita Augspurg and Fraulein Lida Heymann (variously spelled Hayman) who, along with Mrs. Emmeline Pethick-Lawrence (whom she soon calls "Malini"), became her lifelong friends.

At the conclusion of the conference Doty pushed on into Germany, from where she reported for about a month on conditions, namely anti-Americanism, strict food rationing, "an atmosphere of depression and suppression," her Social Democrat friends being spied upon and in danger. "Everywhere you feel the relentlessness of force and the power of organization. . . . Germany will fight to her last man."

Her book contains the account of her trip home via England, where from July to mid-August she found vibrancy and economic well-being but the probability of the introduction of conscription and, among her liberal friends there, concern over the growing centralization of government power. In London she joined Emmeline Pethick-Lawrence in leading a street demonstration against the Pankhursts, who had abandoned the cause of suffrage in favor of support of the war effort. From there she went into France for several weeks, where the plight of so many wounded and crippled moved her to volunteer as an assistant nurse at the American ambulance headquarters in Neuilly. She also got a safe-conduct pass to the site of the first battle of the Marne. In the book (pp.

Emmeline Pethick-Lawrence, photograph by Harris and Ewing,
Washington, D.C.
(Courtesy of Sophia Smith Collection, Smith College)

64–67) she summarized her conclusions from the 1915 trip with this depressed picture:

> Germany — bitter, relentless, ugly and at bay; France tragic, proud, suffering and resolute; England annoyed, reluctant, capable and sure; and all determined to fight the thing through to the finish. . . .I shut my eyes. I see France as she will be in a few years — swarming with cripples. I see young men made old and helpless, sitting in chimney corners silently fingering medals.

The devastation of war had eaten into Doty's usually hopeful heart and mind. In September she sailed for home on a Dutch ship.

Doty's reports during this 1915 trip appeared in a series published by the New York *Evening Post* between 29 March and 22 May, plus three detailed dispatches under her own byline, often printed on page 1. Some of these were later printed in *Century*. The British weekly *The Nation* ran "The Little Commonwealth" about a reformatory she visited in Britain. *Good Housekeeping* on 12 June ran an article by her on Germany and in August of the next year her "Model Reformatory." Doty's article "War Cripples" in the *New Republic* of 13 November 1915 elicited strong objection by the British author Hilaire Belloc in the 25 December issue, criticizing her for picturing the mind of the British and French as turning toward peace. The next year *Atlantic Monthly* on 13 April 1916 printed her "Little Brother," a moving story about how a small Belgian boy carried his baby sister from his German-occupied country into unoccupied Holland in search of refuge.

And so one can see that this chapter 7 as her picture from inside wartime Europe was too important to omit, and that one should read the full account in Part I of *Short Rations*, inasmuch as this summary of necessity is inadequate in covering it.

8
"Snooping Madeleine," the *Tribune* Woman, 1916

*I*T SEEMED A LARGE ORDER after my experience in 1915 to return to Germany, even though the U.S. was not at war. "We want the truth; we think you'll tell it," said the editor of the *New York Tribune.* "Will you print just what I write?" I asked. He promised, and that decided me.

In 1916 the route to Germany for noncombatants was around the north of Scotland to Norway. On the 15th of July I boarded the *Kristianiafjord.* I had never been to Norway. I felt very small and without courage. At that last moment I wanted to desert.

But it was a jolly ship's company; in a day my fears were forgotten. On board were some German Americans, many Swedes, a few Norwegians, and the Dutchman Hendrik Van Loon. It was a calm voyage, with smiling skies and days that gradually grew longer. On the tenth day the sun was setting at 10:00 P.M.

As we neared Scotland we passed the spot where the ship with British Secretary of State Lord Kitchener and his son was sunk this year. We talked of mines and submarines, and got out life preservers. At break of day English officers boarded our ship and took us safely into Kirkwell Harbour. Here we lay for two days while passports, cabins, and our persons were examined. Finally we were allowed to cross the North Sea. Not many of us slept that night, but in the morning we were lying off the Norwegian coast and were soon steaming up the narrow fjord to Bergen.

From Bergen I took a train to Christiania (now Oslo), a three-day trip. In Oslo there was no sign of war. Restaurants abounded in good food, gay music, and interesting people. From Oslo I took a sleeper to Göteborg, Sweden. When I awoke it was in a wholly new land. In my school geography Norway and Sweden seemed one and the same, but Göteborg was as different from Oslo as Berlin is from New York. Sweden was more akin to Germany, well organized, methodical, even militaristic. [In *Short Rations* (p. 85) she wrote it was quite clear that Swedish sympathy lay with Germany.]

My next train took me to Copenhagen. The Danish people, like the Norwegians, were heart and soul with the Allies — not so much because of love for England and France as through hatred of Germany. Nevertheless, professing neutrality, they were giving aid to Germany. Recently it had been found that thin slabs of butter were being sent to the Germans by letter postage. Many Danish merchants were making vast fortunes out of German necessity. But such people were held in contempt.

The atmosphere of Copenhagen was distressing. It was tense. There were many stories of German atrocities. Daily I grew more nervous. It was said a woman who entered Germany was stripped and searched. There were tales of hunger and imprisonment of foreigners. [In her article printed in the *New York Tribune* on 12 November 1916, she wrote that she was told that paper was despised in Germany, so she destroyed her credentials from them and kept only those from the *Chicago Tribune*. She wrote at that time that she was so afraid she could not sleep. "I am shivering, homesick, and terribly excited."]

Only pride holds me to my job. In addition I have an errand of mercy in Germany. "The Christian Work Fund for Starving Children" of the New York Church Peace Union had given me $500 for German war orphans and starving babies, with the promise of more later. I visit the German Embassy at Copenhagen and explain my mission. My credentials are entirely satisfactory, my papers stamped without question. But then come four dreary days of waiting while my pictures and marks of identification are sent to the front. My Danish friends urge me to secure Government permission to carry a small stock of supplies. I purchase eight pounds of butter and a half yard of sausage.

As my train speeds on its way, I study my companions. There is a Swiss woman who speaks English fluently and is very friendly. She is on her way to Hamburg. I ask to join her. If she is a spy, I couldn't have a safer companion. We enter Germany by way of Warnemunde. Taking a German boat from there, we cross this little piece of Baltic Sea. No signs of the German fleet. On landing we are conducted into a long, wooden building. An officer asks me questions and takes down answers. I stammer and stutter; the few words of German I know desert me. I thrust out my papers desperately. These have been translated into German. Their contents are magical. That money for suffering babies softens German hearts.

As the train pulls out of the station, my eyes sweep the countryside. There are no trenches and no soldiers. It looks as if the Danes could walk straight into Germany and vice versa. Dinner on the train was fourth-rate, a total change from the well-run dining car of a year ago. The quantity of food was small, the quality poor, and the preparation atrocious due to the lack of fats and sugar. The pudding cannot be eaten.

In three hours we reach Hamburg. There are no carriages nor taxis at the station. An aged porter carries our luggage to the Reichshof Hotel, which is second class but perfectly appointed, each bedroom with hot and cold running water. German hotel keepers are keeping hotels open at great loss without raising rates.

I am much too excited to go to bed so suggest to my Swiss companion a walk. Through silent, deserted streets we make our way. We come to the great sheet of water in the centre of Hamburg. Bright lights from a cafe send their shimmering rays flashing and dancing across the water. But all is silent and still, as though some great calamity had fallen upon the city.

We enter the cafe, a huge place with hundreds of little tables. Only two are occupied — one by a group all in mourning. We sit down and order coffee. Presently two cups of steaming black liquid are served. There is no sugar, no milk. My companion calls a waiter, "You've forgotten the milk and sugar." He bows politely, "No, madam, I have not forgotten," he says. "We have been *verboten* to serve either milk or sugar." It is coffee 'Ersatz,' coffee mixed with a substitute.

I see the tired, worried soldiers at the station with their lean faces. I look at the little group in mourning opposite me. I taste my undrinkable coffee. Already the suffering of the people is apparent.

Hamburg and Berlin

Early next morning (August 10) I press the electric button and order breakfast. A pale, worried little man arrives with a tray. There is the same undrinkable coffee, a tiny drop of blue watery milk in a doll's pitcher no bigger than my thumb, no sugar, some black, sour, uneatable bread, and a small saucer of marmalade. Irritated, I wonder how I can spend weeks in Germany without proper food. I remember the Danish butter and sausage I have in the hotel refrigerator. But I have the decency not to send for them; the Danish food shall go to a German friend. My traveling companion joins me and we decide to make a tour of the city. Only a few people are on the street — old or very young people and tiny children. Occasionally we pass a silent, dejected group lined up before a meat shop. It is a meat-day. Working women with babies in their arms, or tiny children carrying baskets, or old decrepit men and women, each clutching a Government meat-card, patiently wait their turn. The shop door flies open, three or four are admitted, and a half pound of meat portioned out to each.

Except for people purchasing food, the city seems dead. We enter a book shop and ask for a map. But to sell a plan of Hamburg is *verboten.* So many things are "verboten." Perhaps that accounts for the inactivity. Store windows present a fine display, but the shop is silent and empty inside.

We find a small boat that makes a three-hour tour of the harbour, and take it. The great wharves are empty, no hurrying men, no swinging derricks, no smoke issuing from smokestacks. In the docks lie big and little boats, rusty, pointless, deserted. The great ship *Imperator,* like a towering monster, commands the centre. The paint is peeling from its sides; its brass is dull; some dirty, stained blankets flap on an upper deck. Except for our tug and two others, no vessels move upon the water. There are no whistles, no chug-chug and swish of passing boats, no vibrant, thrilling life.

Faint from want of food, we leave the boat to seek a restaurant. We find one on a hillside directly opposite the Hamburg-American docks. As we seat ourselves on the outdoor porch we notice a long line of women and children filing into the big Hamburg-American buildings. Each bears a pail. When they emerge it is with steaming contents. The docks have been turned into feeding-kitchens. When the women leave, a whistle blows. Then from every direction come old men and young boys. They come running, hopping, jumping, each striving to be first, driven by hunger or by fear that the last may have nothing. The police keep them in order.

The meal furnished us is scanty, but compared to that scene it seems bountiful. Like the day before, our food is watery and tasteless. One can live on it, but patriotism and tempers suffer. When we have finished, we walk to the Bismarck Denkmal. This monument is situated on a small hill, and the gigantic figure is further elevated by a high pedestal, till it towers over the city. There is something sinister in the statue. It is clad in armor and leans on a gigantic sword. It seems to say, "Nothing in the world can deter me. I conquer all." As a work of art it is a failure. It is made of square-cut stone placed on square-cut stone. This endless multiplicity of exactly similar stones, well ordered and arranged, has the effect of massive greatness. But there is no inspired, central vein of strength as in Rodin's figures, for instance. But my companion is enthralled. "Isn't it wonderful?" she breathes. "If only he were alive, how different it would be! Germany would be victorious."

The words have hardly left her lips when we hear voices. A crowd of children is gathering just below. School is out. In the centre of the children we see a woman slouched upon a bench. She is dirty, ragged, and dark in colouring. On the ground at her feet is a baby just big enough to walk. It also is dirty and possesses only one ragged garment. The mother sits listless, gazing at her child. It is evident she is soon to have another baby. I turn to my companion for explanation. "The woman wants to sell her child. She says she hasn't anything to eat. She isn't a German mother. Of course, no German mother would do such a thing."

My eyes travel from the Bismarck Denkmal to this human tragedy at our feet. The Allies are stupidly making women and children suffer, while the military class and militarism flourish.

It is now tea time and we go to a popular cafe. Here at last is a large group of people. There are many well-dressed women, retired officers or officers home on leave. A band is playing gay music. On the surface all looks well. But a line from Whitman flashes through my mind: "Smartly attired, countenance smiling, form upright, Death under the breast-bones, hell under the skull-bones."

There is no chatter and no laughter. The faces are lined with sadness. There are but two topics of conversation in Germany — war and food shortages. The changes have come to the country gradually. One month sugar stops. The next the people must learn to do without milk. Herr Smyth fails one week and Herr Bauer weeks later. This slow decline blinds Germany to what is really happening.

My spirits sink lower and lower. "Look here," I say to my companion, "I've got to have a square meal. We are going to the best and most expensive hotel in town." That evening we dine at the Atlantic and have a meal that is satisfying. By the skillful use of wine, salt, and some stray scraps of fat, the table d'hôte dinner is passable, though the slice of meat served is no bigger than half my hand, brown, and juiceless. Next morning my companion and I separate, and I leave for Berlin.

My inability to speak German is disconcerting. I remember well that in May 1915 English brought angry looks, but now English is tolerated. A year ago there was bitter hatred of America. Today the average person is pathetically eager to be friends. Slowly the people are awakening. For months the newspapers fed them on the triumphs of Germany. But these stories of glorious victories have resulted in what? A lean and barren country, undernourishment, death.

It is early afternoon, August 11, when I reach Berlin. Again no taxis. An aged porter with a pushcart conducts me to the Adlon, Berlin's best hotel. It is Sunday. As we pass the Tiergarten a great throng of people flows in and out about the Hindenburg Denkmal. That figure is made of wood and covered with nails. You pay a small sum and can hammer in a nail. Everywhere there are Denkmals to testify to Germany's greatness. The Sunday crowd is made up of old men, women, and a sprinkling of lean, pale, nerve-wracked soldiers.

Berlin proves to be the busiest spot in Germany. It and the munition districts are the centers of activity. Berlin is more active than it was a year ago. Then the city was crowded but idle, waiting for a quick, glorious victory. A long war was not dreamed of. Now conditions have changed. The assurance and arrogance have vanished. In their place is a dull resignation. All life is centered on mere existence. Germany has declined rapidly in a year.

At the Adlon and other great hotels one suffers little. There is no sugar, but saccharine is served. The government allowance of meat, bread, and butter per person is the same at the Adlon as elsewhere; butter is served only on Tuesday and Friday, the two meatless days. But the meat problem hardly touches the rich. Chickens, ducks, and birds are not called meat and are to be had at high prices. Besides, the poor frequently have no money for meat or butter, so their allowance is purchased by the rich. It is marvelous with what ingenuity the big hotels conceal deficiencies. That is why visitors and reporters fail to see the underlying truth that Germany is cracking for lack of fat.

The next morning I go to the American Embassy. I have a young friend there. I tell him that I mean to talk to everyone I can, including the Socialist leader Liebknecht. "You'll be watched every moment," he says, "and the authorities won't let you see anything they don't want you to."

The idea of spies is disconcerting. The first person I visit is the radical woman [Augspurg?] who was so helpful on my previous visit. I want her to act as my interpreter and to teach me German. I pursue a zig-zag course to her home and elude pursuit. But I soon find this is not always easy. The funny thing is that German spies dress for the part. They are unmistakable. They nearly always wear grey clothes, a soft grey hat, are pale-faced, shifty-eyed, smooth shaven or have a slight moustache, and carry a cane.

One night my friend and I led one of them a chase about the city until midnight. We jumped from one car to another. It proved an exciting game. Once we actually accosted the spy. But spies grow angry when spoken to. German officials have no sense of humor.

One day when I visited my friend we saw a spy standing at the street corner in the rain from three in the afternoon until nine in the evening. He probably still doesn't know whom I visit. Once I got my friend to walk with me to the Adlon. She thinks this is dangerous, but surely one cannot be arrested for talking to a Social Democrat! Sure enough, when we reach the hotel there is a grey-clad spy talking to the hotel porter. As we approach, the porter jerks the spy's arm. "Here she comes," he says. It is terribly exciting! I feel as important as a heroine in a dime novel.

But before I leave Germany the spies get on my nerves. Free conversation is impossible, except behind closed doors. Everywhere are signs: *"Soldaten — Vorscht bei Gesprächen — Spionengefahr"* (Soldiers — In Conversation Be Careful of Danger of Espionage).

For several days I wander about Berlin letting impressions sink in. The people are sombre and thin; there are no protruding stomachs. It isn't that the people have nothing to eat, but they have too little. It is like trying to run a wagon without oil; it begins to creak. Sooner or later a crisis is inevitable. Soldiers as well as the civil population suffer. There is a popular saying among them; it goes as follows: *"Dorrgemuse, trocken brot, marmelade, heldentod"* (Dried vegetables, dry bread, marmalade, a hero's death). Soldiers are everywhere in Berlin. The cripples are not allowed upon the street, but nervous wrecks are plentiful.

One night I went to the station to see a big detachment leave for Vilna. They had all been in war for some time. Their uniforms were dirty and patched. They sat on benches clinging to a loved one's hand, or stood in listless groups. No one talked. They were like tired children. They needed food and beds. The scenes of farewell were harrowing. Here was a young boy saying good-bye to a mother and three aunts. He was all they had — their whole life. Here a father saying farewell to a wife and three children, or a mother in deep mourning taking leave of her last son, or a young wife with a baby in her arms giving a last embrace.

As the train moved out of the station there were no shouts, no cheers, no words of encouragement. Instead, a deadly silence prevailed. The men leaned out of windows, stretching despairing hands toward loved ones. Little groups broke into sobs. They felt the end had come. A man may go once into battle and return, but not twice or thrice.

As I came away I stopped before the big building which manages military affairs. It is known as the "House of Sorrow." On its rear wall is posted the list of dead and wounded. The night was dark and still. By the rays of an electric arc a few stragglers were running anxious fingers down the long lists. I stopped to count the number. The report covered five days' casualties, from August 17 to 21. The total of dead, wounded, or missing was 44,000 — a city wiped out in five days. The Socialists estimate that two-and-a-half to three million men in Prussia have been killed, wounded, or are missing. No wonder the soldiers are desperate.

Such is the fate of the men, nor is life any better for the women. They are to be seen everywhere. In the streets digging and cleaning sewers. On the road with pick-axe and shovel helping Russian prisoners to relay railway tracks. In the subways, clad in bloomers, acting as train starters. On the trams, wearing husband's motor cap and coat. At night they come home to hungry children and empty larders. Their tiny savings go for bread and potatoes. The day labourers cannot frequent feeding kitchens. They cannot afford it. Berlin prepared to feed 35,000, but last winter only 13,000 ate at the kitchens. In summer the number decreased to 8,000. The meal served is a pint bowl of food, which is a cross between soup and stew, usually very edible. It costs about 10 cents. Yet only the bourgeois class can afford to patronize the kitchens.

Everywhere the signs of decline are manifest. In the windows of houses, on the front of empty stores, are great signs: "To Let." For years merchants have been fighting for vacancies on the big thoroughfares of Berlin. Now they are to be had everywhere. But with suffering, a new race is emerging — a lean race with active minds that begin to question German autocracy and militarism.

To an observant person three things are evident, telling an unmistakable story: the flat stomachs, the endless "To Let" signs, and the empty chocolate slot-machines.

The Food Riots and Rebellion

More money had come to me from the Christian Work Fund and I wanted to spend it properly. But Germany abounds in red tape. I struggled desperately to reach Germany's poor. But official Germany denies its poor and hides them.

My lack of success discouraged me. I appealed to a woman social worker. "Very well," she said, "I'll show you what is happening." She took me to the north of Berlin. There little children swarmed, dirty, ragged, barefooted, and pale. This is a new state of affairs for Germany. Heretofore there have always been at least potatoes and clothes; no one had gone hungry. We visited several tenements. A typical family — a mother, nine children, and grandmother — was living in two rooms and a kitchen. Father was in the war. The baby was six months old. It had what is termed "the English sickness," rickets; it could not raise its arms. Since September first only children under six are allowed milk. The allowance is a pint a day. But this family was living on tea and potatoes, even the baby. There was no money for milk.

We visited many families. My companion was a proud woman, but tears ran down her cheeks. She belonged to the official class. She adored Germany and believed everything Germany did was right, but her heart bled for her people. She dashed her tears aside to say, "Do you wonder German women are bitter? But England shall not bring us to our knees. Rather we will give our last baby."

I knew now what was most needed. It was milk for babies. A trust-worthy and well informed Social Democrat told me that in the big hospitals for babies the increase in mortality was 50 percent. I consulted Dr. Kimmule, the head of the German Red Cross. He thought the best investment was goats. The wealthy farmers who sold goats made money out of their country's needs. They asked five times the regular price.

The following items were to be had only with Government cards: bread, meat, potatoes, butter, sugar, cheese, milk, eggs, meal, flour, soap, and cheap clothes. Each person has to trade at the store assigned. The result is long lines in front of every shop at twelve and at six o'clock.

One Saturday evening I went to a big market in the poor quarter of Berlin. At 4:00 at least two thousand people were in line at the potato counter. I stood and watched for three hours and the line never decreased. As fast as some left, others arrived. The crowd swayed and muttered. Women who had worked all day looked ready to drop. At the counter three or four employees were dealing out potatoes and punching cards as rapidly as possible.

Once I left the market and went with my friend to sit on a bench nearby. Close to us were a pale, sickly man and his wife and child. "Have you your potatoes?" we inquired. "No," was the reply, "but grandmother is standing in line. It's going to be all right tonight. Last Saturday we waited three hours. Then we didn't get any. They'd given out." "What did you do?" we gasped. Quietly, without bitterness, came the answer, "We went hungry."

When we went back to the market there was still the same line, but the crowd was getting restless. A rumour was afloat that the potatoes were giving out. Women began to talk in angry tones. Some shook their fists. Then a whisper passed along the line. More potatoes had arrived. A big wagonful stood outside. Only this word prevented a riot.

The wealthy people do not stand in line. Their servants do this for them. Farmers are expected to pool and sell their supplies of milk, butter, and eggs, but they hold back enough for their children. One farmer I discovered greasing the wheels of his wagon with home-made butter; oil was so expensive he couldn't afford it. Now one cake of soap a month is the allowance — and the soap since the war is vile.

I asked the Social Democrats about the food riots. I was told they occurred chiefly in the spring when the potatoes gave out. Then the women in Hamburg had run straight on the soldiers' bayonets in the struggle for food, and several were killed. The following day, a Sunday, the Government had to throw open the Hamburg provision stores to restore peace. Berlin has had several riots. In some cities women have been shot. A Social Democrat told me, "It is quite easy to start rebellion.

Several times we went to the market and urged the crowd to riot. But we stopped that, for women were put in prison for this and the children left destitute."

Germany had not expected the war to last; it had built up an army and laid in food and munitions for two years. But the two years are up. Slowly the German people are disintegrating. In March or April, if not before, unless new food resources are available, the potatoes will give out, and there will be riots. When this occurs, if a hand of sympathy were extended to the German worker, he would rebel against his own government, and militarism would be overthrown. Few people outside Germany know of the extensive revolt carried on by the Radicals. The day Liebknecht[1] was imprisoned (1916), 5500 workers in one munition factory outside of Berlin went on strike for the whole day. There were similar protests throughout the country.

The Liebknecht party grows. The workers flock to his standard. The demonstration that caused his arrest took place in Potsdamerplatz. Several thousand were gathered there. They had come to talk peace. When Liebknecht appeared, a mighty shout went up from a thousand throats. Liebknecht raised his hand for silence. Then steadily, though knowing the cost, he said, "Do not shout for me. Shout instead that we will have peace — now." The crowd took up the cry: "We will have peace now." It went echoing down the street in a mighty roar. But police were already at Liebknecht's side.

The number in prison is large. In Stuttgart 400 are serving terms. There are corresponding numbers in all big cities. But these victims are not suffering in vain, for the military authorities cannot stop the growing popular demand for peace. The major wing of the Social Democratic party has taken advantage of this. Throughout Germany under their auspices peace meetings are being held. Everywhere people are signing a petition for peace on the basis of the status quo before the war. As long as their demands are kept at this level, peace meetings are tolerated. Not to permit them would be fatal. There is a low, ominous murmur rising from the people.

A Tour for Journalists

When I learned there was to be an official tour for journalists, I went to the German Press Bureau, which was under the civil authorities. They are much more liberal than the military authorities and were eager to send news to America. I was told of a nine-day tour which included a visit to two prison camps and was invited to join. These trips were magnificent feats in German propaganda. An intelligent director conducts a group of reporters through the country. All expenses are paid and the journalists feted and feasted. It is hard to view Germany impartially when fed on champagne.

In the very early morning I left Berlin for Leipzig and Karlsruhe. The first part of the journey was in an ordinary coach. This train was bound for the Western front. It was packed with soldiers. They had lowered the light and were crouched down in their corners. For me it was a weird sensation being flung so closely against this evidence of war. By the tiny gleam of light I could just see the outline of these military figures and the knives sticking in each boot. It was a relief an hour-and-a-half later to change trains, even at 1:30 A.M. The next morning, somewhat weary, I reached the Karlsruhe hotel and settled down into the attractive room assigned me, glad of a rest.

I was dressing for lunch when I heard a commotion, a great clattering of hoofs. I hurried to the window. Coming down the square was one open carriage after another. Barefoot children were running beside them. It must be at least the royal ruler of the Duchy of Baden, I thought. But, no, the carriages were stopping in front of the hotel. They were old-fashioned affairs, pulled by resurrected white horses. On the boxes sat aged little men in uniforms many sizes too large. Their silk hats came down over their ears. I chortled with glee. Yes — it was for our party of nineteen scrubby reporters. All this pomp and ceremony was for us.

The gaping populace stood about, while the press alighted with all the dignity they could muster. It was funny and tragic. We were treated like royalty. Downstairs an elaborate luncheon was being prepared. The Chamber of Commerce was entertaining us. There were two gentlemen to each reporter. An excuse for a good meal was a godsend. These gentlemen had spared no expense. We had seven or eight courses, two or three kinds of wine, including champagne. We ate for over two hours.

It seemed cruel, when I remembered Germany's poor. That long swaying line of people in the north of Berlin, struggling for potatoes. Yet it was impossible to be angry with the Chamber of Commerce. These gentlemen were so kindly, so childlike in their obvious desire to be friends with people from neutral lands. Gracious speeches were made, which I did not understand. Perhaps it was well I didn't, for I could clink glasses and drink to unknown toasts. But all the time my heart was aching for the hungry people outside.

There were nineteen press representatives, including myself: four women and fifteen men. We came from Norway, Sweden, Denmark, Holland, Switzerland, Spain, and America. Some of us were quite shabby in appearance. But several of the gentlemen had dress suits. I had a mussy evening dress creased from steady traveling. Starting on the tour we at first found it a little difficult to live up to our surroundings. No money was spared for our entertainment. We traveled in a special railroad car. Carriages and taxis resurrected from the past met us at the stations and conducted us to expensive hotels.

The moment of descent on a new city was thrilling. As the train drew into a station, lined up on the platform would be a group of prominent citizens, retired generals covered with gold braid and medals, wealthy merchants, the Burgomaster and Ober-Burgomaster, and other city officials, while the populace crowded in the background. At such moments I descended from the train as graciously as I could and extended my hand. Often it got kissed. It was difficult to remember we were only reporters.

After our champagne luncheon in Karlsruhe we had set off for the crippled soldiers' hospital at Attlingen. As we walked through the village streets led by distinguished-looking generals, dirty and underfed children sprawled on doorsteps. Through an open door of a big building I saw a long line of patient people buying potatoes.

The Lazarette for armless and legless men was impressive. It had a great stretch of open ground and many well-equipped buildings. The first room we entered contained surgical appliances. Suspended in each machine was a man. One hung by his shoulders, having his neck stretched. Another lay face downward, having a leg pulled. A third endured the twisting of a thumb and hand. Many of the patients were white with pain; beads of perspiration stood upon their foreheads. I shrank back. It was like Mme. Tussaud's chamber of horrors, only these were living men, not wax figures. But the military doctors were urging us forward. With great pride they exhibited their inventions. But as I looked in the men's faces, often I saw anger and resentment.

At one time we were treated to a circus performance. A squad of one-legged men was called to do dumb-bell exercises. Nearly all kept their balance; only one or two lurched and tottered. Then a group of armless or one-armed men were made to jump wooden horses and do kindred stunts. "Don't the men object to being exhibited?" I asked as I viewed the maimed group before me. "They did at first," was the reply, "but we soon broke them in and now they do it quite willingly." At the end of the performance we were taken to the room of false limbs. Here were steel arms with great iron hooks. These were called week-day arms. The Sunday arms were imitations of the real thing. Few but officers have Sunday arms. It was a weird scene, this exhibition of the latest invention in arms and legs. Our little group stood or sat about while the military doctors produced crippled patients and strapped appliances onto them.

The doctor's talk ran as follows: "This one" — jerking a wreck forward — "has one leg off at the knee, and the other at the thigh, but see how well he walks," and the maimed wreck was pranced up and down before us. "Now, this one," continued the doctor with pride, "has had both legs and an arm removed, but you see he is quite satisfactory." I began to feel in a horrible nightmare. It seemed to me in another moment the doctor would be saying, "Now, this man had his head shot off and we have substituted a wooden one. We found the spine controlled muscular action, and he makes a perfectly satisfactory worker!"

Never once in the whole afternoon was the soul inside these tortured bodies considered. The long hospital wards were clean but ugly. There were no flowers, no pictures, no games, no gramophones. These men looked so utterly wretched that I was reminded of my convict friends. When I commented on the need for amusement, the reply was, "It doesn't do to spoil the men; they don't want to work afterward."

At the Baden-Baden station were again open victorias and white horses, and we made our triumphant journey to the hotel. We arrived late at the elaborate dinner-party being put on for us by the city. There were charming red roses at my plate. It was a sumptuous meal and hours long, with everything from oysters to ices and a grand mixture of wines. A German general sat on my right and a prominent citizen on the left. The general confided that he had lost 24 pounds, but added that it was better for his health and that "All the German people are better off for this shortage of meat and fat." But he ate hungrily, as did everyone else. All through the meal a band played gaily. The Casino garden with its lights, its music, and thronging people seemed a fairyland. It wasn't until we left and passed through the iron gates that reality returned. Pressed against the outer railing were the lean and hungry populace. It suddenly became very difficult for me to go on with this life of luxury.

The next morning we were off again, carried by funicular to the top of a two-thousand-foot mountain. From that glorious mountain top the glowing landscape stretched out on every side. It was impossible to believe war was raging a few miles away. There were the shining meadow land with the glittering Rhine winding in and out, the thickly wooded hills, sombre in shadows, fitting their name, "Black Forest," and far off on the horizon dimly rose a church steeple. It marked the city of Strasburg. On a clear day when the wind is right the booming of cannon could be heard. Again the city fed us — this time on the mountain top. Again we clinked glasses and drank toasts. In the afternoon a special electric car took us about the town. We saw parks and fountains and flower gardens and the modern art gallery, and were introduced to the aged and distinguished painter Hans Thoma.

At five o'clock we again set forth. This time for Heidelberg. Here it was the same. I had begun to grow very weary of constant entertainment. Besides, I felt myself a prisoner; I had overheard the gentlemen who danced attendance at Baden-Baden say to my future guide in Heidelberg, as he delivered me over, "Never let her out of your sight."

At Heidelberg there was a quiet dinner in the hotel; then we were given a concert in the park, where more beer and wine flowed. It was a dreary affair. Heidelberg was no longer the alive, little university town I had known a few years before. The university's grounds were empty. No students flocked to the patisseries for coffee and Apfelkuchen. Only soldiers file past, most of them mere boys.

The prison camp at Heidelberg for French, English, and Russian officers and orderlies is a good one, yet depressing. It was the depression of suppression. There is a relentlessness about the German official that to a free spirit is suffocating.

In the afternoon we walked to the ancient "Schloss," a massive, half-ruined castle on the hillside. We sat on broken pillars and listened to an historical discourse on the greatness of Germany. We were then taken to another mountain for another gorgeous repast, given by the city. There were flowers for the ladies, and six or seven courses and unlimited beverages. I began to feel sick of food and drink. No wonder reporters who make official tours and never see anything else of Germany report the land flowing with plenty.

Late that afternoon we went to Mannheim, arriving at seven. Here we donned every speck of finery we had. The city gave us a magnificent dinner in the Friederich's Park. I felt I should die if I drank another toast, but I knew a failure to do so would be taken amiss.

That day Italy and Rumania had declared war against the Reich, but here neither by look or word was there a sign that anything had happened. During the succeeding days it was evident from the newspapers that Germany was concentrating on her new enemy, Rumania, which had great wheat and oil supplies. These must be had.

Next morning I stepped out on the balcony of the gigantic parlour suite given me. It was only seven o'clock and coming down the square was a regiment of soldiers. The men's feet dragged, tired eyes looked out of pale faces, but the band played cheerily. Great God, how long was this horror to keep up! To dine in a rose garden and awaken to such a scene!

That morning our time was divided between a slaughterhouse and a milk depot. These visits were to show Germany's great food supply. In the milk depots there were four great tanks and only one in use. At the slaughter yards were four buildings for animals, but only one was occupied. A bullock was to be killed for our benefit. Reporters from every corner of the globe were thus assembled to see Germany kill one small cow. It was the only creature slain during our hour's stay. The importance of the event demonstrated as nothing else could Germany's lack of food. In fact, the whole trip was evidence of that, in spite of the luncheons and dinners.

At noon there was another elaborate luncheon given by the Merchants' Association, and after that a special treat — a trip on a Rhine steamboat, which was decorated from stem to stern with gay flags and bunting. Ours was the only boat. Women and children ran along the banks and waved to us; to have something happen was a godsend. For two years there had been nothing but death notices.

Smoke came but from one factory in four. Supplies and workers were giving out. There was little leather; children in Berlin were going barefoot. The blankets to go under horse saddles were no more. Linen and cotton for fuses were running low. All the linen in Belgium had been appropriated. Rubber was very scarce. Every family has given all the brass and copper it had. Of what use are outer victories when internally there is only disaster?

On the sixth day of our tour we went to Stuttgart. At the station no citizens greeted us. We went to the best hotel and ate our lunch unheralded. There was no bread, butter, or sugar. That evening we had to be content with our own company, because the Prussian press and its representatives were not welcome in the Duchy of Württemberg. We had been promised a visit to a camp for Russian prisoners, but the Württemberg military authorities flatly refused us admittance. So the next day we meekly inspected the Bosch munition factories instead. Before the war there were 6000 workers here. There was still that number, but now 4000 of them were women, compared to 700 formerly. They were handling big machines; they managed electrically-run engines swiftly and well. Of the 4000 women, 1200 were mothers.[2] The Bosch factories run night and day in eight-hour shifts. Sometimes the same labourers work through two shifts. As we went through the factory we saw a group of one-armed men working. They had the steel arms with iron hooks, the week-day arms.

In a dark corner I saw rubber tubing from hospital douchebags piled high to be turned into munitions. Bicycles in shop windows and on the street no longer have rubber tires. On September first there was no longer rubber for automobile tires. The Bosch family have munition factories in America; it is the same business as in Stuttgart with a common capital. But Bosch in America makes munitions for the Allies, while his relative makes munitions for Germany. When the Social Democrats in Stuttgart got wind of this American connection they had revolted; Mr. Bosch was summoned to court and tried, but the judge exonerated him saying, "Mr. Bosch has done nothing detrimental to the interests of his country." This same judge imprisoned 400 persons for clamoring for peace.

Life did not flow smoothly in Stuttgart. The people were restless. In the evening the workers crowded upon the street. I longed to investigate, but could not escape supervision.

I decided to break away from the journalists' tour. I had agreed to meet my Berlin friend in Nuremberg and I feared to wire a change of plans lest we should never meet. All her letters had been opened. The director of the expedition vigorously opposed my departure. I escaped only by stating where I was going, to what hotel, and what train I should take. I also had to visit the police and lay my plans before them. I boarded the train with a sigh of relief. It was good to be a little bit free again. My heart beat fast as we drew into Nuremberg. Would my friend be there? Anxiously I scanned the long line of waiting people. Then my eye lighted on her. We fell into each other's arms. We went to the biggest and most expensive hotel. Many of the employees in such places are spies so it is a disagreeable atmosphere, but to deliberately live where one can be watched is disarming to authorities.

From Nuremberg we went to Munich. The farther south we went the richer grew the land. And with the increased fertility a corresponding change was noticeable in the people. The Prussians are cold and proud. The Bavarians are warm and friendly; they still possess vitality. But the Bavarians begin to dislike the Prussians. It crops out everywhere. The first morning in Munich the hotel chambermaid unloaded some of her emotions, saying, "It was a sad day for Bavaria when she tied up with Prussia. They are bleeding our country to death. Twice as many Bavarians have been killed as Prussians. We have the worst of the fighting. I tell you the Bavarians hate the Prussians. When our soldiers come back, there will be a revolution. A little while ago two Bavarian regiments were sent to the front. They were fine young men. They were sent straight to the firing line. They stepped out of the cars into the middle of battle. Before they had walked a dozen steps every one was shot down." We heard the same story everywhere, the story of hatred for Prussia. Here the working people are underfed and over-worked. They hate Prussian militarism. The women see their babies go without milk, and they hate Prussian militarism. The women in the factories are paid less than the men, and *they* hate Prussian militarism. This stored-up emotion must have an outlet. With peace will come the reckoning.

Munich, we found, still had animation. People sat at cafes and smoked, and little groups gathered to discuss knotty problems. Spies were abroad, but despite them people talked. One evening I had several members of the Liebknecht party come to the hotel. For two hours we sat in the restaurant and denounced Prussian militarism. When a waiter approached, voices dropped. Still we talked on. This would have been impossible in Prussia.

But Bavaria is torn between two elements — the workers and the aristocrats. The wealthy have been Prussianized but not the workers. In spite of Bavaria's attempts to democratize the food supply, her poor go hungry. As in Berlin there are long lines of people struggling for potatoes, and here too the poor can't afford the city feeding kitchens. Yet Munich is one of Germany's richest cities.

The Social Democrats are indignant over the situation. They sent me to a church to see poverty at its worst. The church belongs to a group of Dominican monks. The friars beg at the street corner for food. Whatever they get they put into a big pot and boil. The liquid mass is served each day free to the poor. The hour of distribution is noon. At eleven, humanity's dregs begin to assemble — tottering old men with white beards and tattered clothes, skinny, bent old women swathed in rags, and barefooted, dirty, ghastly pale children. A little crowd gathered about a stool on which the big iron pot was placed. Simultaneously they drove in spoons and began shoveling down the liquid. There were gurgles and snorts. They were like dogs about a bone. One old man, luckier than the rest, possessed a cup. In spite of his rags he was stately. He filled his cup, drank ravenously, and licked every inch of the cup. I turned away shaken.

Because I still had some money from the Christian Work Fund, I turned to the young Social Democrat with me and said, "I know it isn't solving any problem, but let's feed them." She nodded and her face lighted up. "Suppose we take them to the city feeding kitchen," she suggested. We lined up the little company. They couldn't believe the news. Down the street we went, a row of bowed and bent old people and little children clinging to skirts. We bought meal tickets for each for a week. As the checks were handed out a gnarled and twisted old figure would shoot down the hall to the big eating-room. Youth for a moment came back to those tottering legs. There was no time for thanks. Death was at the door and life had suddenly been thrust out to them.

We stayed with a family with nine children. The father was at the war and the mother ill in bed. Another group of seven had no mother, and the father was in a munitions factory. We bought these families meal tickets for a month. Then I turned over all that remained of the Christian Work Fund and asked my young guide to buy as many meal tickets as possible for unfed school children.

This was one side of Munich. But there was another. Although there were no private autos, Munich kept up its intellectual and art interest. Concert and grand opera were prospering. My friend and I went to hear

Parsifal. Soft music lulled our nerves. The opera was a gorgeous display of light and colour, music and incense. The rich red velvet robes of the *Parsifal* priests, the goblet of wine which turned to fiery red as the Holy Spirit in the form of a dove descended, the singing, the music — everything combined to stir, elate, and soothe the mind and senses. But something in me rebelled. I felt I was being drugged, hypnotized into a disregard of reality. At the end of the first act I said, "I've got to get out and get some air. It's beautiful but suffocating. It's covering up all that ought to be faced."

But Munich was the most interesting spot in Germany this September 1916. The middle class, as well as the unskilled workers, struggle against the relentless organization and militarism. In Munich I found the leaders of the German branch of the Women's International Peace party, who had come to the Hague the year before. They were working steadily for peace. At a meeting of Social Democrats for Peace, when one of the men urged women to bear children, saying, "Remember we need sons for the Revolution, as well as for war," one of these courageous women, Lida Heymann, rose, anger blazing in her eyes, and said, "Never again bring children into the world unless men promise they will not be used as cannon fodder."

Next morning a policeman was at Fraulein Heymann's home. He was a Bavarian and had known her from girlhood. He knew she was a woman of wealth and high standing. He was embarrassed. As a Bavarian he detested Prussia, but he had to do his duty, so he handed out the military order. Henceforth Fraulein Heymann was forbidden to speak in public, nor might she have more than five people in her house at a time, nor could she send any letter or telegram outside the country, and all her German mail was to be opened and inspected.[3]

One night we went to a big peace demonstration. It was under the auspices of the major wing of the Social Democratic party. For peace meetings, in spite of restrictions, are popular. But the military authorities see to it that the peace terms asked for are merely for the status quo before the war. No discussion is allowed. At this meeting there were perhaps two thousand people. The floor was covered with little tables. Beer still flowed. Men predominated; even soldiers in uniform were present. Except for our group, the audience was made up chiefly of factory workers, a keen, alert crowd. The chief speaker said: "The days of *'Gott strafe England'* are over. We hope the time will soon come when Germans are no longer called *Barbaren* and *Boches*. It is essential that peace be made as soon as possible. The government has wholly failed to live up to its promise that women and children should not suffer when their men go to the front."

He called for a standing vote for the proposal that peace be sought at once on terms of the status quo before the war. Everyone, except my friends, stood up. They wanted more than that; they wanted freedom for Poland and a plebiscite vote for Alsace and Lorraine. The audience didn't understand; they thought my companions were averse to peace. Angry people crowded around us. We were pushed and shoved. Several women were shaking their fists. One was yelling, "My husband was killed at the front. How dare you not vote for peace?" We struggled toward the street. Fraulein Heymann's hair was pulled down, and we were considerably mauled before we made our exit. Then Fraulein Heymann turned on her tormentors. She could not speak in the meeting because of the police order, but in the open she risked it. A tall, slender woman with golden hair and blue eyes, shaking her fist, she hurled at the crowd: "I want peace, but I want a real peace. I am more radical than you." A man in the crowd, one of the Social Democratic leaders, came to her side. He told the people who Fraulein Heymann was and what she stood for. Abashed, the people moved on and we slipped off into the cool night.

Yes, German women have courage. They are not sheep. The people are growing restless. There is no easy life ahead for the Kaiser.

There was one other woman I wished to see before leaving Germany: Clara Zetkin. She and Liebknecht have fought side by side for the same ends, she the leader of the radical women as he is of the men. I told my Berlin friend of my desire. She thought it dangerous, but agreed to the undertaking. Clara Zetkin had been imprisoned the previous spring because of her fight for peace. After several months in prison she was released on bail, pending her trial, because of serious heart trouble. She was a woman over sixty, living in Stuttgart — a four hour trip from Munich. It was impossible to make the round trip in a day, but if I left Munich for overnight the passport regulations required me to go to the police and state where I was going. I decided to evade the law. At noon one day my friend and I set forth. We kept our room at the hotel in Munich. We took no baggage. We told no one of our plans. We hoped in this way to avoid detection. We traveled third class because there are fewer spies in the third class.

After a hasty dinner in Stuttgart we took a tram car to the suburbs. When we reached the end of the car line there was still three quarters of an hour's walk through a lonely wood. Darkness was closing in. The sky was overcast. As we started down the road, we noticed a man on the opposite side of the street. A spy. We turned and walked in the opposite direction. The man crossed the street and followed us. We walked until we came to a post office; there we entered and made inquiries about our way. We left by the side door. The man was not to be seen. We started off again down the lonely road. It began to rain. A terrific storm had arisen. There were mighty crashes of thunder and brilliant flashes of lightning; the rain came in great sheets. The one umbrella was no protection. We were soaked, but we trudged on. At last we saw a light; we were coming to a little village. The second house was Clara Zetkin's. She was in, alone, except for a great dog and a maid. Her husband was driving an ambulance for the German Red Cross, and her two sons were surgeons in a base hospital. She was delighted to see us. We had only intended to make a call, but outside the storm raged. Our hostess would not listen to our leaving on such a night. It was dangerous to stay, but better to stay than go. We settled down for a long talk, or rather we let Clara Zetkin talk. Shaken with illness, she fights on. One moment she was pouring out a torrent of words, the next, stricken with pain, she lay white and gasping on the sofa, but in an instant she was up again continuing her discourse. Liebknecht's imprisonment had been a great blow. Imprisonment of nearly all the peace leaders had seriously handicapped the work. "We can do nothing now," she said, "but if peace comes you will see. The thing I fear is *slow* starvation. Half-fed people have no life. If there were *no* food there would be rebellion, but this way — No."

My friend and I spent a restless night, while the storm raged. At daylight the doorbell rang. Surely it was the police! But it was only a tradesman. Early in the morning we made a hasty departure. Going back through the same lonely wood, we reached Stuttgart and took the first train to Munich, where we sauntered leisurely into our hotel, acting as if we had never been away. But our night's absence was known. The hotel employees looked at us coldly.

I had planned to leave for Switzerland the following morning. My American passport included that country. But it wasn't easy to get out of Germany. At least four days before departure you must go to the police, deliver up your passport, and be finger-printed. When finally the day came to pick up my passport, it was an exciting moment. Had my adventure come to official ears? Evidently not, for my papers were promptly delivered.

I had been given much propaganda material on every phase of German organization while on my journalistic tour. I asked to take this with me to America. The officer shook his head. "It can't go," was his terse reply. I shrugged my shoulders. It was silly to let me travel about and yet forbid German-prepared propaganda to pass. In the end a few picture postcards of Bismarck, the Kaiser, some "Denkmals," and some pamphlets on German Red Cross work were allowed and done up in a sealed packet for transportation. This taught me it would be useless to carry journalist notes openly. But how smuggle them through? I ripped open the lining of my dress suitcase and laid my papers inside. I had not spent a voluntary week in prison in vain. Then I bought glue and stuck the lining together. The next morning my friend and I boarded the train for the border. As we sped through the country I had my last glimpses of Germany. I looked at the desolate land with no wagons or motors on the country roads, only now and then a lonely woman in a big field.

In our railway carriage was a soldier, home on a three-weeks' leave. He was a man of means, about forty years of age, and extremely well educated. For fifteen months he had been at the front. "I will never go back. I'll make myself ill or do myself an injury, if they try to send me." "Was it so terrible?" we asked. "Worse than any civilian can realize. I refused to go as an officer and went as a sergeant. The common soldiers weren't given any more consideration than a pack of animals. They were killed off like flies."

I began to worry about my hidden notes. I examined my suitcase. The German glue was a failure; the lining was loose. After much thought I got tissue paper from the lady's toilet and copied the notes onto that. In the toilet I ripped open the heavy seams of the straps of my English raincoat, moistened the tissue paper, laid it inside, and sewed the coat together. It was a wonderful hiding place; you couldn't feel a thing.

At the frontier we were shown into a little waiting-room by the Germans. About twenty other travelers were there and my friend was still with me. At last my name was called. The next minute I was sitting in a tiny room in front of a great white sheet with two holes in it. Eyes were looking out at me through those holes. It was uncanny. Questions were asked me, but all the German I had learned vanished. I sat quite still and tried to look calm, but inwardly my heart was pounding. An interpreter was summoned. My papers were examined. The interpreter made some sarcastic remarks. Then I was led into another room. There was my luggage, spread out on a long bench. I saw I was not to get out of Germany easily. My two valises and carry-all had all been opened. Every item was examined. Each stocking turned inside out. Every scrap of underwear held up to the light and each seam examined. Finally the suitcases themselves were inspected. Thank God I had removed my notes. The soldiers' fingers went over every speck of the lining. I swallowed thankfully as the things were put back. The officer was evidently surprised that they had unearthed nothing. But they still were not friendly; I asked if I might go but they shook their heads. Just then a whistle blew; the little boat that was to take me across Lake Constance to Switzerland was leaving.

Then the door opened and my friend was shown in. I was so glad to see her; I forgot my disappointment at being detained. Hurriedly she explained, "The officer says he has a 'denunciation' against you. He says they have been through all your things and found nothing. That is in your favour, but they aren't going to let you across the frontier tonight."

It was evident some spy who had been following me had told tales. My friend and I exchanged glances but said nothing. I left my luggage with the officials. We went to a hotel facing the lake where we had been commanded to stay. When my friend and I were safely in our room she started to talk. But I motioned to a door leading into an adjoining room. The door had a big crack and a keyhole, and in the bathroom I had discovered two bungholes. By common consent we confined our conversation to clothes, weddings, and babies. Late that evening we went for a walk. Then in whispers we discussed the "denunciation." It was not easy to sleep that night. But fear breeds craftiness. As I undressed I shook out every garment for the benefit of the keyhole.

Next morning we were up early. A boat for Switzerland left shortly after eight. I think it was my cheerfulness and unconcern that won the day. The officers had grown friendly. They had come to the conclusion I must be harmless. This treatment made my conscience prick as their suspicions of the night before had not. I was not personally examined nor was my luggage re-examined, but passed through the roped-off enclosure. I was not allowed to speak again to my friend. I stood on the boat's deck, and she on the shore. Now that I was off, I hated to leave her. During my stay in Germany she had understood and protected me. She loved her country as few do, so much so that she could see its faults.

But as the boat drew close to the land on the other side, a flood of joy seized me. I had not realized how exiled I had felt. One wireless message three weeks old had been my only connection with America. It was an almost deserted village at which we landed. Was it really Switzerland? I put the matter to the test; I made for the nearest restaurant. For a solid hour I consumed bread, butter, coffee, cream, and sugar. I hadn't known how I missed them. It was exactly like getting oiled up. My tense nerves began to relax.

In a short time my train arrived. Then as it sped on through the country I saw I was indeed in a new world. Cars were on the country roads. At the stations were crowds of men, *young* men in business clothes. I couldn't take my eyes off them — nor off the milk cans! I noticed my fellow-passengers had fat hands and great fat stomachs. To my unaccustomed eye they looked enormous. They laughed and talked. Their eyes were bright and they had rosy cheeks. In the dining car we had a huge meal, six courses, two kinds of meat, and a salad reeking with oil. But suddenly I couldn't swallow. It all seemed wrong. I wanted to cry out, "Don't you understand? A nation is starving."

After Berne we passed from German into French Switzerland. My destination was Geneva. It was good to be in a land whose language I could speak. But I discovered life in Switzerland was distressing. The land was deluged with spies. Wherever I went some man followed me. There were German spies and French spies, for in the First World War part of Switzerland was for Germany, the other for France.

All that is best and worst in mankind was here in evidence. On the one hand the Swiss Red Cross worked day and night, nursing wounded soldiers, protecting war prisoners, and offering to trained nurses from the belligerent countries a two week's vacation in the best hotels free. On the other hand greedy merchants, who fatten on wine and good food, were busily taking money for munitions designed to destroy their countries. German merchants sold war material to the French, and the French to the Germans. Poor Switzerland! It was being squeezed between these two forces. It was not a haven of rest.

I wanted to get away as quickly as possible, but I did not want to go back through Germany. My escapade in Stuttgart made it dangerous. I didn't know what to do, for Americans were not permitted to travel from one belligerent country to another. The American Embassy was adamant: I must go back the way I had come. I decided to appeal to the British and beg for a pass through France. At the British Embassy I found a fine young captain at the head of the Intelligence department. To him a woman who had been through Germany was a curiosity. I explained my predicament. "I simply can't go back through Germany, and the American Embassy won't help me. What shall I do?" The young captain was sympathetic. "Don't worry. I'll see you through," he said. Soon we were chatting gaily. "I want to hear more about Germany. Couldn't you dine with me?" he asked.

Suddenly I remembered the German spies. "Spies follow me everywhere," I said, "and if I have to go back to Germany and I've been seen dining with the British Embassy, what do you think would happen to me?" He laughingly agreed it wouldn't do. But after a few minutes he said, "Suppose we elude the spies? I'll be in a taxi at X street at 7:00 P.M., and you come along and take the taxi."

The situation of trying to foil the spies appealed to my sense of humour or adventure. That evening I slipped quietly out of my hotel and down a deserted street. At the corner stood a taxi. I opened the door and popped in. It was the right one. We had a great laugh and felt we were acting the leading roles in a new movie. We went for dinner at a country club.

Here I poured out my story, "The German population is like prisoners; they only become enraged by punishment. There are only two ways of treating Germany," I said. "You can crush her or you can offer her a square deal if she will overthrow militarism. Why not appeal to the radicals? Drop literature instead of bombs. Tell the German people we want to be their friends." "We've thought of that," he replied. For the captain was well informed on Germany. He knew of the food shortage. He hoped for signs of collapse. This English officer wanted Germany defeated, but he was not vindictive. It was amusing to watch him study me. When we parted that evening, he promised assistance. He said he was taking a risk, but he trusted me.

In three days he handed back my passport. On it was written: "Seen at the British legation in Berne, September 22nd, 1916. Miss Doty is personally known to me. Good for London." In addition I was given a letter in French for use in France. I destroyed all my remaining identification papers including those from the *Chicago Tribune* and a precious note from Romain Rolland, in exile in Switzerland. That night I took the train for Paris. At the French frontier I was full of anxiety. Had the captain the power to protect me? First my luggage was examined. Then a soldier stepped up and took my passport. It was covered with official German seals. He was staggered. He hurried me into the next room. For two hours I was passed from official to official. Endlessly I repeated my story. When they had finished I was turned over to a woman, who conducted me to a large closet and asked me to undress. When that ordeal was over, I was allowed on the train.

I was very tired and crept quickly into my berth. But in the midst of dreams of Paris there came loud thumps at the state-room door. It was flung open and in walked the French police. They examined my passport. The chief officer was suspicious. "How long," he said, "have you known Captain X?" I replied carelessly, "Captain has an American wife. We dined together." That settled it. Dining with the British Embassy gave me a standing. The officer withdrew. When again I opened my eyes, it was to hear the porter say, "*Paris dans une demi-heure.*"

What would I now find in Paris since my visit of a year ago? The station was packed with people. More was happening in Paris in five minutes than in a whole month in Berlin. I knew at a glance that Germany could never defeat this country. I went to a little sidewalk cafe for breakfast. Streams of people passed — girls on their way to business, crippled soldiers, rushing ambulances, flying taxis, delivery wagons, English officers each with a French girl clinging to an arm. I wanted to stay in Paris, but I'd promised the British captain I wouldn't. He feared I would get into trouble with my German-marked passport. But it was Saturday, and there were no train reservations to be had until Sunday.

I soon found much of the idealism of a year ago had vanished. There were other signs too that were distressing: France was beginning to copy Germany. She was growing militaristic. Yet the victory of the

Marne was not won by a relentless military system but by a united and idealistic France. To go from Germany to France is like going from a land of poverty to one of plenty. The Allies have all the resources. They have the raw material, workers — 70,000 Chinamen, for instance, — food, and munitions, while Germany's supplies diminish. But as long as Germany has a speck of food or a man to fight she will not give in.

On Sunday I took the train for Le Havre. As I gazed from the car window I saw that the country teamed with activity. Smoke poured from factories. At one point we came to a military centre; here the construction of gigantic new buildings was in progress and railroad tracks were being laid in every direction. Le Havre was the temporary seat of the Belgian government and was crowded with Belgians. There would be no boat to England that night because a U-boat had been sighted. The chances of accommodation were small. There were no porters or carriages at the station. An old postman offered me his services. He swung me up onto the high front seat of his wagon and we tore down the street at a mad pace. I secured the last room to be had; it was at the top of the hotel, six flights and no elevator. But I was thankful for a bed. The next night I boarded the Channel steamer, where I had to tell the English officers of my trip through Germany. It was two hours before they released me. The steamer was frightfully hot; every porthole was fastened down. The decks were in total darkness. There wasn't a sound except the swish of the water as our boat moved through the silent night. But I was more afraid of capture than bombs. What would the Germans do to me if I were made prisoner?

We reached Southampton in the early morning, without breakfast and without sleep. My passport was taken from me, and I was told to go to Scotland Yard to pick it up as soon as I reached London. That city was quieter than a year before. The gay enlistment posters had vanished; the bands no longer played. At night the streets were pitch-black. Given the fog and the short, winter days, London was dreary. A spirit of relentlessness and hardness had grown in the land. The people believed that Germany had stored up goods to destroy them commercially after the war. So they wanted Germany smashed. Slowly England was dividing into two camps: those who only wanted to fight for freedom and the rights of small nations, and those who wanted to destroy the enemy. The latter class now prevailed in both England and France. They both grew militaristic. I stayed ten days in England, again with my great friends the Pethick-Lawrences. I felt I had no right to linger. My pass had been given me by the military authorities. On October 11th I sailed from Liverpool; it was safer than going through the English Channel. On the ocean trip homeward my thoughts ran riot. I had seen both sides. I had no doubt about the outcome — Germany would eventually be beaten. But a prolonged struggle might mean spiritual bankruptcy for the Allies. Was there a way out?

I had learned much on my trip. My prison experiences had shown me that convicts are just ordinary folk, both good and bad. Now I had been shown the same thing about nations. In each country were good and bad, irrespective of nationality. The dictatorship governments were the trouble, greedy persons who wanted to own the earth. I closed my eyes and dreamed a dream of how America would change in the next 50 years to lay the foundation for permanent peace. In this dream we wished to make reparation, to aid with war indemnities, and we contributed a million dollars for the reestablishment of Belgium. The establishment of small nations was insisted on, and in cases of dispute a plebiscite vote decided the nationality of the disputed territory. An endeavour was made to give to the uttermost, instead of take to the uttermost. "So the foundations of a permanent peace were laid."

Was it a dream? I woke with a start. I was lying in a steamer chair and we were drawing into New York harbour. There at the dock were my beloved father and mother. My mother held high a book for me to see. It was my book about my prison experiences. It had just been published by the Century Company and was called *Society's Misfits*.

It was good to be back in America, but I could feel the growing tension. My prison book did not receive much attention. All thoughts were centered on the European war. But many notes about the book came from unknown persons, which gave a great satisfaction, including one from the author Eleanor Gates, who called it "profoundly moving and inspiring."

My articles on Germany for the *New York Tribune* had to be written from the precious notes hidden in the lining of my coat. These articles began to appear every week in the Sunday *New York Tribune*, often on the front page with big headlines.

Mrs. Amos Pinchot, one of the most ardent peace workers, felt I should go to Washington and tell the President my story. She was a friend of Woodrow Wilson and arranged the interview. We traveled together to Washington. Wilson received us in his sitting room quite informally. There were just the three of us. He, poor man, had a frightful cold, but was eager for information and asked many questions about Germany. Even then I could see how tormented he was. The pressure for U.S. participation in war was great. He was torn between his desire for peace, the need to help England, and the sacred duty of protecting the rights of citizens, particularly the right to the freedom of the seas. He had just been reelected on the slogan "He kept us out of war."

Back in New York I continued to work with the Woman's Peace Party and helped edit a little paper called "Four Lights:" "Then he showed four lights when he wished them to set full sail." Jane Addams was still with us and as firm in her stand as ever. She too had seen Wilson. And letters came regularly from my two great friends Malini Pethick-Lawrence in England and R.R. in Berlin. I had lived through great experiences with them; each though so-called enemies of each other was fighting for peace and freedom. I found in these friendships the affection I needed, and greedily lapped up their love. Intimate friendship with men brought complications, which close friendship with women did not.

My *Tribune* articles soon brought me considerable fame and many invitations to lunch and dinner. Concurrently with the *Tribune* articles, the English weekly magazine *The Nation* was printing my story. The editor, Mr. Massinghane, was writing me: "Thank you for your admirable work. It has been much quoted . . . and had a considerable influence on public opinion." In Paris also my articles were appearing in a French newspaper, *La Populaire.* Jean Longuet, deputy de la Seine and a leader in the socialist party, had asked to translate the articles and print them in his paper.

But the voice for war was growing louder than the voice for peace. Wilson feared the inevitable. On 22 January 1917, to ease his conscience, he was proposing a League of Nations and a "peace without victory," that there be neither conquerors nor conquered.

In March my articles on Germany appeared in book form under the title *Short Rations.* The press notices were extremely good. An editorial in the *New York Evening Globe* of 11 March 1917 said: "It is amusing to discover that of all the war correspondents a woman seems to have brought the most interesting and convincing news out of Germany." *The Philadelphia Press* said: "Lurid, fair, vivid, impassioned but without prejudice, sympathetic but without sentimentality — a pen picture which may well last beyond the conditions that inspired it."

Then on 16 March we woke one morning to hear there had been a Russian revolution and the Czar overthrown. This was exciting news, for in those days we believed kings, czars, and Kaisers should be eliminated everywhere and democratic government established.

Coincident with this news was another event of lesser value but of great importance to the feminist world. Jeanette Rankin had been elected to Congress, the first woman Congressman, one woman among about 430 men. The event was especially interesting because women had not yet obtained the vote. A big breakfast was given Jeanette Rankin by the united women leaders of both right and left, at the Shoreham Hotel the day Congress opened.

But these happy events were of short duration, for the war clouds were gathering fast. Germany had renewed her policy of sinking neutral as well as enemy ships. Three American ships were sunk; the overt act had been committed. President Wilson went before Congress 2 April 1917, to ask for war. His words:

> It is a fearful thing to lead this great and peaceful people into war, the most terrible and disastrous of wars . . . but right is more precious than peace. . . . The world must be made safe for democracy. . . . We have no selfish ends to serve. We desire no conquest, no dominion. We seek no indemnities for ourselves, no compensation for the sacrifice we make. . . . We dedicate our lives, our fortunes, everything we are and have with the pride of those who know the day has come when America is privileged to spend her blood and her might for the principles that gave her birth. God helping her, she can do no other.

On 6 April Congress voted for war. The Senate was almost unanimous, but there were 50 votes against war in the House. One of these was Jeanette Rankin's, who with tears on her cheeks and with a choking voice said, "I can not vote for war."

This vote was to blight her career for many months to come. For overnight the whole spirit of America changed. There sprang up a campaign of hatred for the Germans; one had to hate a German to kill him. The pacifists continued their campaign, but it was hopeless. *Short Rations* was no longer spoken of. It had no value. It took six months of growing hatred and then my book was banned as unfit for soldiers to read. This in spite of the fact that the German press in the *Cologne Gazette* had been calling me "Snooping Madeleine. She writes like a journalist, with no lofty point of view . . . her political views are the most superficial imaginable. She understands nothing of our political situation. . . . We wonder that this foreigner has been permitted to visit our prison camps and industrial centers. Evidently we should always vigorously supervise American women who travel among us." [The *New York Tribune* in 1917, full date missing from clippings among Doty papers, ran a story about this under the headline: "GERMAN PRESS ANGRY AT MADELEINE DOTY. Tribune Writer Denounced for Exposé of Conditions in the Empire." It continued, "The German press, evidently angered by the revelations of actual conditions in the Central Empires through Madeleine Doty's recent articles . . . has taken to 'strafing' the writer."]

Fortunately the condemnation of *Short Rations* did not come at once. For I had won a place as a writer, and now *Good Housekeeping Magazine* asked me to go around the world for them. Mr. Bigelow, the editor, was careful to state, "We don't want any articles on the suffering of women and children in this war. We want to be looking ahead and that will have to be the ground work of whatever you do."

To travel abroad with the United States not at war was one thing. To go around the world with America at war quite another. It was my Dad who gave me courage. He said this was far too big a thing to miss. This, in spite of the fact that tears were rolling down his cheeks as he bade me goodbye.

But I went well armed with every sort of endorsement as a correspondent. I even had a letter from Secretary of War, Newton D. Baker, which said: "I cannot under the proprieties of the situation give you a formal letter of introduction since you are not attached to the military establishment. But I can at least let you take this letter, to show to anyone interested . . . that I feel it an honor to have your friendship and would be glad to have any courtesy extended to you. . . ."

Around the World to Revolutionary Russia in 1917:
Japan, China, and Across Siberia

HERE IS A GREAT FASCINATION about warring Europe. Across the seas a world drama is being enacted. One cannot stay away.... This was my third trip [during the war]. This time I was to go around the world.

I knew that parallel with the physical battle that engulfs us runs a great spiritual struggle. I tried to discover the dreams and plans of the women of the future.... I made no attempt to acquire facts and figures. In superficial details [the resulting] book[1] [*Behind the Battle Line*] undoubtedly has inaccuracies. It is merely a bird's eye view of a mixed-up world, with a glimpse of the new spiritual order which arises out of the muddle.

My voyage began at the Grand Central Station in New York. Then by the Canadian Pacific Railway part of the trip was through the Canadian Rockies, with their magnificent gorges and towering mountains. It took four days and nights to reach Vancouver. From there I would cross the Pacific, visit Japan and China, cross Siberia, go through Russia, Sweden, and Norway, cross the Channel, visit England and France, and cross the Atlantic back to New York. It seemed a formidable undertaking. The next morning from Vancouver, on 26 September, I boarded the S.S. *Empress of Russia*, a steamer of 18,000 tons.[2] To my joy I found my cabin companion was a lovely young English woman, Florence Harding, whose husband was a secretary at the British legation in Peking, her father a missionary in China.

The ship was crowded. People headed for Russia, India, China, and Japan were streaming across the Pacific. It was safer than crossing the Atlantic. Yet even the Pacific had reminders of war — a coat of grey paint covered the ship. It looked like a monster cruiser. But gay music floated from the salon; a Fillipino band was playing a two-step. The menace of German submarines seemed remote as Florence and I paraded the deck. The passengers were merchants, bankers, government officials, and missionaries. The latter were numerous; they

165

gathered about the piano and sang hymns, while on the deck below fox-trots and cocktails were in progress.

As we steamed north the air grew cold. In ten days we were approaching land. But even as we sighed with content, little black clouds appeared in the sky. The wireless told of two typhoons raging off the China coast. We tossed and moaned; we had caught the edge of the storm. But with evening the clouds broke. Far off on the horizon were a golden sunset and the dark blue hills of Japan. On land I found a new world, or rather an old one. For Japan in 1917 was still back in the eighteenth century. Her government was autocratic; her Emperor was worshipped as a god. The most radical institutions were the YMCA and the YWCA.

Florence Harding had agreed to travel with me through Japan. We did not linger in Yokohama but went on to Tokyo. Here for two weeks we lived in a Japanese inn. This gave me the flavor of the country and its unique charm. We loved our bright, airy room; with the lattice screen rolled back the whole room was exposed to sun and air. We sat on silk mats and slept on wadded quilts on the floor. Our meals were served on a lacquered tray on a table a few inches high. The bathing facilities were a drawback. In the common wash room were brass basins all in a row. Here one scrubbed and cleaned one's self, men and women side by side. When lathered one stepped into a tank full of sizzling hot water, both sexes. Usually men and women did not see each other before marriage but bathing together naked was quite correct. However, we persuaded our little kimono-clad maid to shoo off intruders while we bathed.

The beauty of Japan was often marred by western innovations. A crude electric light with common white shade spoiled the delicacy and charm of our room. Everywhere was this mixture of charm and ugliness. Japan on the surface had accepted modern inventions without assimilating them.

Japan had no conception of the meaning of democracy. This was particularly evident in the treatment of women. The women were voiceless. They could not attend political meetings. When they appeared in public they stood not beside the husband but to one side. The husband was lord and master. A girl's education was not the same as a boy's. The women who worked in the factories were literally sold to the employer for three years. They ate and slept in the factory. The marriage customs were often degrading. Marriages were arranged by the parents, the wife became the husband's possession and serving maid, she had little control over the children, and infant mortality was enormous. The women were still living in the middle ages. I felt Japan would never be a great nation with such a handicap. For two weeks

Florence and I journeyed through the land, enamoured of its painted gardens, tiny lakes, gnarled and twisted trees, the smell of sandal-wood and incense in our nostrils. We both said good-bye to this dainty land with regret.

After a night of tossing on a small Japanese boat, we landed on the Korean shore. Gone were the miniature loveliness and the smooth-running life of Japan. The Korean peninsula was a stretch of flat, sandy waste with mountainous ridges, the little town of Fusan [now Pusan] unspeakably dirty, the buildings crude and ugly. The population was a mixture of lean, tall Chinese in shirt and trousers and of short, black-haired Japanese in kimonos and big Koreans in long baggy white bloomers and short, white, Eton-shaped jackets.

The Korean, unlike the yellow man, is brown-skinned. He looks like an ancient patriarch. It seemed a sacrilege that the tiny Japanese should be ordering this venerable patriarch about. But Japan intended to dominate Korea [a dependency of Japan 1910–1945]. The best railway that Japan possessed was in this peninsula. Besides the daily expresses, there was a weekly *train de luxe*, containing drawing room cars, observation cars, and two-berth sleeping compartments, whereas in Japan itself there was no such elegance in travel. Halfway up the peninsula was Seoul, the capital, where we spent a couple of days. The official, Japanese-run hotel, like the train, was superior to any other in the Far East. It had elaborately tiled bathrooms, smooth running elevators, central heating, and electric lights. In addition, it had typical, screened Japanese rooms for the Japanese. Thus in 1917 I was seeing a struggle going on everywhere between the old and the new — between democracy and autocracy — between mechanical inventions and ancient customs.

It took two days and a night to travel through the sandy wastes and mud huts of Korea. When we arrived at Mukden in Manchuria we had passed into Chinese territory. Immediately a great change took place, for the Chinese and Japanese are as unlike as the Russian and the German. The neat, orderly little Japanese stations with brass basins where one washed disappeared. The Chinese railroad station was a shack. It was dirty and overflowed with humanity. The air was filled with shrill chatter. The crowd poured into the train gesticulating and eager.

For a day and a night we joggled and bounced over a bad road-bed in our shabby Chinese train. At night a bundle of bedclothes was tossed in, and we spread these on the slippery seats. There were no regular sleeping cars. At ten in the morning we pulled into Peking. I was disappointed when I passed under a great wall and stepped into paved streets with high walls and European not Chinese buildings. The first mile of the city belongs to foreign embassies. It was a European world. The British Section was indeed lovely, with its smooth lawns and green trees and low buildings, like a bit of England dumped down into a high-walled enclosure, with Hindu soldiers at every gate. Florence had invited me to visit her. She had a charming English home with three Chinese boys to do the work.

Not until the second day did I discover the real Peking. I journeyed in a rickshaw to the Forbidden City and the Palace of former Emperors. A high wall shut out the palace buildings, but the tiled yellow roofs rose above the wall and glistened in the sunlight. Then I passed under that wall that separated the palace from the city and was at last in China. Such life, such activity! Hurrying in every direction were thousands of rickshaws, little human horses pulling their two-wheeled carriages. On the narrow sidewalks moved throngs of people, men, women, and children, all dressed in trousers and skirts. Lining the road were small shops wide open to the street. There was the hum and chatter of a thousand voices. And China seemed more modern than Japan, for one sat on chairs, ate at tables, reclined on couches.

In 1917 China seemed to possess at least the seeds of democracy. The mass of the people were still ignorant, superstitious, and procrastinating. The women were everywhere the inferior of men. The man could have as many concubines as he pleased. Half the women still had bound feet. But in practice these things were becoming obsolete. The Empress Dowager at the close of her reign had begun to make reforms. The Chinese were beginning to absorb the spirit of democracy. They were fighting for their freedom and looking to the future.

The country is vast. There is a greatness about China. Nothing is static. Out beyond the city of Peking is the Temple of Heaven. Its tiles are a deep penetrating blue. Close up it is dingy and shabby, the wood is warped, the paint chipped. But at a distance the largeness of design and the beauty of color are extraordinary. I sense an analogy here: on the surface China wallows in dirt, but inwardly there is a beauty of spirit, a love of freedom. China cannot be conquered. It is said all her conquerors eventually became Chinese. One felt this would always be true.

My stay was all too brief. I hated to leave Florence. The Embassies in Peking advised strongly against my departure. All sorts of rumors were coming out of Russia. The Russian Embassy said it was extremely dangerous to go around the world. Yet I could not give up now. I must fulfill my agreement. With aching heart and much misgiving I set forth.

I left Peking [the last week of October] and returned to Mukden and boarded a comfortable, Japanese night train to the frontier, where the next morning I boarded a dingy, dirty, Russian train.[3] Despite the dirt,

From dust jacket of *Behind the Battle Line* showing some of the
travel permits required on her 1917–18 trip around the world
reporting for *Good Housekeeping*.

I felt I had left the East and was back in the West. The Russian language was just as unintelligible as the Chinese, but it has a familiar
note. The rough log houses in place of mud and stone huts, and the long,
belted, fur-lined coats and fur cap instead of the pigtail and shirt
brought one back to a crude but modern civilization.

At seven in the evening we reached Harbin. Here I was to catch the
Vladivostok de luxe express for Petrograd. The temperature had
dropped 30 degrees; it was dark and cold as I stepped into the large
waiting room. I was grateful for the warmth of the place, but the air
was foul. Sprawled over the floor, on the benches, in the chairs were
hundreds of Russian refugees. There wasn't an unoccupied floor spot.
Women and babies lay flat upon their backs with their bags as head-
rests. Dirty Russian soldiers sat upon curled-up legs and smoked, spat
upon the floor, and littered the place with cigarette butts. Rough-
looking Cossacks with unshaven faces, armed and knived, pushed their
way in and out of the crowded room. The Russian revolution had
descended upon me. I shrank back frightened. All around me was the
babble of voices, but not a word could I understand. It was seven, and

I had had no food since one o'clock. In the far end of the room was a refreshment counter, but the crowd was too dense for me to reach it.

Two hours crawled by. The Petrograd train was many hours late. I could not endure the discomfort so struggled to the door.

It was dangerous to leave the station. Stories had reached me in China of the disorder in Harbin. There had been shooting in the streets, and hardly a day passed without someone being killed. Chinese, Russians, and Japanese filled the town, no one was in control, the foreign consulates remained out of sight. But bad air, hunger, and fatigue drove me forth. I hailed a rickshaw and climbed in. There is one word common in all lands. "Hotel," I said. Soon I was at Harbin's one hotel. That place, like the station, bulged with humanity. Beds filled the corridors. Russia was spewing forth an endless stream. Even here my English tongue brought no response till a young man in European dress stepped forward. I had asked for the British Consulate, for there was no American one in Harbin. "Let me take you there," he said. "I have an automobile." Trust is necessary in a warring world. I gladly accepted. A quick, breathless ride in the winter night set me before the house of the English consul. But my reception was not at all cordial. He felt I should not have come; a strange woman was an added responsibility. Life was difficult and dangerous. At eleven he insisted on seeing me to the train. We deserted the sidewalk and walked on the snow-covered road. He said it was safer because there had been much shooting lately. It was a mile to the station. When we arrived we learned to our dismay that the train was still hours late; it wouldn't arrive before two A.M. I was faint from hunger; reluctantly my companion set out with me for the hotel. A hard piece of bread, a stale egg, and a weak cup of tea gave me back a little courage. We returned to the station, crowded into the packed building, and found standing room near the door. One o'clock came and went. Rough-looking Russian soldiers gazed suspiciously at the neat khaki-clad Englishman beside me and brushed rudely against him. He swung his cane nonchalantly and looked uneasily about. Minute after minute crept by. Two o'clock came, then two-thirty and the shrill whistle of a train. I bade my companion goodbye and staggered up the steps of a first class car. Would my berth reservation be correct? A thick-set man in a Russian blouse unlocked a stateroom door. I was too tired to notice my surroundings. The grimy dirt of the floor, the gray sheets went unheeded. My heart rejoiced at the empty stateroom. I flung off my clothes and dropped into the lower berth. The seclusion and rest were heavenly, but a wave of loneliness and fear swept over me. Was there anyone on the train who spoke English?

It was six A.M. when I awoke with a start. My door had been flung open. The Russian porter was showing in a Cossack soldier. I sat up in my berth and let forth a flood of English; I gesticulated wildly, but the Russians only shook their heads. Then the Cossack dismissed the porter, closed the door, and locked it. Tales of Cossack brutality surged through my mind. I felt for my money under my pillow. My heart beat violently. The soldier was distinctly disagreeable. He saw my discomfort and enjoyed it. He gathered up my scattered garments and flung them into my berth, slowly took off his coat and shoes, and climbed into the upper berth. I listened breathlessly till all was still; then I stealthily began to put on my clothes. When dressed I crawled out of the lower berth and stood up. The soldier was lying above me with eyes wide open. He had a cigarette between his lips. He puffed at it leisurely and grinned. A wave of resentment seized me. I picked up my comb and brush and began quickly to do up my long hair. My hand trembled. Then suddenly I remembered the note of the editor of *Good Housekeeping* magazine, the last sentence of which read, "We vouch for the character of the bearer of this note and will be responsible for her actions and conduct throughout the journey." Laughter surged up. I thought he should see me now! My nerves relaxed and fear vanished. I gathered up my possessions, unbolted the door, flung it open, and in a moment was out in the corridor.

It was dark night outside. Dawn did not come until 9 A.M. Every compartment door was closed and locked. I stood in the swaying train corridor and waited for morning. My courage oozed. I wanted to turn and run home.

At ten the doors began to open. I wandered up and down, inquiring, "Do you speak English?" and "Parlez-vous français?" At last I found a Russian who spoke English. He told me there were two American boys in the rear car. Joyfully I hurried back and timidly knocked on their door. In a moment a sleepy boy stuck his head out. I explained my predicament. "Don't worry," was the cheery answer. "We'll be dressed in a minute." And presently two boys from New York City and a Serbian soldier, who spoke English fluently, were listening to my story. It was the Serbian who took command. "We three are traveling together for an American firm," he said. "We have two compartments between us. There is an unoccupied berth in mine. You'd better come travel with us." Gladly I consented, and soon my luggage was beside the Serbian's. We then went to the dining car, where I saw there were a few Russian women on the train, but they knew no English. The passengers were Russian merchants, army officers, and soldiers. The American boys were young, shy, and inexperienced. It was hard to keep up my courage. Petrograd seemed a long way off. Twelve more days and nights of travel — an eternity!

It was the Serbian soldier to whom I turned. He was young, only twenty-five. He had black hair and burning black eyes, a pale face full of restless energy. He had been in the Serbian Army since 1912 and in the great retreat [from Austrian troops in 1915]. Wounded and nerve-racked, he had been discharged. For a year he had been in America. His friends called him Nick, and soon I followed suit. Nick could speak Russian like a native. From him we learned that my adventures of the night before were the subject of conversation among the passengers. I did not receive much sympathy; to the Russians I seemed finicky. Life for them had gotten down to the elementals; there was no room for conventions. For a woman to object to sharing a compartment with a man was being fussy. I swallowed hard and tried to adjust myself to new standards. I could see that even Nick thought me overly sensitive. But he was kindness itself and gave me his compartment and went to sleep in the room with the Cossack.

It was a queer, rushing world into which I had come. Even that first day there were wild stories afloat — Kerensky [Premier of the Provisional Government since a revolution that had overthrown the czar the previous February] had fallen or he had not fallen but was in possession of Petrograd and fighting rebellion. Smoke and talk filled the train. Cigarette butts and ashes covered the floor. The air grew foul. People sneezed and coughed, but no one opened a window. There is a prejudice against fresh air in Siberia and Russia. Many of the car windows were nailed down; the only ventilation was the opening of doors at stations. At night the air was cold and rank, in the day hot and fetid. My throat grew sore; I began to cough. The station stops were a godsend. Flinging on our coats we marched back and forth on the platform. At each stop the entire train turned out. Every man was armed with a tea kettle, because at the stations were huge samovars or big tanks of boiling water. Once the tea kettles were filled, the passengers rushed back onto the train. Then from every compartment floated the odor of tea, the smell of cigarettes, and the babble of voices.

All day and most of the night this went on. When the evening of the first day came I was half sick and utterly weary. The next morning I woke with a splitting head and aching throat. I could scarcely breathe. When Nick appeared I begged for air. He wrestled with the window and managed to open it a little. But the respite was brief. When the porter discovered the open window he slammed it shut with a torrent of angry words. He was an ugly youth, a Bolshevik. To him we were all hateful capitalists. I knew no Russian words with which to make friends. I had not learned to say "Tavarisch" — comrade.

At each station we hurried to the platform to learn the news. Conflicting stories poured over the wires. Now that it was there, there was

rioting and bloodshed in Petrograd and Moscow, that the Bolsheviks
were in the ascendant, again that Kerensky had moved on Petrograd
with an army and quelled the uprising. When the news for the Bolsheviks was bad our surly porter grew more and more ugly. He took my
drinking glass from me; then he removed my electric light. I began to
fear him and sat with my door locked. I had difficulty in keeping Nick
from smashing the fellow's head.

All the time our train moved steadily forward, and to my amazement
I discovered that Siberia was beautiful. There were hills and great
woods and rushing rivers. Though it was November, many places had
no snow. When we drew near Irkutsk, there were snow-covered mountains and the great Lake Baikal. Siberia had much of the grandeur of
Canada. But the villages were crude, the houses chiefly log huts. The
peasant huts have but two rooms; sometimes as many as twelve people
sleep in one room.

The Siberian women, like the men, were strong, rough creatures.
They wore rubber boots and short skirts and had shawls tied about
their heads. They worked in the fields with the men; their labor was the
equal of theirs. Sex differences were not considered. At one station a
Siberian woman boarded our train for Petrograd. She went as a
representative of the women of her village to demand that clothing be
sent to her town in exchange for the foodstuff being sent to Petrograd.
She was full of tales about her village. Two deserting soldiers had just
visited her town and raped a young girl. The women had risen up in
wrath and beaten the men and thrust them out. It was a crude,
elemental world, full of hot passion, into which I was rushing.

As the days went on my cold grew worse, until finally I could only lie
in my berth. Through the long, weary hours Nick talked on and nursed
me. When my cold threatened to go into my lungs, he hunted up a young
Russian soldier who was a medical student. They sat beside me and
discussed my needs. Heroic measures were adopted by my young
"doctors." It was the method of the trenches and soldiers. I was to sweat
my cold out. Army coats were piled on top of me, my window closed
tight. At the stations Nick bought bottles of boiling milk. This he sternly
poured down my throat. Minute by minute my discomfort increased. My
body ached; sweat poured from me. But Nick relentlessly stood guard.

Then he began to tell me stories — the tragedies of battle. Nearly all
his friends had been killed, his best friend before his eyes. A shell had
severed the head from the body. Between the bursting bombs Nick
crawled out onto the battlefield, tenderly gathered up that headless
form and bore it back to the trenches. Blood from his friend's wounds
infected open cuts in Nick's hands. For weeks he tossed in high fever.
But the infected hands and arms were not amputated, and in time he

recovered. As I listened to these tales my own suffering seemed small, the endurance of men enormous. The next morning I was weak, but my cold had broken.

Now the stories we heard at the stations grew alarming. It was evident a great revolution had taken place in Petrograd. Still our train rushed on. But the stops grew tense with excitement. Men huddled together and felt for their pistols. The car doors were locked. This express train with its first-class carriages and sleeping compartments was a sign of the plutocracy that had been. Any moment we might expect to have the windows smashed. Nick tried to keep the news from me, but the American boys came with their stories. I ceased to be afraid, for one could not think in terms of the individual — life was moving too fast. But sick fear crept into the hearts of the Russian merchants on board. They stormed and raged.

And now the last day of the trip had come. Russian soldiers had begun to crowd onto the train. They slept or stood in the corridor. But there was no violence. At some of the stations we saw that there had been rioting. Windows had been smashed and houses burned. But no move was made against the train, and at six one morning we pulled quietly into Petrograd. There was a great stillness over the station, no hurrying porters or calling cabmen, none of the bustle of arrival. We filed silently out into the street. It was like the dead of night. A few people lurked in doorways, but the big, snow-covered square was empty.

It was Nick again who came to the rescue. He suggested I'd better go to a hotel across the way because people keep off the street in the dark. At the hotel a sleepy porter showed me a room, but there was no heat, no hot water for a bath, only one electric light, and nothing to eat until nine A.M. I sat in my big cold room and from my window looked out on the empty square. There was an ominous silence. Shivering, I waited for the dawn. What would it bring?

Life Inside Revolutionary Russia, 1917–1918

At 7:00 A.M., two hours before sunrise, I could see from my window weary, ragged soldiers forming in long lines before tobacco shops in the square and women with shawls over their heads and baskets on their arms standing outside provision shops. A few trams began to move. They overflowed. Soldiers had climbed to the car roof and sat there while civilians struggled for a foothold on the steps below.

By 9:00 A.M. there were masses of people in the square. Great processions of men and women passed arm in arm under flying red flags, singing through the street. There was the beat of drums and now Bolshevik *Kronstadt* sailors surging by. It was my first glimpse of revolutionary Russia. Throughout my stay of over two months it was the picture that remained with me: gigantic processions of men and women like a mighty river coursing through Petrograd. A great force had been released and nothing could stop it. Three days before my arrival Lenin and his followers had taken control of Russia.

Freed from the pogroms, beatings, and starvations under the Czar, the people wanted three things: bread, peace, and land. Anyone who promised them this they were ready to follow. The moderate socialist leader Kerensky with the Provisional Government did not promise this, and the militant Bolshevik leader Lenin did. Therefore the peasants, city workers, and soldiers were for the Bolsheviks. For two-and-a-half years the soldiers had fought bravely at the front. Many were now without guns or shoes. They could fight no longer. They had gone over to the people. The Provisional Government had been overturned, Kerensky had fled, disguised as a sailor.[4]

So Petrograd had come into the hands of the Bolsheviks with Lenin and Trotsky in control. They had ordered the streets leading to the railroad station barricaded with barrels, wagons, and automobiles; soldiers with bayonets guarded the barricades. The State Bank and the telephone and telegraph stations had been seized. The Winter Palace, where the Provisional Government sat, was fired upon. In a few hours it had been forced to surrender and the Ministers were seized and imprisoned in the Fortress of Peter and Paul. Meantime the Council of the People's Commissars, an all-Bolshevik cabinet, was set up with Lenin as President, Trotsky as Commissar for Foreign Affairs, and included the lesser known Stalin, all of whom had spent at least a year in prison or exile. The Council made Smolni Institute, formerly a girls' school, the seat of government, issued a statement to the effect that they were now the central government, and added, "We are standing before an experiment unheard of in history, of creating a government with no other aim than the wants of the working men, peasants, and soldiers."

The Russian society had been turned completely upside down. Now on the underside were the monarchists, capitalists, and landowners; on the top were the soldiers, peasants, and workers. Cooks and waiters had become the aristocrats; lawyers, bankers, and professors, the riff-raff. That is why the people went singing through the streets. They thought a new day, a new life had dawned. They did not know that a change in leaders changes little, that violence and power only pass from one group to another, and that the new group of strong men would soon exploit others for their own end.

I shivered in my room as I watched from the window. The cold I had contracted grew worse. I tried to get a doctor but most doctors had fled or were in hiding. When one finally arrived he was of small assistance. Drug stores were closed so it was impossible to have a prescription put up. I telephoned the American Consulate, which was still open. They sent me a Russian nurse who spoke English. She kept me in bed for a few days. But I soon realized a capitalist hotel in a communist world was no place to be. Each day I feared the hotel would be seized. My nurse offered to take me into her home; her family had an apartment in a quiet street.

I bought fleece-lined shoes and rough clothes, and from then on had no difficulty. Often I was on the street until midnight, but no one molested me; I had only to smile and say "Amerikanski Tavarisch." I got caught in great crowds and was unafraid. Many foreigners experienced great hardship in Petrograd and went home with wild stories, but much of the trouble was of their own making. For it wasn't wise to wear a high silk hat, a fur coat, and a diamond ring and expect an unfed, ill-clad Bolshevik to be polite. Every day on nearly any street corner a fur-coated gentleman and a soldier could be seen in hot argument. Sometimes on dark nights the fur coat changed hands, but usually the men merely parted in hot anger. One night the American correspondent Jack Reed was held up and robbed.[5] He knew a few Russian words and explained he was an American and a Socialist, whereupon his possessions were promptly returned and his hand cordially shaken.

Certainly Petrograd was not a place to live if you wanted a peaceful and luxurious life. It was a continual fight to get the bare necessities. On the day there was heat, there was no electric light; if the light worked you ran short of food. The temperature stood on an average at twenty degrees below zero. The tram cars were often so crowded that one had to walk miles in the snow-covered streets. The buttons got pulled off my clothes and remained off. I ceased to feel baths were a daily necessity. I grew thankful for coarse but nourishing food. There was plenty of tea, a fair amount of black bread, coarse meat, and quantities of vegetables. There were never any sweets or pastry, but sometimes we had butter and usually four lumps of sugar a day. It was a case of survive if you can, and if you do you'll grow strong.

But there was great joy about life in Russia. It was thrilling and interesting for me. You could not get bored. Every day the Bolsheviks issued some new decree. One day all titles were abolished; the next, judges and lawyers were eliminated. I confess to a wicked delight on that occasion, being a lawyer myself and knowing how little justice there often is in the law.

Such deeds frightened the Monarchists and Conservatives. They would come out of hiding and make a show of resistance and then scurry back. Day by day the Bolsheviks grew in power. Petrograd became a city of working class people. In the few automobiles rode collarless working men, while on the street trudged an angry and puzzled banker. A duchess and her ladies-in-waiting wore aprons and wrapped shawls about their heads to hide their identity. The Bolsheviks had not yet had time to seize the personal possessions of the rich.

In the midst of such a topsy-turvy world the Bolshevik government had no easy task. It had let loose the elemental force of Russia. As always, it was the greedy brute who caused the trouble; he looted happily and thoroughly, while the government struggled desperately to bring about order.

My first experience of looting I shall never forget. I had been out to dinner and could hear shooting at a distance. It was when I started to return home about 11:00 P.M. that the fatal thud of bullets grew unbearable. Then there came shouts and cries of distress. I confess I was a coward. I shamelessly begged Jack Reed and his wife, Louise Bryant, to see me home.[5] With great difficulty we secured a sleigh. The driver was very loath to go in the direction we ordered. He said the shooting came from the Winter Palace, that soldiers were looting the Czar's wine cellar. It was a wonderful night, bright with stars; our sled glided swiftly over the hard snow. It seemed impossible men could be killing one another. Then a sleigh dashed past us. It evidently carried a wounded man, for he kept crying out, "Help, comrade. Help!" Then we came to the great river Neva, so white and silent in its winter coat of ice. A little way below the bridge we were crossing stood the Winter Palace. The shots had grown very loud now. We could see the soldier guards running away. Their guns had been taken from them. They were shouting and screaming. Our sleigh passed close by them, but they made no move toward us. My companions said something about going to see the excitement, but I wanted to get home and bury my head under the bedclothes.

In the morning I had more courage. The shooting had ceased. I walked from my house toward the Winter Palace. When nearly there I saw bright red drops on the snow. It was too red and thick for wine and there were splotches of red on some of the buildings where a wounded man had been leaning. All over the road and on the frozen Neva were smashed bottles. I picked up one; its label bore the Czar's coat of arms and was a choice brand of Madeira. When I reached the Winter Palace I found it was guarded by a ragged crowd of factory boys in civilian clothes, carrying bayonets. They were part of the Red Guard and at least were sober. What had happened the night before was that thirsty soldiers got into the Czar's wine cellar and held an orgy; other soldiers came to drive them out and remained to drink. Quarreling broke out. *Kronstadt* sailors [who had turned against the Provisional Government] and Red Guards arrived, but the drunk and half-drunk refused to leave. Firing began, tempers rose higher and higher, and a small battle ensued. In the end the hose of a fire engine was turned on, all the bottles in the cellar were smashed, and the place flooded. Three soldiers had drowned in the wine and water, between twenty and thirty were killed, and many more wounded. But with daylight had come order and shame and repentance. [According to Reed (p. 364) these "wine pogroms" occurred "Toward the end of November."—Ed.]

It was difficult in these swift moving days to see clearly. But one thing was apparent — in a bloody revolution where force is the basis, as in a bloody war, everything fine gets pushed away. Art, science, and social welfare vanish. A small group of radical intellectuals leading the working class fought for power and became dictators. They ruled not by the vote but by force. The class hatred was as great as before. They were failing to live up to their ideals of brotherhood, fair play, and freedom. It is always so in a revolution. There was no spiritual regeneration.

Maxim Gorki in his paper was protesting, declaring: "The working class must realize that Lenin is experimenting with its blood and trying to strain the revolutionary mood of the proletariat to the limit to see what the outcome will be." But few listened to the warning; events were moving too fast.

One of the first places I visited was Smolni Institute, now headquarters for the People's Commissars. I walked up the broad driveway between snow-covered lawns to a large, white wood structure, with a chapel at one end. Only a few weeks before students, young girls of the aristocracy, were going in and out of that school. Now Red soldiers stood in the columned porch with fixed bayonets and machine guns pointed threateningly. Inside soldiers halted me. I must have a pass. Two girls behind a table were handing out passes. They couldn't speak English but I made them understand I was an American journalist and with a smile showed them my credentials. One of them tore from a tiny notebook a scrap of paper and stamped it with a rubber seal bearing the date. Anyone could have faked the pass!

As I turned down the long white corridor, it was crowded with soldiers and workingmen moving in and out. Cigarette smoke filled the air; cigarette butts and ashes covered the floor. Only a short time before little girls had paraded these corridors, clean dormitories had been filled with little white beds, the big schoolrooms had buzzed with childish talk. Now the fate of a nation was being decided within these walls.

There were long tables in the corridor piled high with radical literature. There were pamphlets on anarchism, socialism, and syndicalism. All extremists here had a hearing. The place had the atmosphere of a working class meeting. It seethed with intense emotion. It was unlike any seat of government ever known. There was no formality or order. On white doors down the hall the name of the committee occupying the room was written on a slip of paper tacked to the door. The rooms of the Commissars were equally haphazardly designated. Scribbled across a sheet of paper was the simple statement "Commissar Trotsky's Office" and stuck in the door with a pin. It was hard to believe this was the official Government of Russia.

Thanks to Jack Reed I was introduced to Lenin and Trotsky. But the meeting was brief. Lenin was very businesslike; too much was happening for personal talk. When he had crept back into Russia unknown a month before, he had shaved off his moustache and little beard as a disguise; now these were growing again. His head was large for his size and he was bald; he had a strong chin. He wore conservative clothes and looked more like a banker than a radical. Not until I heard him speak in an outdoor mass meeting did I realize his power. He began so quietly. He had no oratory, but he put profound ideas into simple words. In ten minutes he held the whole audience in the hollow of his hands.

Trotsky, on the other hand, looked the part of a revolutionist. He had a well shaped head with a mass of bushy hair, which he kept pushing back. He had a moustache and beard, wore an open-neck shirt and black, flowing tie. When he spoke it was with passion and many gestures. He was a fiery orator.

Such were the two men in whose hands lay the fate of Russia. They had declared the Dictatorship of the Proletariat. They had declared all men equal. They had no doubt about their cause. That was their strength. And they needed strength, for it was a rushing, turbulent world. Plots and counterplots were unfolding daily, food was running out, transportation was breaking down. The city was in a state of upheaval. The Bolsheviks were having a hard time. They had gained control of the central government, but the Liberals, the Kerensky group, still had control of the city government at the time of my arrival.

The members of the Petrograd Municipal Duma, an elected advisory group, were liberals and some socialists, but no Bolsheviks, so conflict arose between the city government and the new Central Power. The Duma refused to recognize the All Russian Congress or Soviet, composed of the radicals and soldiers. Thus the Central Government had angrily declared the Duma dissolved and ordered new elections. When the Duma refused, the Council of People's Commissars (or cabinet) was not to be defied. Soldiers with fixed bayonets entered the Duma, turned out the members, and closed the hall. The irate members were helpless. They had no soldiers to defend them. They met secretly and declared publicly: "Down with autocratic Commissars. Down with stranglers of liberty. Down with the saboteurs of the city administration. Long live universal suffrage, direct, equal and secret. Long live the Constituent Assembly." But Petrograd did not rally to the support of the Duma. The soldiers, deserting from the crumbling front against Germany, and the workers remained faithful to the Bolshevik Government. Meanwhile the liberals had hoped for a counter-revolution and depended on the peasants, many of whom had not yet joined the Bolsheviks.

After the Municipal Dumas were abolished, local soviets or councils were organized — district, city, and village Soviets, autonomous in local matters, but their decrees had to accord with the fundamental principles laid down by the Central Power.

Slowly the working class government took shape. It began to issue decrees. Property was the main object attacked. The right to private ownership in land was abolished. It was to be confiscated and parceled out to the farmers according to the needs of each family. But the distribution was slow, and the peasants often took the law into their own hands. In Petrograd I met a maid servant, one who still worshiped her landed employers. When I asked her what had happened in her village, she replied angrily, "The hooligans seized the big estate. They murdered the family, even the five-year-old child. They found wine in the cellar and got drunk. They destroyed the house, divided the furniture, and seized the land. They had no right to other people's things. The land belongs to the peasants, but not the house and furniture." I asked if she was a Bolshevik. "No," she said fiercely, "for they say things but they don't do them."

Another interesting decree of the Bolsheviks dealt with the town houses and apartments. These were no longer to be private property, but the former owner might continue to live in his house provided he occupied only a small portion, not to exceed a rental of a thousand rubles. This worked out in practice to one room per person. Such a decree was not carried out in the early days because there was not sufficient machinery to enforce it. But when the Government needed extra rooms, they went to a rich man's house and took possession.

Still another decree dealt with clothing. This was not to exceed a certain value. No man might have more than one fur coat, and the number of blankets was limited. Everyone was requested to make an inventory and surrender the extras to a soldier at the front or a shivering mortal at home. Of course lies were told. It was impossible to enforce this decree.

The Bolshevik government daily grew more unfriendly to the Constituent Assembly. The one hope the conservatives, liberals, and socialists had was the Constituent Assembly, which has been elected during Kerensky's regime. The people had been taught to regard the

Assembly as the culmination of all hopes. It was to meet on 11 December. The Bolsheviks felt the Assembly had been supplanted by the All Russian Soviet Congress, but they did not quite dare suppress the meeting, for public opinion still demanded everyone have a voice. Shrewdly the Communists let the well-loved socialists Chernov and Zeretelli speak. These two men believed in revolution by the vote, not by the sword. Their power was great. The peasants believed in them.

Several days before the date for the opening of the Assembly I went to hear Zeretelli speak. The meeting was in a great arena that held six thousand. It was jammed. Zeretelli had spent seven years in penal servitude in Siberia and given his life to the cause of Russian freedom. He was pale and thin; his eyes were sunken. He was dying of consumption. No one ever doubted his honesty and sincerity. With passion he declared the time was not ripe for a working class government. There must be a coalition first; socialists and capitalists must unite. This speech brought thunderous applause — but the audience was made up of doctors, lawyers, bankers, school teachers, and shop keepers. There were no factory workers and only a few soldiers present.

On 11 December a parade was organized as a demonstration in favor of the Constituent Assembly. I was out early and wandered the streets. I saw no violence. There were perhaps ten thousand in line, whereas a Bolshevik demonstration would have brought out fifty to seventy thousand. The marchers were all well dressed; none of the proletariat had joined. They swept to the Tauride Palace, the meeting place of the Constituent Assembly, but Bolshevik soldiers guarded the entrance and turned them back.

I watched three men with particular interest. They were lawyers or bankers. They wore fur coats and fur caps. They and others with them were singing the "Marseillaise." Over their heads waved a red flag on which was written "Land to the Peasants." On the sidewalk factory workers and unshaven soldiers stood and jeered. Surely I had gone crazy! It wasn't possible that those of the moneyed class were marching under a red flag singing the "Marseillaise," demonstrating against the Government, and shouting for freedom!

When the Assembly met the next day, I went back to the Tauride. Only 194 of the 800 delegates had arrived in Petrograd for the meeting, and of those only thirty or forty attended. Now eight thousand soldiers had been placed in the neighboring barracks. Inside several correspondents gathered in a corridor to talk. Immediately soldiers stepped up and told us to move on. The Commissars had cleverly let the Constituent Assembly meet to show that the latter no longer represented the proletariat. The Commissars grew bolder and now issued two decrees: one declared all liberals are enemies of the people and demanded they be arrested immediately and brought before the Revolutionary Tribunal; the other decree granted the right to new elections and gave the power of recall. At a meeting of the Bolshevik side held at Smolni Institute Lenin defended these decrees saying: "In the midst of a civil war one must not make a fetish of the Constituent Assembly. It is the bourgeoisie and the liberals who have dragged us into strife. Around them all counter revolutionary elements gather." After he spoke Trotsky sprang to his feet and added: "It is impossible to collaborate with elements against whom we are obliged to send troops. Russia is divided into two camps, the bourgeoisie and the proletariat. It is not immoral to achieve the fall of the bourgeoisie. You are indignant at these terroristic methods, but, if they are not used, methods more menacing will have to be applied within a month. It will become the terror of the French Revolution. For our enemies it will not be the *fortress* but the *guillotine.*"

Feeling was now at white heat. An exciting meeting of the Soviet Congress was to be held at Smolni Institute to debate the question of the Constituent Assembly. I determined to attend. Unfortunately no trolleys were running because the electric wires had been tampered with, thought to be the work of some counter revolutionary. I was four miles from Smolni Institute, but I plowed through the snow. The school's ballroom was the Soviet headquarters. A gay chandelier flooded the place with light. The Soviet delegates were out in full force. Most were in dingy uniforms, both factory workers and peasants. No extra reverence was shown to the Commissars; they mixed with the delegates. Trotsky and Lenin pushed their way to the platform. Trotsky spoke first; he spoke with passion and played upon this audience's emotion. His feeling about the Assembly was bitter. His words came thick and fast:

The right of immunity of the Assembly members is raised. But there is another right that is higher, that is the right of the revolutionary people. In declaring the Liberals our enemies we have only made a beginning. We have not yet executed anyone. (There were cries of "We oppose the death penalty.") Yes, that is true, but if the conspiracies of the Liberals disorganize the country, not one of us can guarantee that in their legitimate anger the people will not turn against the bourgeoisie. No one of us can say that the people exasperated will not raise the guillotine in the public square in front of the Winter Palace.

At this point Trotsky's voice was drowned out. The room was in commotion. Everyone talked at once. A Socialist Revolutionary sprang to his feet, order was restored, and he spoke against such extreme threats, reminding them of the fate of Robespierre and what came after. "In this chamber there should not only be words of hate but also words of love. Our revolution before all else was waged in the name of justice."

Thus the battle of words raged. But in the end Trotsky's proposal won by a big majority. All liberals were declared enemies of the people. The Assembly's fate was sealed.

I left before that vote was taken because I knew there would also be a battle royal in the Peasants' Congress, which was also meeting to debate the future of the Assembly. Another correspondent and I made our way to the town hall. The tram cars were still not running. We were both dead tired, but by a bit of luck we got a sleigh. We mounted the steps of the Duma building, the Nevsky Prospect, entering by the back way because we knew the place would be jammed. No New York East Side Socialist gathering ever equaled that crowd for emotion. The place throbbed with the life of the whole of Russia. The Peasants' Congress still retained Chernov and his faction; they sat on the right, the Bolsheviks on the left. Chernov stirred his group to new endeavor, his great head with its mass of hair waved and tossed, his fists pounded the desk. The room when I entered was in the throes of a debate on whether Lenin should be allowed to speak. He had pushed his way through the seething people to the platform. There were hisses, cries, bursts of applause, a maddening uproar. Chernov called for Lenin's ejection; he had no right in the Peasants' Congress. Marie Spiridonova, a tiny wraith of a woman, controlled the left. She was adored by the peasants; her years of torture in exile had made her a god. Amid the hot words and hisses her tiny hand quelled the peasants. "Let the other side speak," she kept saying. Finally a vote was taken and by a large majority it was voted Lenin should speak.

He started in like a college professor reading a lecture. He didn't pound or rant. But in a few moments the crowd was still. Each word came liquid clear. It was like a stream that started small and clean and grew to a deep, swift-running river. The man was sincere, a fanatic without humour but an idealist. I found myself swept along with the same emotion as the great rough peasants, though my reason was against what was being done. I didn't believe in force and dictatorship. I believed in democracy; surely what was *right* could be risked to the decision of the whole people. Yet in spite of my belief I found myself shouting and clamoring with the Left. It was infectious. After all, the peasants had been beaten and abused and underfed and left to fight the Germans with naked fists. The moneyed class had betrayed them. The aristocracy had allowed Germans to flood the land, monopolize the Government, and seize the business. With a mighty effort this beastly tyranny was being overthrown. Now the peasants were being told that even the Liberals were betraying them. Well, then, down with all Liberals.

Through all this surge of feeling, gradually the words of Lenin stood out:

> Only people without consciences can say the Bolshevik Government is a menace to the peasants. It is just because the power of the Soviets rests on the mass of the people that no force in the world can go against them. The conspirators must succumb wherever they are, even if they are members of the Assembly. . . . It does not reflect the opinion of the masses. You have not hesitated to take the land from the capitalists, why should you hesitate to take from him his vote?

For a moment there was quiet. Then came tumult. As Lenin walked from the room, the Left rose. They shouted, they stamped, they cheered. It was deafening. The hisses of the opposition were drowned. But Chernov was on his feet demanding a hearing. He spoke heatedly, but somehow his words misfired. His oratory was unconvincing after Lenin's simplicity. He seemed to be hurling rocks into a rushing stream without effect. When he finished, men sprang up all over the floor. Hot words flew back and forth. One peasant on the left cried out, "Long live the Constituent Assembly, but if it goes against the will of the workers this is the last time I will utter that cry." At 11:00 o'clock Trotsky entered the hall. But the auditorium was in no temper for another speech. The right had grown ugly; they hurled taunts at Trotsky. "Down with the drinker of blood. Put him out," they yelled. When a motion was made to demand the immediate opening of the Assembly, a violent struggle ensued but the motion passed by a vote of 360 to 321.

That night I trudged back to my house full of conflicting emotions. Russia and Russia's problems were not easy to solve. There was only one light on each street; they lacked fuel for more. It would have been difficult to see but for the glistening snow. I hurried into my residence. To be out after midnight was neither safe nor comfortable. I was weary from my enforced walks and fell promptly to sleep. Then — bang, bang. I woke with a start. Another bang. I sprang to the window. The street was empty, but I saw a couple of people running, stooping low. They dashed into a doorway of the telegraph office opposite. Then more shots. Instinctively I knew what it was. The soldiers were looting the wine shop on the corner. If they stuck to the wine it would be all right, but a drunk man loses all reason. Violence spreads like wild fire. Suppose they took to looting and killing. Suppose they broke into buildings, smashing windows. Excited voices rose from the street. I crept back to my bed in fear and trembling. Suddenly I realized the pain of the rich as they cowered in their palaces. But presently the shooting ceased and all was still.

I wondered what would be the outcome of all this. Changes had come too quickly. The pendulum had swung too far to the left. It could not remain there. It must swing back; that is the law of nature. Russia had swung clean out of the twentieth century. Whether she will come back with counter revolution or gradually slow down and stop in the center, like a pendulum, was a question hard to answer. What could save Russia from further bloodshed and turbulence? Progress can only come by a slow and steady march onward. As yet there has been no race of men great enough to achieve the perfect balance. What Russia needed was not more force, but men wise in understanding, sympathy, and love.

Editor's Supplement

Besides the preceding chapter on Russia, Doty wrote two more chapters in her autobiography, one titled "Revolutionary Justice" written for Atlantic Monthly, *and "The Germans in Petrograd," both also in her book* Behind the Battle Line. *In addition, that volume contains a chapter on "The Women of Russia." For the sake of brevity, yet to let the reader know of her experiences and the history related therein, there follows this editor's summary of the highlights, in which summary direct quotes are clearly indicated.*

"Revolutionary Justice"

"'Stop off and have afternoon tea with the Czarina,' the American magazine editor had said as I left the United States." — But that was back in late September 1917. By the time Doty reached Petrograd she learned that "the Bolsheviks held the Royal family in hiding. There was no hope of my finding out where she was. . . . But I could at least visit their palace. The Winter Palace in Petrograd was a disappointment. Outwardly it was impressive, but inside callous use robbed it of its glory. There were marks of ill use and muddy feet, silk hangings had been torn down to wrap around the freezing soldiers, royal bedrooms had been turned into offices; one had the impression that the czar was long since dead and buried," though he and the czarina were not murdered until the following July 1918.

During her stay of over two months in Russia Doty made a train trip from Petrograd to Moscow, which took 24 hours one way, in hopes of seeing something of what was happening to the Kremlin and the beautiful and elegantly furnished palace of the deposed Czar Nicolas II. She found that, though the palace gate had been smashed and the outer walls battered with bullets, inside little damage had been done by revolutionaries. Thus she could imagine the splendor and pomp of life there not long before, though the palace was now cold and uninhabited. She was shown about by an old, former caretaker for the czar, who had treated the caretaker well, he told her.

On the train to Moscow she shared a compartment with a woman of the aristocracy, who traveled in a Red Cross costume as disguise out of fear of being attacked as having been wealthy. Now that her money and jewels were frozen in the bank she predicted she would have to hire out as a domestic in order to survive. Doty learned that some wealthy women had become nurses during the war against Germany; one with whom she talked had served as a nurse in a dugout at the front until it was struck by a shell which instantly killed the seven other nurses with her.

Although excited by the prospect of more voice for the common man in Russia, Doty also saw the evil of power in the hands of uncontrolled, impassioned mobs. She described the brutal and fatal beating of a fifteen-year-old boy whom the crowd incorrectly thought had robbed a woman. Many thieves and murderers had been released from prisons in the early days of the Provisional Government; so the wary crowd had little sympathy for anyone caught preying upon another. When the accusing woman returned to announce too late that she had made a mistake, for she had found her purse, the mob turned on her, beat her to death and tossed her into the canal along with the lifeless boy. The people only knew brute force, Doty wrote, because that is what they had experienced under the czars.

Because of her interest as a lawyer she looked and found that "judges and lawyers had been abolished. Overnight legal learning and ancient precedents had been cast into a scrap heap." With considerable difficulty she obtained a permit for herself, with a young woman as interpreter, to enter the Fortress of Peter and Paul, then being used by the Bolsheviks to imprison the bourgeoisie, professionals, upper classes. By persistence and her persuasive power she slowly befriended the soldier-guards over a cup of tea with sugar, butter, and black bread to which they treated her. The soldiers were curious about her and poured questions upon her: "'Why has America gone to war?' 'Has President Wilson sold out to the capitalists?'" Through this she even obtained permission to interview some of the prisoners. Among them was a former Minister of Finance, who, she read later when back home in America, became probably one of the two ministers reported stabbed to death by a night guard. Among other prisoners she interviewed was "a Social Democrat, a man who had fought for Russian freedom and was a well-known economist." She guards his name to protect him from reprisals. He bitterly denounced the Bolsheviki:

> Go back to America and tell them what is happening here. Tell American Socialists that the Bolsheviks are imprisoning their fellow Socialists. Nine times I was imprisoned by the old regime, and since the Revolution I have been imprisoned ten times. . . . Both the Czar and the Bolsheviks are dictators. There is no democracy. . . . In here it's the uncertainty that's so terrible. Personally I'm not afraid. They don't dare hurt me. But the others are afraid; they are going to pieces. Every day they expect to be lined up and shot. It is unbearable.

In each cell the story was similar. "Dire deeds were said to go on behind the green walls of the Fortress. Here ministers and generals languished in cells formerly occupied by ardent revolutionaries. Each day a wholesale killing was predicted. But the government was trying to suppress mob violence by setting up Revolutionary Tribunals, people's courts with workingmen for judges administering a crude justice."

Doty visited one of those Revolutionary Tribunals "to see how law without law books and precedents was administered." It met in the Nicolai Palace, former residence of the Grand Duke, its halls now swarming with angry crowds, its marble floors damaged by muddy feet and cigarette butts. The trial that day was of Pourishevitch, a monarchist and general in the Czar's army and one of those who aided in the assassination of Rasputin. The court was four hours late in starting, the judges were overwhelmed, the audience was openly ridiculing one side and then the other.

> Again I felt like Alice-in-Wonderland. . . . Cooks and duchesses, soldiers and resplendent generals, collarless workmen and bewigged and begowned judges had changed places. Even the gaudy ballroom, by the wave of a magic wand, had become a dirty human meeting-hall.

> When the court decided to retire for deliberation, it was eight o'clock. I was faint for want of food and decided to leave. As I pushed my way out, I realized again the same intense emotional atmosphere I had seen elsewhere. Faces were flushed and eyes angry. Hot, eager talk spurted up. There was the same desire on

the part of each to dominate. Only the judges had been calm. They were pitiful in their simplicity, their struggle to understand, their attempt to be fair.

From that trial Doty went to the apartment of her old friends since 1906, Maxim Gorki and his wife; about him she wrote this in admiration:

He was the one intellectual who, though he had not deserted the Bolsheviks, criticized and condemned them and tried to help those who suffered. Each day his paper *Novia Jizm* told the faults of the Bolshevik government. Hourly he was in danger. But his fairness made his home the refuge of the oppressed. Workingmen and countesses came to him for aid. It was only the voice of Gorki that rose above the maelstrom, pleading for moderation, for patience, and for spiritual regeneration, as well as economic equality.

From one of his articles, in which he questioned whether the Revolution had brought change in men's mean spirit, she quoted these ominously predictive lines, " 'Are the brutalities still in existence? . . . . There is no poison more dangerous than power over others. We shall become cannibals worse than those against whom we have fought all our lives.' He was too popular to be liquidated, but his voice was soon silenced."

"The Women of Russia"

In Doty's book the brief chapter about Russian women began by saying that her intent and assignment by *Good Housekeeping* "to study the woman's movement in the midst of a revolution was difficult, especially in Russia where there is no feminist group." She explained that women there did not stand out as women because for years they had taken on the life of the men — in the fields, in the city, in exile, as good comrades. They had not devoted themselves to home, school, the vote, or social welfare; rather they gave themselves to the men's fight for freedom. Now in war time women trudged through the snow and kept the cities going by such work as shoveling snow off car-tracks in sub-zero weather, hour after hour. And, as always, the peasant women shared the heavy farm labor.

When the Provisional Government had been set up the previous March at the overthrow of the Czar, the women fully expected to get the vote like the men. But when that was not forthcoming the All Russian

League for Women's Franchisement headed a demonstration of 40,000 women, who marched to the Tauride Palace, where the Council of Workingmen and Soldiers Deputies was meeting. The women would not leave all day, despite being wet and hungry, until they were assured an equal vote. This they obtained on 19 March 1917. But no women's movement had continued after that. They disbanded and again "merged their identity with that of the men," each supporting her husband's political stand. During the next tumultuous months "the wealthy women, the intellectuals, and the bourgeoisie sided with Kerensky and the Provisional Government; the peasant women and factory workers were with the Bolsheviki." Although in meetings the women did not generally speak out, there were two ardent Bolshevik women who did stand out — Madame Kollantai and Mlle. Maria Spiridonova,[6] both of whom Doty interviewed. Writing about these interviews in *Behind the Battle Line* (pp. 119–125) she said Kollantai was a refined-looking woman yet had "spent nine years in exile and for twenty years has been a revolutionist." In the summer of 1917 she had been imprisoned by Kerensky for openly supporting the revolutionists but was soon released. When Doty questioned her she had become the Minister of Social Welfare. That made her the only woman in Lenin's cabinet and, according to Doty, the first woman minister in the world. Kollantai told Doty that to date she was able to do very little in her new position because the employees in her department were from the old regime and would not follow her instructions. Known as a leader for the rights and protection of working women, she told Doty she was also anxious to open up institutions for orphans.

Spiridonova, of whom Doty wrote briefly in the preceding section, was a revolutionist under the Czar and had killed the Lieutenant Governor of a province because he was flogging and brutally ill-treating the peasants. Doty wrote, "For this she was imprisoned for years and finally exiled to Siberia for life. During imprisonment she was abused by the keepers. Her body was beaten with sticks and burned with the soldiers' lighted cigarettes. Today she is hardly more than a wraith, but her power over the peasants is enormous. . . . At their great meetings she can stir the sturdy peasant to a frenzy of passion with a sweep of her hand, or quiet him as though he were a child."

"The Germans in Petrograd"

In her chapter under this title in her autobiography Doty gave an inside view of the difficult and tenuous negotiations going on in December and January, while she was there, between the German and Russian delegations to end the war between them, talks which were to culminate in the Treaty of Brest-Litovsk, signed in mid-March 1918, after her departure and when the German army was advancing on and bombing Petrograd. Doty described the divergence between the motives of the two sides and the growing disintegration of unity among the Bolsheviks over the issue of whether to make peace with their German enemy.[7]

She wrote that the Bolshevik Commissars had promised peace. They knew the masses would no longer fight; seven million Russians had been killed or wounded in the war, military equipment was running out, the soldiers were defecting. The Commissars loathed the German imperialists; yet, because Karl Marx had been a German and because there were uprisings and strikes in Austria and Hungary (which the Communist propaganda there had tried to stimulate), the Bolsheviks thought Germany was near collapse, and therefore they hoped that with peace the Communist revolution would spread to Germany and to the workers of the world. Lenin and Trotsky had even prepared a manifesto to be distributed from the air into the German trenches urging their "brothers" to join with them in peace and world socialism.

> About this time a big meeting [the Second Congress of Peasants' Deputies] was held in the Alexander Theatre in Petrograd. . . . The members of the All-Russian Soviet, the representatives of the Peasants' Congress, factory workers, soldiers, and Red Guard were present. . . . A pass was necessary; I had only the statement from the American Embassy that I was an accredited correspondent . . . with its impressive red seal. . . . [Finally an armed soldier/guard let her in and lead her via the back stage toward a seat.] In another second we were out on the stage. The curtain was up, the place was jammed, the speakers were already on the platform. But this didn't trouble the soldier. Straight across the stage he went, right in front of Commissar Trotsky, Mlle. Spiradonova, Mme. Kollantai, and the other speakers, and I trailed along behind. Each moment I expected to hear jeers from the audience. . . . When we were safely across the platform the soldier deposited me in the front row of the orchestra where the correspondents were assembled, and I settled down to watch proceedings.

Soon a speech by Trotsky brought hot debate. Doty wrote that this is part of what he said about the peace negotiations:

> The same causes which brought about the revolution in Russia will cause uprisings in other countries sooner or later. Certainly our situation would be better if the people all over Europe would rise and if we could talk, not with General Hoffman and Count Czernin, but with Liebknecht, Clara Zetkin, Rosa Luxemburg, and other German Socialists. . . . If the Kaiser finds the means of marching against us, then I do not know whether we have the strength to fight, but I think we have. . . . We certainly haven't overthrown the Czar and the bourgeoisie at home to kneel before the German Kaiser and implore for peace. But if because of economic conditions we are not able to carry on the war and must renounce our fight for the ideal, we will say to our foreign comrades that the battle for our ideals is not finished, it is merely suspended, as in 1915 when the battle against the Czar was not won, but was merely put off.

The Germans were seeking peace with Russia because they needed new food supplies and badly needed their soldiers for the western front. Doty described the growing intensity of discussions in Petrograd, while at Brest-Litovsk little progress was being made. "The Kaiser hoped to dictate his own peace terms." Again she was swept along in a workers' demonstration called to show Russian strength. And she attended more contentious meetings. "When it was known that the Allies would not join in peace negotiations and that the Ukraine and Finland had split off from Russia, the Germans grew arrogant and superior, though they still continued to negotiate. Daily the Russian hope of a German revolution dwindled." Those in the Soviet were enraged by the demise of parts of their nation. German propaganda flooded their land; at the same time the German press was telling its own people that Russia was falling to pieces from riots and bloodshed, that the Allies, especially England, were making secret treaties to take over numerous other nations, and that if the Germans made a revolution their country would fall prey to the imperialistic greed of the Allies. This line had the desired effect of increasing fear among the German people, with consequent increased support for their armed forces and reduction in the number of strikes.

While Germany was expanding its influence in the Baltic, Scandinavia, and the Ukraine, Doty attended another meeting which broke into a frenzy against the Germans. "The majority of the Assembly wanted to arm and fight, to annihilate the German despots." One man sprang to his feet and urged that they go to the hotel where the German delegates were staying and cut their throats. Hourly the tension between Germany and Russia grew greater. But when reports came that the Russian Army had broken down and that Finland and the Ukraine, where the upper classes were pro-German, were welcoming the Germans, and that Germany was extending its sphere of influence sending aid to Poland and Lithuania, the Russians believed themselves helpless and signed the German peace proposals.

Doty's analysis of these events in her 1918 book, *Behind the Battle Line*, differs from that in her autobiography written much later. In the book she gave a cautious warning: "This compromise with Germany, the suppression of the press, the arrest of moderate socialists, and like intolerant acts were causing dissension among the Bolsheviks. It was making a break in support, a break that may prove fatal to revolutionary Russia." Doty, still the idealist, hoping and believing democratic ways would win in Russia, clearly felt in 1918 that the Bolsheviks had made an unnecessary mistake in capitulating to the Germans, that they had failed to hold to their ideal, but, like Trotsky, she thought that the Russian submission was only temporary. "We Americans believe in self-government. . . . Surely then we ought to believe in it for the Bolsheviks. Little by little Russia will right itself. . . . Beside a strong, free Russia, imperialistic Germany cannot stand" (p. 118).

However, by the time she was finishing her autobiography some 35–40 years and another World War later, she was less sanguine. History had shown her that totalitarianism under Lenin and Stalin grew out of the instability and chaos that usually accompany and follow revolution and harsh peace terms. When writing her autobiography she recognized that Russia and Germany in 1917, as in 1939, "faced each other controlled by a small minority on the top who were dictators. The German dictators were determined [to impose] *'Deutschland uber alles.'* The Russian dictators demanded world revolution, material well-being and brotherhood of all the workers, and the destruction of the rich. . . . The [Brest-Litovsk] treaty signed was outrageous. It gave the Germans hundreds of thousands of square miles of Russian territory and three-fourths of the country's coal and iron and many other things. It naturally bred hatred, made peace in the future impossible."

The Long Way Home, 1918

T WAS HARDER TO GET OUT OF RUSSIA than to get in.[1] In order to go to England my passport had to be visaed by both the Bolsheviks and the British military authorities — a difficult combination. Whom to go to first? I decided on the Bolsheviks. My career as an "Americanski Tavarisch" was satisfactory. My passport was quickly stamped, but then, oh then! I was asked to carry a small, sealed envelope to Sweden. "We'll make you a Russian courier," said the amiable Russian official. "If you take this letter to Sweden you can take out your own papers unopened. I tried to smile appreciation, but my heart sank. What would the British say? Russia had been an ally during the war, but Communism was hated. I hurried around to the British office. "What shall I do?" I asked. "Take the papers, of course," said the friendly British captain. "If you didn't take them, some one else would, and we can keep track of *you.*" So I tucked my press notes, covered with many red seals, into my bag and made ready.

It took a week to get all the visas. Besides the British and the Russian, I had to have the American, French, Swedish, and Norwegian permits. It meant hours of waiting in dingy rooms among struggling and desperate people.

There were no short cuts to England. One had to go to the northernmost corner of Finland, cross a river and then down the length of Sweden, across Norway and the Channel to Scotland. From Petrograd to Stockholm it was a journey which took me five days and nights.

I left in a driving snowstorm. The thermometer was 20 degrees below zero. The train was two hours late in starting. A snowplow went ahead of us. When we reached Finland two hours later I began to notice a difference. Things began to be orderly. A dining car was put on; the food was scanty but well served. I felt the white tablecloth and napkins with pleasure. It had been so long since I had seen clean linen. We reached Torneo at the top end of Finland late at night, too late to cross to Sweden. Our train pulled up on a siding. Torneo consists of a vast stretch of snow, a few wooden buildings, and a church. That night there were no sheets, I slept in my clothes and rolled up tight in the one blanket we were given. In the morning we moved on to the station. The thermometer now stood at 40 degrees below zero. We had a great breakfast and three cups of coffee, the first coffee in many a day.

All morning we wrestled with the Finnish authorities. When we had been passed, we collected our luggage and got into a sleigh. The Finnish sleighs are like beds; there is no seat except for the driver. The bed part is covered with straw. On this you lie three in a row, covered by a great fur rug. It is the only way to keep from freezing. By this time the temperature was 50 degrees below zero. As we sped along I peered out from the fur rug and my eyebrows were instantly white with frost. We were crossing the frozen river which separates Finland from Sweden. There was nothing to see but a flat, white world.[2]

At the Swedish border we were shown into a spotless room with an operating table and a doctor and nurse in white. After a hunt for germs — instead of literature — we were passed on. System and order had descended upon us.

The majority of passengers on the train had to sit up all the way to Stockholm. In Sweden a train cannot start until the car temperature is 60 degrees. Fuel is scarce, the wood green. The train was scheduled to leave at 7:00 P.M. It left at 1:00 A.M. At six the following morning we were awakened by great excitement. The steam pipes in the adjoining car had burst. For hours the passengers had been without any heat. When they were ordered into our car, there weren't enough seats to go around. Then that night the heat in our car gave out. Before we reached Stockholm the heating system of the entire train had broken down. We had to change to a whole new set of cars. On the fifth day after our departure from Russia, at one in the morning, we reached Stockholm. We stepped out of the station in the middle of that beautiful city; it lay there under the shining stars in absolute peace. But Stockholm was crowded with refugees from Russia and Germany. With difficulty I got a room in the Strand Hotel.

The next morning when I woke, it was some moments before I realized where I was. Then I lay there exultant. The bed was so soft, the sheets smelled so sweet, the room was so clean. It was marvelous to have a telephone that worked, an electric light that turned on, a bell that brought a smiling maid in white cap and apron. I felt like Cinderella turned into a princess. No longer should I have to sleep in my clothes, go without baths, be covered with fleas, and hear rifle shots and machine guns in the street below.

For twenty-four hours I reveled in the peace, beauty, and order. Then I began to miss something. Life was so still. Everyone dressed alike. The men wore frock coats and high silk hats. Their faces were set and unsmiling. They didn't seem alive. I missed the crowd, the passionate street-corner arguments, the pulsating life.

The opening of the Riksdag or Swedish Parliament occurred the day after my arrival. It was held in the Palace and the King made a speech. Through the courtesy of the American Embassy I was given a card of admission. When I arrived at the Palace, two or three hundred people stood in the snow waiting for the great gate to open. The crowd was visibly excited. They were going to see the King. Again I had the feeling I was living in a dream. The change was too sudden: in Russia, Maxim Gorki was considered a conservative, and in Sweden I was to see a king on his throne. How could the world get together with such diversified ways of life?

When the Palace gate opened there was a rush for seats. Most of us stood at the end of the long hall opposite the ermine-covered throne. After a wait of an hour the members of both houses of Parliament filed in and occupied seats on either side of the long hall. It was 11:00 A.M. but those ladies wore evening dress, and the men dress suits. Then there was a flare of trumpets and the royal family appeared in their box. The Queen wore a very low-necked, black velvet evening gown, a diamond necklace, and a diamond headdress. When the royal party was seated, there was another flare of trumpets and a lot of generals and courtiers arranged themselves around the throne. Then there came a burst of music, and the King's bodyguard, followed by the King, marched in. The soldiers formed two long lines down the hall. They were dressed in chamois skin and wore great shining coats of mail and helmets. They looked exactly as though they had stepped out of the British Museum. They drew their swords from their scabbards with a great flourish and held them solemnly before their faces. Then the king read his paper.

I had come too recently from Russia. I couldn't take the proceedings seriously. I felt in a Gilbert and Sullivan opera. The ceremony didn't last long. In an hour we were out in the street among the ugly tenements for the poor.

War has been a tragedy for Sweden, for she had reached the state of Germany in 1916. In the hotels only one electric light is allowed, and the temperature is kept at 60 degrees. There was little fat or food that had substance. Yet Sweden still clung to luxuries. It was possible to buy at exorbitant prices poor pastry, cream for your coffee, and a tiny bit of candy, although there was no butter, the bread supply was low, and all necessities were rationed. The rich were thriving at the expense of the poor.

From Sweden I went on to Norway, through Christiania [Oslo] to Bergen. Two-thirds of my journey around the world was over. But the danger was not past. Fifty miles from Bergen a snow avalanche had crashed down the mountain side. The railroad track was destroyed. Two houses and their occupants had been caught by the rolling snow and swept into the fjord. Fortunately our train escaped injury, but it was two days before we could go on.

When I reached Bergen my boat for England had left. The Germans were keeping track of the boats going to and from England, though the English tried to keep the dates secret. The Channel was full of sub-marines. The sense of danger and intrigue was nerve-wracking. Norway was unbearable. Bergen dripped moisture; the land was covered with melting snow; the houses were damp. The people were hungry. It was impossible to get a square meal. The Allies had stopped supplies, and the Germans had nothing to give. The friendly little land had grown morose.

Day after day dragged by. There were endless stories of ships that had been sunk. Finally after ten days we were told we could leave in a few hours. Two ships were being sent over escorted by two heavily armed British cruisers. The English boats were small and the North Sea very rough. When we got out of the fjord we began to toss like an egg shell. I had crossed the ocean without seasickness, but in a few seconds I was leaning over the rail. Then I staggered to my berth and for thirty hours I never moved. I didn't care how many submarines attacked us. With two exceptions, everyone was ill.

Not until we were steaming into a Scottish harbor did I have the strength to rise. It was nine in the evening and very dark. Only a few lights shone along the waterfront. But the smell of England, or rather Scotland, came to my nostrils. The air was soft, the bleakness of Norway had vanished. The smoke from soft coal fires poured from the chimneys. Something within me broke. The strain was over. I was safe at last. Food had been poor in Russia, worse in Sweden, and lacking in Norway; I was half starved — here the tea, bread, butter, and jam were delicious.

The next morning, after the night at a queer little seaman's inn, I took the train for London, wearing the same clothes I had in Russia — a fur hat and fleece-lined shoes. I was literally ragged and dirty. But the Pethick-Lawrences received me with open arms. I was hurried into a lovely warm bath. I was back in a normal world. I found my spirit as well as my body were healed. From the windows of their apartment in Lincoln's Inn in London the only evidence of war was two newly ce-mented squares in the roadway where German bombs had recently dropped. But neither the nearby church nor houses were injured. I soon adjusted to the air raids. They occurred so frequently that the popu-lation had grown hardened to them. The subways had become campingut grounds. After dark mothers with babies would descend there; blankets and rugs were spread down and babies put to sleep, while the mothers sat with their backs to the wall and knitted or gossiped. The air raid signals were picturesque. After the boom of an explosion a police man on a motorcycle dashed by calling in solemn voice, "Take cover, take cover." When the raid was over there was the gay note of a bugle; then the bobby dashed by calling "All clear."

In Britain I saw that neither black dresses, nor shortage of butter and sugar, nor air raids and the anguish of war could blot out the triumph of spirit. And at the centre of the spiritual regeneration stood the women. They had done much war service, made magnificent sacrifices. They had undertaken the hardest jobs and done them well. They had acted as motormen, laid railroad tracks, worked in munition factories, run ambulances at the front, and nursed the wounded.

Such service could not be ignored. A bill had just been passed through Parliament on 9 February giving the vote to women 30 years of age or over. Malini [Emmeline Pethick-Lawrence], who had given her life to the cause, was a leading figure in the new enfranchisement. A great Woman's Crusade was organized. Women paraded through the streets. So dominating was their spirit that men stood respectfully on the sidewalk and occasionally cheered. Malini sent out a message to the Woman's International League saying: "The attainment of the vote is not the end. It is only the beginning. Women as citizens must make good their claim to freedom.... They must enthrone life above machinery ... They must awaken to their collective responsibility for the happiness of the human family."

I spent three weeks in London and found it a wonderful place; a spiritual revolution had swept through the land. The average work-a-day man and woman had reached new heights. They were prepared to give all for a cause they believed in.

I attended the first suffrage celebration over having won the vote, held not in a hall but in a church — St. Martin's-in-the-Fields in Trafalgar Square, London. Women with grave faces poured in, rich women, poor women, professional women, and factory workers. The place was filled to the last niche. A thrilling silence filled the place. Singly down the main aisle of the church came the women leaders of the different suffrage organizations, each bearing in her hands the banner of her cause. The bishop stepped forward and amid tense silence read the names of the women now dead who gave their lives to the day that had come. And we all knelt and chanted a new litany written by women, each line of which ended with the line "We thank Thee, Lord":

For the new power entrusted to women
for the shaping of the national life —
For all who have toiled and suffered
for the enfranchisement of women —

For the passing away of ancient tyrannies
and prejudices and the growth of a new spirit
comradeship and respect between men and women —
For the hope that fills our hearts
as we look forward to the future —

Then we stood and sang a hymn. With the last words I turned to Malini, who stood beside me. I saw she was white to the lips. We had seen a great vision way beyond our own lives.

In America the enfranchisement of women was also in the air. My Dad wrote me, "It looks as though the federal amendment for Woman's suffrage would pass, and the politicians are tumbling over each other to be in at the finish." But the 19th Amendment did not become law in the United States until 1920.

My travels had shown that the women in Japan lived in the dark ages, and in China they were awakening. In Russia there was no feminist movement; there men and women worked side by side for a common cause. In Sweden the struggle was for sex freedom in marriage and divorce. In Norway the women had the vote — the first country to grant it. In England the enfranchisement had come as I arrived. That made a fine climax to my articles, which had begun to appear, for I had been sending them back to *Good Housekeeping*.

Next there was France still to visit before my tour around the world was complete. I hated to leave England. It had been a glorious time. With Fred Pethick-Lawrence, a Labour member of the House of Commons, there had been tea on the terrace and dinner in the House of Parliament. I had tea also with H. G. Wells, who wanted to talk about Russia, and another tea with Bertrand Russell.

To reach France the Channel had again to be crossed. The evening I left it was full moon, a time when submarines reap their harvest. I spent the night on deck, wrapped in a blanket. In the morning we were in Le Havre. Old men in blue blouses helped us disembark. Soldiers were everywhere. The train from Le Havre to Paris was packed with them. I had suddenly been flung into the world war. In most of the countries I had visited, except England, there were but three topics of conversation: food,[3] clothes, and how to keep warm. Here it was different. The battle field was a few miles away. Hospital trains moved back and forth. Yet curiously enough in this land of the conflict the civi population thrived. Physically France was better off than any of the other countries. Paris had plenty of food.

It was the first of March when I reached Paris. A strange Paris — Italians, Serbians, Moroccans, and, above all, American boys in khaki crowded the cafes. Life moved hot and fast. Taxis flew hither and thither, women packed the stores, and soldiers occupied every sidewalk chair and smoked and talked. One heard every known language. At night as I walked home through the darkened streets I would hear an American voice behind me saying, "Gee! How I'd like to see Broadway. Say, wouldn't the lights look good?" In the restaurants I continually ran into American boys struggling desperately with the menu, and when I brought my French to the aid of one, we fell into conversation. "How are you getting on?" I asked. "Great! Say, this is the life. You know, we fellows will never be the same after the war. The little Western town I come from looks pretty dull. And, say, these French women are corkers."

The days in Paris were hectic, with air raids almost daily. Early in March the big drive began and the Germans concentrated on Paris. Nearly every evening the air raid signal sounded. Sometimes the enemy didn't get across the barrage. But on moonlight nights between 8:00 and 9:00 the alert always came. At 8:40 the fire engine dashed past, blowing its shrill siren, and everyone dashed to cover. The subway trains stopped, the people crowded into the métro stations, and the street lights went out. In the hotel we hurried into the underground cellar. Here the gas was turned off to prevent explosion; there was only candle light. The first night I found myself in a dim recess with six Moroccans, guests of the hotel. They wore long, flowing robes and great white turbans. My companions were nervous and excited. Somehow a subcellar with six Moroccans did not seem safe. I decided to risk my life on the floor above. In the front hallway were two or three American soldiers. It was their first air raid, but they were cheerful. We pushed open the front door. A bomb crashed to earth. There was a great flash of light. We hastily stepped back into the hall, but after a little our courage rose again. We peered out into the bright moonlight and saw the French aeroplanes come low, skimming over the top of the houses, darting about clearing the sky of enemy aircraft.

Between 11:00 P.M. and midnight the fire engine again dashed by, sending forth a gay triumphant bugle call, all was well. Immediately there was wild rejoicing. The world poured up from the underground. Supper and drinks were in order and a paean of thanksgiving went up. Paris treated lightly the forced exodus to the cellars. With characteristic pluck and good humor, the French dressmakers even designed models for underground wear.

In the morning there was a mad dash for the papers, but they never told where the bomb had dropped. Fortunately few bombs had fallen on buildings. Notre Dame gazed as proudly up at the sky as ever. It was factories and apartment houses in outlying districts that suffered most. When a cheaply built tenement house was struck, the bomb crashed through to the ground.

The methodical Germans had at first timed and planned the air raids. The signal came regularly between 8:00 and 9:00 P. M. Then some *Boche* got original. At one o'clock we were routed out of bed by the alert. We could no longer sleep in peace, and this got on our nerves. We grew cross from want of sleep. Then for a couple of nights there was a lull. But soon the nightly air raids began again. It was late before the signal came that all was clear. I had hardly closed my eyes when bomb —bomb — bomb. The fire engine went tearing by. I stepped out onto the balcony. It was early morning and a glorious day, the birds had begun to sing, the sun was already warming the great boulevards. It couldn't be possible that the enemy was flying over Paris in broad daylight! Then there came another thud and crash. It was near. The people in the street below scurried into the doorways, windows were slammed to, and iron shutters rolled down. I dressed hastily and ran downstairs. Guests were hurrying from their rooms: women in negligees, with hair twisted in hasty knots, and nurses carrying half-dressed babies. It was a disgruntled crowd; they were angry rather than frightened. It was an outrage to be gotten out of bed before *petit déjeuner*. The Germans were going too far! It was all very well to be raided at night, but to be bombed before breakfast!

The thuds continued to come regularly at 20- or 30-minute intervals. We stepped out onto the sidewalk. On the Avenue de l'Opéra people were already moving back and forth. On the street corners little groups gathered to gaze up into the shining blue. During that whole day with each thud we scanned the sky. I had a morning engagement and at 10:30 was walking up the Avenue de l'Opéra. The stores were closed and the shutters down. Transportation had ceased. The *métro* trains were not running. But many people were on the street. When a thud came we paused a moment, shivered, and then walked on. I finally secured a cab and went tooting across the Place de la Concorde, over the Seine, past the Chamber of Deputies, to the house where I had my appointment. When I alighted, the taxi driver asked, "Aren't you afraid, Miss?" I shrugged my shoulders and said, "I suppose I am. But there isn't much use. I am an American and there is still the ocean to cross. *C'est la guerre, que voulez-vous?*" He smiled appreciatively.

I soon found the family I had come to see. As the daughter and I were walking back across the Seine to keep a luncheon engagement, we paused on the bridge to gaze at the city. Then bang. The earth shook. It was a terrific thud. We knew the explosion was near. Later we learned the Tuileries garden had been struck. It was uncanny, unreal. It couldn't be true that under the bright blue sky bombs were dropping on the city. We little dreamed that a long-distance gun was bombing Paris. We went to see what damage had been done. There was a hole in the ground the size of a dining-room table. Fifteen feet from the explosion a soldier had been asleep on a bench, but he didn't get a scratch. Some dirt was thrown into the eyes of a baby in a baby carriage, but not a soul was injured. It was marvelous how little damage the big gun did elsewhere that first day. The toll was 10 killed and a few injured.

With the setting sun there was a respite, but at 9:00 P.M. the alert sounded. This was a real air raid by planes. It was midnight before it was over. But with the daylight again came the bomb — bomb — bomb. Now we knew it was a long-range gun. We didn't fear it as we did the air raids; the chance of its killing you was infinitesimal. The second day of the bombardment Paris went about its business as usual, stores were open, the trains ran, and the sidewalk cafes were as crowded as ever. I went to the Grand Hotel for breakfast and had my coffee at a little table on the sidewalk, facing the Opera House. It was ten o'clock; people were streaming in and out of the *métro* station. Then suddenly there was a terrific explosion. Just beyond the Opera House a shot had torn a big hole. Everyone seemed paralyzed, but only for a second. Then the laughter and talk spurted out as before. Not by the quiver of an eyelid was Paris going to show it cared a cent for the Germans and their long-distance gun.

One night I went to the *Theatre Français* with a friend, Valentine Thomson, the woman who edited the paper *La Vie Féminine*. The play was by Anatole France, and at the end of the first act my friend took me to his box and introduced me to Anatole France. He was an old, grey-haired, grey-bearded man of 70, but his eyes were still young. He was wholly absorbed in his play. It was about the struggle between a mother and daughter, really about the conflict between life and religion, between the young and the old.

It was a momentous evening. As if to emphasize the struggle in the play, a battle raged outside. In the middle of the second act there were two heavy thuds. The airplanes were over Paris. The explosions were so heavy the theater rocked. It was the worst air raid Paris had had. With the first thud people rose all over the house. Then one of the actors came to the front of the stage: "If you are willing, we will continue with the performance. Of course those who have children and feel they must leave, please do so." There was a little pause. Then the mothers rose and left, and the play continued. Anatole France sat serenely on in his box. The play held us more deeply than before. Only, with each thud we breathed a little quickly and leaned closer together.

At the end of the play the bombs were still falling. It was utterly black outside; an occasional flash from a bomb was the only ray of light. My hotel was only two blocks away, so I said good-bye to my friend. But I couldn't see where the sidewalk ended and the road began. A man brushed against me. I asked the way to the hotel. He said, "Permit me" and led me there. I have no idea who he was or what he looked like. But in those days it was safe to trust strangers and safe to be out on the totally dark boulevards in the late evening. Once a man accosted me with an improper proposal, but I had no fear and a bright idea flashed through my head. Chuckling I said, "You had better wait until you see me under the electric light before you make further proposals." I heard him scurrying off in the dark.

One day I took the train and went up toward the Front because I had heard that my friend, the surgeon who had operated on me for appendicitis, was in charge of one of the big, British base hospitals. When I had asked to come, he had written: "You probably ought to see a British general hospital. . . . It has been difficult in the past to get permission for people to come, but I think with the letter I enclose you will make it. . . . I hope you can manage it. It is a long time since I have seen a familiar face." It was intensely interesting to be within a mile or so of the front-line trenches and within sound of the battle. My friend had achieved wonders with a hospital largely built of tents. I could see in what respect he was held, though he declared the hospital was not much to see and said, "I have been chiefly concerned with keeping my people fit and seeing they were properly looked after, rather than polishing brass."

It did us both good to meet on this basis of friendship and work.

It was now time to turn homeward. I was glad to go; life had been very strenuous. In Japan there had been a hurricane and a small earthquake. In Russia a revolution. In Norway a snow avalanche. Then back and forth across the Channel strewn with submarines, air raids in London, and both air raids and bombardment in Paris. Yet there was still the Atlantic to cross, where submarine attacks were common.

I sailed for home on a French boat. It left from Bordeaux, a safer port than Le Havre. [Permission to leave France through Bordeaux to return to the U.S. was dated 27 March 1918, stamped on her passport, some seven months before the end of World War I.] There was a thin, drizzly rain when we started. The sea looked grey and desolate. We paused at the outer border for gun practice, where for a day we attacked imaginary submarines. The long wait was varied by life-saving drills; we strapped on life preservers and hurried to our respective life boats.

Cabin passengers and steerage mingled indiscriminately; war travel removes social barriers. Our boat was a second-class steamer, the *Chicago*, but in 1918 one took any boat gratefully. The passengers consisted of the Countess de Preyas and her sister, 500 Spanish day laborers, some French and Italian officers, and a dozen American YMCA men. Silk sweaters and ragged coats, white sport shoes and clumsy leather clogs walked side by side. As I lay in my bunk at night, I thought about my trip around the world. And beneath all the struggle and the differences, the good and the ill, I saw the spirit of man slowly emerging.

When I went on deck we were making preparations to put out to sea. A friendly grey cruiser dashed up beside us and then hurried on, beckoning us to follow. All day we sped over the grey sea, the two boats so close to each other one could call from deck to deck. When night came every porthole was darkened; not a glimmer showed on deck. To walk about was impossible. I gathered up my blankets and, wrapping them about me, stretched out in my steamer chair. By my side lay my life preserver. But fear had gone out of my heart and wonder entered in, wonder at this great, on-rushing world with its incessant upward-striving. All night I lay there, sometimes asleep. And when I slept I dreamed:

I saw a group of women gathered about a council table. And the women came from all the lands, and they were of all ages and nationalities. But in the eyes of each was understanding and tenderness. And their talk was of the children, of their day, and of the peace to come. And no woman spoke of "my children," but only of "our children." From their talk it was plain war still existed. Dictatorship had not vanished, internationalism had come but class still fought against class. From time to time a man would burst into the council chamber waving his arms and shouting, "Come, comrades, you must not sit here. We too have your ideals, but this is a time for action. Come, fight with us the bloody fight of revolution, draw your sword and slay the monster greed." And from the midst some women would rise and answer, "This man is right; class must not fight against class. Those who have not must slay those who have. There is no other way to rid the earth of lust and greed." But wiser women shook their heads. They wept as the man and that woman went forth, because they knew that the sword in their hands would in time breed again the greed and cruelty they sought to slay, that evil methods destroy fine ends. But how this new world was to be brought about my dream did not reveal. For I had not yet learned that a changed world means changed men and women, that man without God is helpless.

The next night, as I leaned against the ship's side in the darkness, a war correspondent recently back from the Front stood by my side. He pressed close and asked for something more than talk. And the evil in both of us, lust without love, was strong. I said no, but the weakness of desire was there.

The next day when daylight came I saw the cruiser had turned back and was steaming toward France. We were far out at sea and each moment the danger from submarines grew less. Steadily, day by day, the ship plodded on. It went slowly, for the ballast, it was said, had rolled to one side of the ship and we listed badly. We walked on a slanting deck as the ship limped into New York harbor. And there at the dock were the dear faces of my father and mother to greet me. What a joy to be home, to have long, sunny, quiet days at Sparta where I could finish my articles.

It was my Dad's extraordinary love that often gave me strength to go on. He was so very humble, and I needed love. For it was not a happy world to which I returned in the U.S., now fighting in the war a year. Intensive propaganda had created mass hatred for Germany. Even German music could not be played. Attacks were still being made on my articles on Germany. The *Manufacturer's Record* in the July 1918 issue declared: "The Century Company has done America and all civilization a great injustice in the publication of *Short Rations*. Miss Doty denies that the book was intended as pro-German and all through it there runs a constant criticism of Kaiserism, but also an increasing sentimental flow of gush about the dear, suffering German people."

There was a whole page of such attack. My articles on Russia were also coming in for criticism. *Good Housekeeping* magazine had advertised my articles in posters in the subway, but now came a letter from the editor, Mr. Bigelow, saying, "The advertisers are already suggesting that *Good Housekeeping* would do well not to use Miss Doty's work in the future."

How could one be a pro-German imperialist, a pro-Russian communist, and an ardent pacifist at one and the same time? It was difficult to understand. But in war, common sense and justice seem nonexistent.

On the other hand, the *Atlantic Monthly*, which had taken an article on Germany [printed in June 1917], now asked for one on Russia [published in their July 1918 issue under the title "Revolutionary Russia"]. The editor, Mr. Ellery Sedgewick, wrote, "I read your paper with intense and ever-increasing interest. . . . To me it is perhaps one of the most illuminating documents that has come out of Russia." And it is interesting that a young soldier, a lieutenant, should have written me: "Will you accept words of gratitude for your splendid Russian article. I thank you because you painted Russian pictures true and full of sympathetic understanding and because I could find no such pictures in the narrow, prejudiced, and colored articles in the press."

From many sides came praise, in spite of the attacks. Macmillan published my articles in a book entitled *Behind the Battle Line: Around the World in 1918*. I also had many speaking engagements, because pacifists could talk though the press was censored. *The Masses*, the Socialist magazine of the intellectuals, edited by Max Eastman, was indicted [for conspiracy to obstruct conscription]. George Kirchwey wrote me: "I planned to run in to see you today but I got into *The Masses* trial [begun in April 1918] and couldn't pull myself away. Max Eastman has been on the witness stand all the afternoon, and I don't know whom to admire most, Max as a witness or Morris Hillquit as an advocate."

Perhaps the person who was struggling hardest for his ideal at this time was Woodrow Wilson. He was fighting for his Fourteen Points and the League of Nations, not only with the Allies but with our own narrow-minded men in the Senate and the House.

But as the days went on, America's strength was turning the scale. The war news grew better and better. And in the middle of it all I went camping with Roger Baldwin, and that changed the current of my life.

Part V
Post–War Devastation. Marriage

Introduction to Chapters 11–12

*T*HE ROGER BALDWIN (1884–1981) whom Doty describes in chapter 11 became the well-known director of the American Civil Liberties Union (ACLU) from 1920–1950.[1] He was a co-founder of the ACLU, along with Clarence Darrow, Felix Frankfurter, Jane Addams, Helen Keller, Norman Thomas, and John Dewey in 1920, a time when civil liberties were under increased attack during the "red scare." Baldwin also was Secretary, President, and trustee of the American Fund for Public Service (the Garland Fund), which gave grants to liberal causes, such as workers' and minority rights and peace. The fund's records show that Doty and Jane Addams would later borrow from that fund for publication of *Pax International*. The day after Baldwin's death the *New York Times* carried a full-page account of his life as a "crusader for Civil Rights" (27 August 1981, D 18).

Both the ACLU and the Fund for Public Service — and therefore Baldwin and Doty — were to come under continuous suspicion and investigation by the FBI, as verified in its files on Baldwin, now available under the Freedom of Information Act. These security reports charged that the ACLU "is made up largely of Communists, Socialists, and radicals . . . its activities show clearly that it is nothing more than a front for the Communists" (1941, File No. 100–3267).

Similar suspicion of both of them for their connections with the American Fund for Public Service and with the Birth Control League is found in an FBI file on 1930 hearings before a House of Representatives Special Committee to Investigate Communist Activities in the United States, in which a Walter Steele presented "voluminous" printed material of evidence against the American Fund as Communist and favoring birth control, charging that it was started in this country by "the anarchist crowd" and "Margaret Sanger, . . . a friend of Roger Baldwin and also of his wife Madeline [sic] Doty, who is secretary of the Women's International League for Peace and Freedom [WILPF] in Geneva and who in one of their bulletins chronicles a visit from their friend Sanger" (FBI file on Baldwin, pp. 268–69). In another file (no date) both were named on a chart of 126 men and women as "Favoring

Recognition of the Soviet Government of Russia," she for belonging to the Woman's Peace Party and the WILPF, he for affiliation with five pro-peace and civil liberties organizations.

In fact, neither Doty nor Baldwin became Communist, though he was very sympathetic to and at times supportive of Communist objectives. Despite this constant investigation, by 1976 Roger Baldwin had gained a respected reputation. Arthur Schlesinger, Jr. described Baldwin as "the wise, robust and humorous man who in one lifetime transformed America's attitude toward civil liberties." And Alan Reitman, at that time Associate Director of the ACLU, wrote that Baldwin is "the man who personifies America's struggle to make its practices match its pledges of liberty."[2]

In the chapter 11 Doty writes of their love affair and her decision to go to examine and report on conditions in post-war Europe. She recounts experiences on this 1919 trip, her fourth to Europe within five years, as she traveled this time to England, Ireland, and France en route to Zurich to attend the second Congress of the Women's International League (at which her friend Fraulein Heymann of Germany spoke out against war crimes and against the terms of the Brest-Litovsk Peace Treaty). Then Doty writes movingly of the devastation and starvation she saw as she traveled on into Austria and Germany.[3]

Doty's warning about the lesson to be learned from harsh peace terms is particularly pertinent today at the beginning of the twenty-first century as we fearfully watch unrest, civil wars, and national, ethnic, racial, and religious rivalries on every continent, causing starvation, massacres, and possible world war. As recently as March 1993 former Soviet President Mikhail Gorbachev, in a *New York Times* syndicated column, warned those who love democracy and peace: "People like stability. . . . People are prepared to obtain order and tranquility by giving up other values, for example, democracy and freedom. This dangerous temptation has not disappeared, even in our own day."

During the period 1919–1925, of which Doty writes in Chapter 12, various records show that she was involved in numerous civic activities and volunteer services other than those she mentions here in her autobiography. Among her various speaking engagements, for example, was a talk titled "The German Revolution," given on 18 May 1920, at a meeting of the Pennsylvania Branch of the WILPF held at Swarthmore College. She does say in her autobiography that later that year she was in Washington, D.C., supporting the Maternity Bill, introduced by Representative Jeanette Rankin, and writing of that bill in *The Suffragist*.

But again the matter of intrigue emerged when the place of Doty and that of Crystal Eastman appeared on the infamous Spider-Web Chart, compiled in the Chemical Warfare Department to expose and connect pacifists with Socialism and Communism. It was the period of growth of post-war nationalism, fear of "Bolshevik-led" strikes, and paranoia. This chart was circulated in 1923–1924 and got the attention of J. Edgar Hoover of the F.B.I. It named as suspect 29 women leaders in 15 women's organizations, including the YWCA, the Women's Christian Temperance Union, the PTA, the League of Women Voters, and the WILPF. Doty was named twice, Jane Addams ten times. Lines criss-cross the chart to show these women's interconnections with suspect organizations; indeed, most lines run from individuals to the WILPF. One entry read, "Miss Doty (wife of Roger Baldwin the intellectual anarchist) active worker of the WIL. Courier of Russian Soviet Government." Another box on the chart sought to condemn her further for having seconded the "ultra-pacifists' Slackers' Oath" at the 1919 Zurich convention of the WILPF, which oath declared its signers would do nothing to aid any war, not even help the Red Cross nor buy war bonds. Not long afterward the Women's Joint Congressional Committee, founded several years earlier by the League of Women Voters as a lobbying group of ten women's organizations, forced the War Department to withdraw the chart.[4]

By contrast, the *Washington Times* praised Doty for her work for the 1924 Congress of the WILPF held in Washington, D.C., the first time their international conference met in the United States. For this meeting Doty had been active in procuring money to bring Augspurg and Heymann over here from Germany and was asked by Jane Addams to help set up speaking tours for them.

The next year at the annual meeting of the American Section of the WILPF, held in Chicago on the topic of economic imperialism, Doty was in charge of the program and gave a report as the editor of the national WILPF Bulletin.[5] Also at this time she was serving as Executive Secretary of the New York branch of the WILPF.

On Getting Married

Roger Baldwin in an interview with his biographer Peggy Lamson some 55 years later told her that in his earlier love affairs he didn't like being in love. "I hate being possessed." In the Lamson book he tells how he met Doty and that "she introduced me to the most astonishing group of people I had ever met. . . . They were the advance guard of social reformers known as the Liberal Club.[6] We would dine at some Bohemian restaurant in the village, some thirty or so socialists, feminists, free lovers and free thinkers. . . . So our fast friendship grew and blossomed until it was more than a friendship."[7]

After their marriage *The Evening Mail,* on 15 September 1920 printed an interview with Doty by Beulah Powers which exemplifies Doty's feminist stance as well as some of the public attention being given her at this time. It ran four half-columns in length with a 4-by-5-inch photo of Doty, under the headline "HUBBY PAYS WIFE FOR HOUSEWORK IN HAPPY DOTY-BALDWIN MARRIAGE." Later that year she wrote an article for Hearst which ran under the headline "WHAT IS BETTER THAN MARRIAGE" — not subservience, but love and understanding to encourage each other in their work.

In chapter 12 the reader learns that even in Roger's wedding vows he expressed fear of loss of freedom in marriage.[8] In his vows he also quotes two words, which were to prove very prophetic, namely "Virtues" and "Realities." Certainly Roger Nash Baldwin, conscientious objector, lifetime champion of civil rights, and Madeleine Zabriskie Doty, lawyer, reformer, columnist, and international reporter and peace worker, both exemplified extraordinary "Virtues" by their public lives. But because of differences in *personality* and in *needs* they were soon to face less than ideal "Realities" in their private relationship. His understanding reminiscences on their marriage can be found here in the Addendum.

11
Love and Post-War Europe, 1918–1919

*R*OGER! HOW CAN I DESCRIBE HIM? Once when we visited Smith College together, President Neilson said that I had the most interesting man in America to live with.

I met Roger back in 1910 when he was chief Probation Officer of the St. Louis Children's Court. But I hadn't seen him since. Now [1918] he was in New York working with a prominent group of pacifists in an organization called the American Union Against Militarism. Roger had offered his services and been given the job of running a Civil Liberties Bureau. His group soon became independent of the parent organization. Most of his time was spent defending the right of conscientious objectors. Roger himself was an objector. It was our common belief in pacifism that brought us together. Roger was a radical. He was thrilled with the struggle of the Russian people for freedom. I was full of my experiences in Russia. I was writing an article on "Revolutionary Justice" for the *Atlantic Monthly* and the *New York Times* had asked for an article on the Russian Soviets.

Roger wanted to know everything I could tell him. He invited me to his camp for a day of canoeing. It was a great experience to be with him in the out-of-doors; he knew all the birds and flowers by name. He was gay and handsome; his charm was irresistible. He came from a conservative background and was a Harvard graduate. But the people who really influenced him were Thoreau, Whitman, Tolstoy, and Kropotkin.

We had several canoeing trips together and he often visited me in my studio. It was impossible not to be impressed by this man who was fighting as ardently for peace as I was, whose philosophy was "I oppose the use of force to accomplish any end." Such a position was dangerous when the United States was at war. The Civil Liberties Bureau was raided on charges of encouraging resistance to the draft; Department of Justice workers were assigned to ferret out any treason. But no sedition was discovered.

Just before this event, Roger's own draft number had come up. All men up to the age of 35 were drafted. He was ordered to present himself for physical examination for military service. This he refused to do. There was little likelihood that he would be sent to the front, for already defeat for the Germans was in sight. But he felt he could not evade the moral issue involved. He refused to obey and was immediately imprisoned in the Tombs in the city. It wasn't an easy time for our growing love. My telephone was continually tapped. Our private conversations became public property. He wrote me before imprisonment: "And now when we find ourselves, to have to be cut off. Oh, Lord! But I shall have the more strength to will myself through it though I shall not dance into jail with joy." [On 14 October Baldwin wrote Doty of his "conviction and ideal for which I would die."]

Roger refused legal defense, but while he was in the Tombs I acted as his attorney. I tried to look important and carried a briefcase. As his attorney I had the right to see him at any time. Frequently I found myself locked in the cell with him.

At last the day came for his trial, October 31, 1918. A heavy cold kept me in bed, which was a great grief. But friends and newspapers told me the story.

He made a memorable speech before Judge Julius M. Mayer. It was widely printed and used later as the expression of man's right to freedom of conscience. He and the Judge looked at each other with respect. Roger left no doubt as to his position. He said:

> I am uncompromising in my opposition to the principle of conscription of life by the state for any purpose whatever in time of war or peace. I not only refuse to obey the present conscription law, but I would in the future refuse to obey any similar statute which attempts to direct my choice of service and ideals. I regard the principle of conscription of life as a flat contradiction of all our cherished ideals of individual freedom, democratic liberty, and Christian training. . . .

> Personally I share the extreme radical philosophy of the future society. I look forward to a social order without any external restraint upon the individuals save through public opinion and the opinion of friends and neighbors. I am not a member of any radical organization, nor do I wear any tags. . . .

> I know that as far as my principles are concerned, they seem to be utterly impracticable, mere moonshine. They are not the views which work in the world today. But I fully believe they are the views which are going to guide in the future.

The Judge in reply said:

> I believe that obedience to the law is the bulwark of the Republic, that a Republic can last only as long as its laws are obeyed. . . . It may often be true that some man or woman has greater foresight than the rest of the people and it may be that he who seems wrong today may be right tomorrow. . . . You have not made my task an easy one. You are entirely right; there can be no compromise on either side. There is nothing left for me to do but to impose the full penalty of the law, one year's imprisonment.

A little note from Roger from the Tombs said: "It is over — the formality of being handed a sentence to fit the criminal. . . . And I shall skip over in a few days to the Essex County [N.J.] jail for a year's vacation. . . . I understand as a jail it isn't half bad, but I am prepared *for anything.* The Judge was decent, almost sympathetic, and friends were altogether too generous. I don't deserve commendation for so simple a virtue as standing by what I believe. . . . Now let's forget it. It was painful not to have you there. Your father faithfully stood by and I felt your presence by proxy."

It was almost with gaiety that Roger went to the Essex jail. It was Armistice Day and the excitement over that was terrific. Broadway was a howling mob of people blowing horns. Inside, Roger soon made friends. The detectives who arrested him sent him 500 cigarettes at Christmas. The prison warden, an Irishman, immediately made him his cook, which gave Roger many privileges. He was given the run of the prison. He was allowed to go outside the jail to mail his letters. One night he got locked out and had quite a hard time getting in. He wrote me from the Essex jail: "Well, this is a real place, infinitely better than the Tombs, clean as a hospital, light, airy, and sunny. . . . I am allowed all my things and there are no restrictions except that outgoing letters are read. . . . I have no complaints. We had a celebration last night and I played the piano and helped with the singing." Then followed a long list of things to do for him. It was the end of the letter which brought comfort, for he said, "I cannot tell you in an inspected letter all I have to say of what you have been in these days and are every moment — of reliance, of faith, and of great hope."

Soon I was visiting Roger regularly. The warden permitted us to meet in the prison greenhouse. But it was not easy.

We both felt the frustration and even Roger's cheerfulness was put to the test. He wrote: "I don't know what is the matter. I never heard of a love so dumb. I am full of feelings I cannot voice. It's not only jail . . . . It isn't anything you have done or are, for you answer more completely

Roger Baldwin, photograph by Underwood and Underwood
(Courtesy of Sophia Smith Collection, Smith College)

my underlying and essential needs. I think it's just the difficulty of accommodation in personality.

As I look back, I marvel at his courage. For his was not a religious objection to war. He had no definite religious belief. He never went to church. He simply believed man should do what his conscience said was right. I now know how incapable of such bravery I would be without God's help. However, at that time I too was not seeking God's guidance about my actions; in fact it was the period in my life when I was farthest from God. I had come to believe, as Roger did, that a change in economic conditions would create a new world, that if man's environment was right, all would be right. I had nearly joined the Socialist Party. I was eager to organize and reform, believing the mere will to put things right was sufficient.

Roger's whole life had been devoted to the fight for freedom and human rights. His love for all sorts and conditions of men was extraordinary. In the cell next him was a young fellow imprisoned for unlawfully carrying loaded firearms. Freddy was in his early twenties. He was a born comedian. Roger woke on his first morning in jail to hear Freddy remarking in loud tones, "So this is Paris." From that moment Roger's friendship began and Freddy was to loom large in our future.

As the weeks passed, the strain on our relationship grew. Roger had already asked me to marry him. But we agreed it would be silly to do so under the circumstances. Moreover, we were the products of the age. Neither of us was keen on the marriage ceremony — Roger because of his ideas of freedom, and I because of my feminist principles. We looked on the ceremony as something to be endured because of our families and because if we did not accept it we would be hampered in our work. In other words, our relation was to be that of free comrades, each supporting himself and independent of each other.

This meant of course I must earn my living. It was time for me to get to work. I could not spend my days in the Essex jail. I suggested to Roger I make another trip to Europe. I wanted to see the condition of the world as a result of war. I also wanted to attend the Congress of the Women's International League for Peace to be held in Zurich. War had prevented all contact since the 1915 Hague meeting.

Roger readily agreed to my departure. But two difficulties confronted me. I was no longer the popular reporter, for the attacks on me as pro-German and pro-Russian had had their effect. And now I was associated with a conscientious objector. My passport was in question.

By chance, the British Intelligence officer in Switzerland who had given me a pass through France when I came out of Germany in 1916 had arrived in America. He came to call and I explained my difficulties. "Don't worry about the passport," he said. "I am on my way to Washington and I think I can arrange it." True to his word, he did. He told the State Department that I was one of the persons who had given the most valuable and useful information about Germany. Another difficulty was that (because of the country's mood) I could secure no contract in advance with the magazines, but several of them gave me letters of introduction and agreed to take articles if they liked them.

I set sail on the British S.S. *Saxonia*, glad to be making the trip. I was six years older than Roger. I was not sure our marriage was right and I wanted him to think things over.[1]

I arrived in Liverpool February 14, 1919, and went straight to the Pethick-Lawrences in London. Malini had written me of the great happiness that had come with the Armistice. She had read President Wilson's speech in Manchester in December and wrote: "I was greatly impressed with what he said and the way he said it and with every expression of his personality. He will be a very great man if he can direct the course of destiny during the next few weeks." England and all Europe seemed to have gone wild over Wilson. No man ever had greater adulation. But at the time I arrived in England he was having a bitter battle over the creation of a League of Nations. Between the wily and subtle European diplomats and the intransigent little group of U.S. Senators, he was fighting a losing battle.

Soon after my arrival I spent a week with Malini at Babbecombe, Devon. I shared with her my letters from Roger. His first letter said: "It was a long time ago you sailed away. . . . I didn't know until you went how much I relied on your being close by and how much my subconscious was engaged to you when my conscience was on strike. The greenhouse is empty now and I am leveled to a routine. . . . Mother even knows I have lost something real, and sister and brother, who called on me today, alluded to your going as if you were the family attorney."

Roger wrote me in England that he had started a prison welfare league, saying "Jail is getting too interesting to leave. It is a human laboratory of new ideas and excitements daily. Our organization has been started with boundless enthusiasm by the boys, and I expect to have it in running order in a week. I am meanwhile attaching myself to several charming youths, all without proper guardianship and ideals, and I foresee you as the lady proprietor of a house for Roger's stray crooks. But they are fine boys and I love them." One of the number was of course Freddy. Roger spoke of putting up a shack and teaching the boys agricultural arts, and added, "Aunt Ruth says you will need an assistant, marrying a gang."

In Europe. The Aftermath of War

In London early that spring of 1919 I found no hatred of the German people such as existed in America. England distinguished between the people and the government. Here I was under no suspicion. My writing was accepted at its face value as an honest statement of what I had found. The English intellectuals were more than ready to meet me. My first encounter was with Henry Nevinson, one of England's leading journalists. We had tea together, and he told me of a trip he was planning to Ireland. A revolution was brewing there, for Ireland was demanding independence. He suggested I go with him. He thought there was some danger, but if need be we might escape by airplane. I had seen the beginning of a revolution in Germany, lived through nearly three months of one in Russia, why not add Ireland to my list? So one night before very long I found myself crossing the Irish Channel.

Back in 1916 the insurrection of Easter Week by Sinn Fein rebels for Irish independence under the command of Eamon de Valera had occurred; Sheehy Skeffington and James Connolly had been killed. Ireland was put under martial law and de Valera was sentenced to life imprisonment by Britain. The severity of England had reinforced the opposition. The Irish Labour Party grew stronger and more radical, but this group was small. The vast majority were Sinn Feiners and members of the Catholic Church. The movement was wholly concerned with the separation of Ireland from England. To compare Ireland with Russia was grotesque. The Bolshevik revolution was economic, a changing of the social and economic order. The Irish struggle was political; it was for self-determination. It was not a swing from constitutionalism, but only an endeavor to shake off English constitutionalism. In 1918 the Irish revolutionary Labour Party and the Sinn Feiners had come together on the basis of nationalism. Separation from England was inevitable. The Celts and the Anglo-Saxons were so different.

While I was in Ireland, de Valera was released from prison. He was to make a triumphal march into Dublin to attend a reception for him as President, to be held at the Lord Mayor's house. Through Nevinson I had an invitation from the Lord Mayor to attend the welcome. It was not stated what he was to be president of, but the English authorities believed it to be a recognition of de Valera as President of the Irish Republic, so they decided to suppress the demonstration. All Dublin was in a state of excitement. English soldiers poured into the city. Men with rifles and machine guns were stationed on many buildings. The triumphal procession was called off. No shooting occurred and de Valera was privately received by the Mayor.[2] There was no violence during my ten days in Ireland. The Irish people, I discovered, were a race apart. They were not internationalists. They were not concerned with world affairs. As Celts they were a people who delighted in poetry and fairy tales and were devoted to the Catholic Church.

Through Nevinson I met in Ireland the leading intellectuals, a fascinating group. There was Yeats, the poet, and the Abbey Theater, which produced his plays and sometimes those of Bernard Shaw. Another very popular man was George Russell, known by his pen name as A.E. He was at the head of Plunkett House, a sort of social settlement. His philosophy of life was based on the love of all men as brothers. His open letters to the newspapers were famous. He exposed the low wages, the miserable housing, the frightful condition of the workers. Such were the people who clamored for independence. Wilson's demand for self-determination, one of his Fourteen Points, was taking root everywhere. Right in principle, it was nevertheless stirring up hate and revolution. It was a pity that nations could not live together in harmony, like organs in the human body, separated but united. Each side had so much to give. Their very differences made life rich.

When I returned to London, I found Malini and Fred campaigning hard for Irish independence. In addition, a post-war problem about which Malini and other women were deeply concerned was the blockade. There were stories of the frightful starvation among the women and children in Central Europe. The Allies' blockade of enemy countries was bringing death to the innocent. All Wilson's promises of a peace without victory, no conquerors or conquered, were being wrecked. The English women, with the help of Nevinson, had sent rubber nipples to Germany and Austria, where there were none. At least the babies had nipples on their bottles, but the content was not milk but ersatz coffee.

A big demonstration to demand the lifting of the blockade was planned for April 6 in Trafalgar Square. I went to the meeting with Malini. It was a warm spring day; thousands thronged the streets. At 2:30 the speakers mounted the stone foundations at the base of the monument. They spread their great banners about them on which were inscribed "Save Starving Europe," "Raise the Blockade." No police came to hustle the women away, for England believed in free speech. I stood on the stone coping and looked down at the crowd. Fully 10,000 packed the square. There were women speakers on three sides of the monument. Malini was one of them. Many soldiers were present. At first some were rude and yelled, "Let them starve." But the crowd would not have it. Gradually the soldiers grew silent and even respectful. As the horror of what was told penetrated the people's minds, tears were in many eyes. They pushed up close to the platform. When the meeting was over, they did not leave. They stood there muttering. Finally someone said, "We want action; tell us what to do." Then another voice was heard: "Let us march to the Foreign Office, let us demand the blockade be lifted." The women hesitated; then Malini came forward. "Very well," she said, "let us go." A great shout went up. In a moment

I found myself between Malini and another woman speaker leading the procession. Behind us surged the crowd. Police reserves were called. They cleared the way for the oncoming crowd. Two years ago women would have been arrested. But today they were voters. The police were very courteous. At Downing Street the procession halted because a cordon of bobbies was drawn across the street. But five women were allowed through. Up the steps of Bonar Law's house they went, while the crowd cheered and sang.[3] Bonar Law was not in, but his secretary made an appointment to receive the deputation the next day.

That night women, with the help of men, carried paste pots and posters and plastered the city with the posters which read, "English people, will you permit your Government to starve thousands of babies? Can you bear the shame? Protest!" But it was a long, hard fight, and I was to see much starvation in Austria and Germany before the blockade was lifted.

Those were vastly interesting days in London,[4] but I could feel how the people had suffered. Physical damage to the country was small. Rather it was the loss of their young men. At an afternoon tea with H. G. Wells he said, "It will be ten years before great writers will again appear. Our best young men have been killed. Materially we are bankrupt." He was not, however, pessimistic. He felt a better world was coming. He invited me to spend a week-end at his country place, the home he has described in *Mr. Britling Sees It Through*. When I stepped out of the train there, I was met by Mr. Wells and his famous car. Automobiles were still in their infancy. I was bumped over the road and run into hedges quite after the manner of Mr. Britling with his guests. When we arrived at the house, I was greeted by his charming wife and two sons. Lunch was served on the lawn. Then a game of cricket was in order, just as in his book. In fact, to know about Wells' country life one has only to read about Mr. Britling. We talked much of history. He was deeply interested in the book he was writing, *The Outline of History*, which his wife helped him write. His philosophy is that man can be saved if *he will*. He must fight if he wants salvation. He wrote: "Everlastingly you may conquer and find fresh worlds to conquer. . . . If you have courage through the night of dark and the present battle bloody, nevertheless victory shall be yours. Only have courage. On the courage of your heart all things depend."

One day I had lunch with Bernard Shaw and his wife in their attractive apartment in Adelphi Terrace. He too said, "We have lost five years out of English literature. In time of war and crisis, artists cannot create. We cannot know what we have lost in the death of so many of our promising young men." Bernard Shaw I found to be a shy man, sensitive, and not easy to talk to. He did not pose as anyone great. He was simple and alert and his mind was as flexible as his body. He liked to draw people out, and he began on me. He had read my articles in the English *Nation*. "They were good," he said, "but of course they weren't true. They were much too good to be true." Shaw, without doubt, was one of the greatest analytical writers of his generation. He showed up the hypocrisy of the age in which he lived. Unlike Wells, he did not make any predictions of the future.

From London I went to Paris. France had suffered even more than England, for the war had been fought on her territory. There had been much destruction. France was bitter and full of hate for the Germans. They wanted the last drop of blood exacted. It was evident war had not brought prosperity to the conquerors.

I came to Paris largely to see my younger brother Ralph. He had run away at age 17 and joined the army. He had driven an ambulance during the war, was now stationed with the army of occupation at Coblentz [as Quartermaster Sgt. Senior Grade], and had a leave of absence for several days. Unfortunately he had become a periodic drinker, largely due, I felt, to an inferiority complex acquired in childhood. We had a good time together, visiting Versailles and going to a musical show. But all the time he was drinking heavily. When his leave was up I feared he would not go back to his outfit. This was serious and might mean court martial. On his last day I decided on a desperate remedy. When we left the hotel I said, "Let's go and have a drink." We did. And at the next cafe I saw I said again, "Let's stop and have another drink." This I continued to do until he grew furious. The lack of opposition brought him to his senses; he rushed back to the hotel. That night he managed to get on the train, and a week later I heard from him. He thanked me for understanding what he needed.

From Paris I went to Switzerland. The Women's International League for Peace and Freedom was meeting in Zurich on May 12 [while at the same time heads of state were debating terms for the Versailles Treaty]. We women had not seen each other since the wonderful Congress at The Hague. What a relief it was to be in a country where there had been no war for a hundred years. The only reminders were the ration card and an occasional flock of airplanes overhead. The blue lake shimmered in the sunshine. Spring sweetness filled the air. Little rowboats bore gay parties out upon the lake. The snow-capped mountains towered above. Gladness filled our hearts. War was forgotten. American and Austrian women walked the street arm in arm. Switzerland, with its mixed population of French, Germans, and Italians, made a fitting background.

The women from Central Europe at the Congress were thin and pale, with haggard eyes. Smiles came rarely and laughter not at all. The women of the Allied countries caught glimpses of their own vigorous bodies beside those of their undernourished sisters and turned away ashamed. We were pathetically eager to make amends. At one of the first business sessions two young German girls were seen munching cake and chocolate. The glad light of youth was in their eyes. "Forgive us," they said, "but it is the first time in three years we have had anything sweet."

But, though national enmity was forgotten, there was a great difference in intellectual conviction. A left and right soon developed. One woman from Germany asked, "How is it that President Wilson made such wonderful speeches that we made a democracy in my country and now America is no longer democratic?" About 150 women attended the Congress, representing 15 countries, including 65 delegates from the Allied countries and 35 from Central Europe. The largest delegation came from the U.S.[5] The American delegation was the most conservative of the group.

It was Mrs. Philip Snowden of England, wife of the man who was to become Finance Minister in the Labour Government, and Mrs. Pethick-Lawrence who were the outstanding personalities, though many English delegates disliked their passionate speeches — emotion was not quite good form. And over all our differences presided Jane Addams, gentle, wise, serene. No matter how deeply we disagreed, she insisted that everyone be heard. Her quiet sense of humour was delightful. And there was one thing on which we were all in accord: we all denounced the Versailles Treaty. Long before men diplomats came to doubt its wisdom, the women at the Zurich Congress had picked it to pieces. It was Mrs. Snowden, with her clear, brilliant intellect, who tore to shreds the humbug of diplomacy. With eloquence she laid bare the meaning of the peace terms. She declared that Wilson's Fourteen Points had been violated from end to end. She pointed out that Germany was to pay 5,000 million British pounds in two years, which for a starving people was impossible. And even if it could be done, that was not enough. On May 21, 1921, the Central Powers were to be told what further was to be exacted. All Germany must submit to total disarmament, while England and the U.S. continued to build up their army and navy. She ended saying, "Women, as long as we content ourselves with tears and poetry, we will do nothing. Democracy by this treaty has been thrown into contempt, idealism reduced to dust. We must not tolerate it."

The Congress, quite swept off its feet, passed the following resolution:

> We declare the peace terms proposed by Versailles, guaranteeing the fruits of secret diplomacy to the conquerors, tacitly sanctioning secret diplomacy, denying the principle of self-determination, recognizing the right of the victors to the spoils of war, and creating all over Europe discords and animosities, can only lead to future wars. [6]

The women from Austria and Hungary told us harrowing tales of the general decline of the race, of children half their normal size, with big eyes and clawlike hands, of children dying in the hospitals, of aged people left unfed.

Jane Addams closed the meeting with these words:

> The value of the life of one child is as great as that of another. It may be that the only way to heal the wounds and reconstruct the world is to get back to primitive needs. It may be these needs will hold us together. The distribution of food may be a holy thing. Let us take up this task in the spirit of humility, and out of it may grow new friendships and affection.

A resolution was passed to this effect, and it was agreed a deputation with Jane Addams at its head would present it to the national leaders in Paris [and would request that the Allies' blockade of the Central Powers be lifted].

That was perhaps the high point of the Congress, though a dramatic moment occurred when a French delegate from the devastated French territory arrived. She had gotten through at the last moment. She made an eloquent speech about the suffering of her country and begged that French and German women stand together in order that such things never happen again. Fraulein Heymann, stirred beyond control, left the platform and went to Mlle. Melan and grasped her both hands. They stood there, hand in hand, French and German, personifying a love that transcends hate. Then Emily Balch of the U.S. sprang up and stood between the two women and, raising her right hand, said, "I pledge myself to return to my country and as long as I live fight against war." And the entire Congress rose spontaneously and offered the same pledge.

While we in Zurich were denouncing the peace treaty, Clemenceau and Lloyd George were each fighting for their national interests. Wilson, in a vain effort to secure at least a league of nations, made compromise after compromise. All the seeds were laid for a future war and revolution. Some of the provisions made were due to lack of foresight. For instance, the total separation from each other of

Czechoslovakia, Austria, Hungary, and Yugoslavia, right in principle, was in fact fatal. A federation which granted independence with union might have saved much suffering. For each new state selfishly began to raise tariff barriers and restrictions against its neighbors. Austria became almost a dead country; two million people in Vienna and no hinterland. Where was it to get its food? Hungary would not sell its products; Czechoslovakia put such a high tariff on sugar that it was cheaper to get it from the U.S. It became evident that treaties could not bring peace to the world without understanding, compassion, and friendship.

One day a trainload of little waifs from Austria had arrived in Zurich, a group of Swiss women having agreed to receive a hungry child. I went to the station with the women. The kiddies had been checked like express packages. Around each little neck was a string with a label giving name, address, and condition. They came from all classes, the starving bourgeoisie as well as the starving workers. There were four or five hundred of them. There wasn't a laugh or even a smile; only occasionally a tear slid down a hollow cheek. At first one was deceived by flushed faces. But the color was from weakness. All the boisterous vitality of childhood was dead. Near me was a young Swiss woman of 25, herself a picture of health, but with tears rolling down her cheeks. Clinging to her hand was a tiny creature, who was like a fairy with golden curls and blue eyes. She looked to be five years old. She was too exquisite to be real and too weak to speak. The young woman showed me the little skeleton hand and arm. Every bone showed through. "She is ten years old," said the woman. After that I looked at the legs and arms of the children and turned away aghast. It was the women who were sobbing. They knelt and clasped the frail little creatures to their hearts.

From Zurich I took a train for Austria. [Doty had obtained a pass which allowed passage through Allied-occupied territory.] George Landsbury, editor of the *London Daily Herald,* had asked me to write articles on both Austria and Germany. He even suggested I go again to Russia and thought I might get an airplane from Hungary.

The moment the Swiss border was crossed into Austria, tragedy was everywhere visible. Desperate, hungry mobs crowded trains to Switzerland and were sent back. The resources of Switzerland were not great enough to receive them all. "We are done for. It makes no difference whether we sign the peace, treaty or not." These were the words uttered on every hand by rich and poor, conservative and liberal.

It took all day to reach Innsbruck, which was still under Italian military control. My breakfast at the hotel consisted of imitation coffee and imitation marmalade. There was no sugar, no butter, no bread, no milk. From there I went on to Salzburg by train. In the "Personenzug" the plush coverings had been cut off the seats for clothing; the leather straps were gone from the windows. At the stations barefooted children crowded under train windows. They begged not for pennies but bread: "Brot, bitte, Brot." One of the few pieces of chocolate I was allowed to bring through I gave to a small boy. He grasped it, gave a quick look around, hid it in his blouse. He didn't thank me but moved off, his hand clasped over his shirtfront. When he thought no one was looking, he put a crumb in his mouth. It was the real thing. He looked at me as though I had been giving him a gold piece. He feared I would discover my mistake; he couldn't believe his luck. Then he turned and ran, ran recklessly, his hand clasped over his treasure.

At Salzburg it was the same. Hollow-cheeked, listless people moved slowly like sick flies. Children released from school tried to play, but rickety legs would not hold them up. At the hotel the concierge gave me a food allowance list. It was one 1 oz. of bread a day, 4 oz. of meat a week, 1 lb. of sugar a month. But the poor often could not afford to buy even these rations and sold them to the rich.

After much difficulty I reached Linz and from there took a boat down the Danube to Vienna. The boat was crowded but not with holiday seekers. Each man, woman, and child had one deadly purpose: to find a scrap of food at some farm. It was dark when I reached Vienna; every good hotel was full. The hotels were in touch with smugglers. And anyone with money could, at enormous prices, live with some comfort. I had to content myself with a third class hotel. In the morning my breakfast was imitation tea, no sugar or milk, and imitation bread made from a field flower called *kokles*, which has little nourishment. In a few hours such bread grows hard as stone. I still had some chocolate, and with hot water made myself a cup.

The plight of Austria was beyond description, dismembered and crushed. Statistics in the mayor's office showed 400,000 out of 500,000 children were half starved. America for three months after the armistice gave aid, but much of the food was seized by gamblers and speculators and sold to the rich. Now there was nothing. Children, whose bones were like rubber, ceased to walk, then to crawl, and at the last lay panting on a bed. A nation was dying and the world went on. The words of Christ kept ringing in my ears: "Inasmuch as ye did it unto the least of these little ones, ye did it unto me."

In striking contrast to Austria was Hungary. The rich farmlands still supplied food. In late March Hungary had come under Communist control with Bela Kun at the head of the government.[7] Hungarian women had demanded that children be fed first and the Hungarian Soviet had agreed. The majority of the people were not Communist, but as long as there was food they didn't rebel. I lived in the best hotel in Budapest and was adequately fed. It was the headquarters of Bela Kun. His wife was having a glorious time frequenting the hairdresser and manicurist and buying new clothes. But little wars were flaring up all over the country. The Whites were fighting the Reds. Bela Kun was having a hard time in Hungary, though the Russian revolution seemed to be prospering. One morning I saw a car in front of the hotel with a machine gun back and front. I was told Bela Kun was off to a battle. I waited in the corridor until I saw him coming downstairs. Then I rushed to him and cried, "Take me with you!" Much surprised, he said, "Where to?" "Anywhere," I replied. Then it dawned on him I was a reporter. He grinned and said, "Impossible."

I went out to the airport to inquire about a plane to Russia. It seems two had tried to cross the mountains and crashed. The plane I saw was a rickety affair, a warplane with just room for the pilot and a passenger. It was making a trial flight over Budapest, and the pilot offered to take me. A woman friend who had traveled with me watched as we took off. Afterward she told me she had kept saying to herself, "What shall I do with the body? What shall I do with the body?" That trial flight convinced me it was unlikely the plane would ever reach Russia. The risk would be enormous. I decided to give it up. I had a father and mother and Roger waiting for me.

There was nothing I could do in Hungary, so I took a train back to Vienna, planning to go on to Germany. I left in the evening and we had hardly proceeded an hour when the train halted. A battle was raging just ahead. We had to wait until morning.

When I reached Germany I found my prediction of 1916 had come true that the land would crack and crumble for lack of fat and grease and that there would be a revolution. Besides the war casualties and epidemics, between 1916 and 1917 some 763,000 had died of starvation, and tuberculosis had increased 50 percent. In 1917, 50,000 children between 1 and 15 years of age died for want of food.

On the surface, life in Berlin seemed normal. Food could be had at enormous prices. But beneath were rank misery, hunger, and despair. The first person I visited was my friend who had been my companion and interpreter during my 1916 trip. We had had no communication since. No letter could get through. With beating heart I rang her doorbell. Was she alive or dead? Then I heard footsteps. There she was, with her massive head and her shock of grey hair [Augspurg?]. But her face was lined with sorrow. When we could speak I asked, "What has happened to the revolution?" She bowed her head. "Temporarily it is at a standstill. We have been imprisoned and killed until there are none left to fight." "But," I ventured, "the talk is of a Socialist republic in Germany." "It isn't true," she said. "There isn't an atom of Socialism. What we have is a capitalist republic, which is even more relentless than a monarchy." Then she told me her story: in November 1918 the uprising came, the Kaiser was deposed, the people swept everything before them. At first the power of Karl Liebknecht and Rosa Luxemburg was electric. The masses flocked to them. Then the day came for the election of a National Assembly. Liebknecht advised the Socialists and Communists to join sides in the election. But 60 out of 75 of the delegates refused. Liebknecht gave way to the majority. That was the signing of his death warrant. He and Rosa Luxemburg were seized and led before the Chief Army Staff, the Prussian militarists of former days, and were immediately sentenced to imprisonment. As Liebknecht stepped out into the street he was hit on the head with the butt of a gun and became unconscious. He was then put into an automobile, and by the time they reached the Tiergarten he had regained consciousness and was ordered out of the car. As he staggered to the ground, he was shot in the head and died instantly [January 16, 1919].

Rosa Luxemburg left the military tribunal 15 minutes after Liebknecht. As she stood in the doorway, soldiers rushed upon her and beat her head with their guns. She was put in a car. When it was found she was dead, the soldiers stopped to get some barbed wire. Her body was bound round and round with this and thrown into the canal. It was a long time before the body was recovered. The people were enraged by these murders and became more revolutionary than ever. When the military leaders saw they had accomplished nothing by killing these two leaders, they turned on the people. They gave up all pretense of socialism and decency. In the Kaiser's time there were at least trials, but the military tribunal imprisoned thousands without trials. My friend went on:

On March 28, 1919, eight soldiers came to my door and seized me. They searched and found nothing. I have never preached violence. They had no evidence but they carried me off to jail. It was my first prison experience. I did not know it was so horrible. I was ill with bronchitis. They made me take a hot bath and then put me in a cell with the window wide open and gave me no covers. For seven days and nights I did not sleep and became very ill. My daughter, a doctor in a big hospital, was allowed to see me. She is not a Socialist. Through her influence I was sent to a sanatorium and after several weeks allowed to return home but forbidden ever to speak in public. Such is the situation in Germany today. It is useless to do anything. Our leaders are imprisoned or dead. The people are not ready for either Socialism or Communism. The Government knows it, but pretends we are. Two armies are forming: the militarists, the Prussians, the White Army versus the army of the workers, miserable, half-fed, but filled with rage. We who might have quieted the people are being killed. What will be the outcome? The Kaiser was overthrown by the people, and now the reactionaries are trying to make a counter-revolution. The Germans are not like the Russians; they do not hunger for personal freedom. All their tendencies are toward socialization and centralization. What they want is State Socialism. But the workers are being pushed further and further to the Left by their treatment. The middle class, those of us who want democracy, are caught between the extreme Left and the extreme Right. It is difficult to predict the future. But the treaty must be signed. The people will have peace. Otherwise there will be another uprising.

The National Assembly was to meet in Weimar. I told my friend I wanted to attend it. There was a strike on the railroads, so no trains were running. But a plane left Berlin daily for Leipzig to deliver mail and newspapers. I arranged to be flown on to Weimar. The plane was a small open cockpit with two engines, used in the war. At 5:00 A.M. a car came to the hotel and I was whirled away to the airport. Here I was given a heavy corduroy suit, all of one piece, a fur cap buttoned tightly about my ears, and big goggles for my eyes. The pilot helped me into the plane. He had flown in the war. I settled down on a bundle of the *Berliner Tageblatt*; there wasn't room for a seat. The pilot sat directly in front of me. There were just the two of us. At 6:30 we were off with a deafening roar and a terrific rush of air. We mounted higher and higher until we were 3000 feet up. Once there we didn't seem to move. It was like floating on a cloud. The pilot turned and smiled at me. The noise made speech impossible. The sense of being up in the air was exhilarating. I looked over the side of the plane to the earth below. At the outskirts of Leipzig we came down in great swoops at 8:00 A.M., delivered our mail, and were off again.

But soon I was conscious of little jerks and sputters. Something was wrong. My calmness vanished. I saw the pilot had turned about and was heading again for Leipzig. We landed safely and the pilot explained he had forgotten to fill the gasoline tanks. He suggested I might prefer to continue some other way. But I had paid for the round-trip ticket to Weimar and wanted to go on. We arrived there without incident at 10:00 A.M.

In Weimar a big public building had been turned into an assembly hall. I walked through the corridors, but alas the meeting closed its doors to reporters. To pass the time I went to call on Count Bernstorff, ambassador to the U.S. just before the war. I had met him in 1916 when I made my trip to Germany. Now he was very thin; it was evident he had not had enough to eat. He sat beside me on a sofa in friendly fashion. His days of being a Count were over. I asked him what he thought of the peace treaty. "It must be signed," he said, "otherwise there will be a revolution. The people will have peace. There are provisions that are impossible of fulfillment, and I suppose," he added grimly, "if we fail, it will be said Germany again signed a scrap of paper." "What provisions would you change?" I asked, and he replied, "First, Germany should be admitted to the League of Nations. Second, the amount of indemnity should be fixed. Third, there should be self-determination for the territories formerly belonging to Germany. Without that there will be another war." "And what about the Kaiser?" I asked. There was a hardly perceptible quiver before he answered, "Germany should deal with the Kaiser. I am willing to acknowledge our mistakes, but it is for us to rectify them. What I cannot understand is why America isn't satisfied. She wanted a democracy in Germany and Germany is now making one."

It was late afternoon before the pilot and I set out for Berlin. As we flew back, it grew dark and began to drizzle and the lights had come on before we landed. If Weimar was quiet, Berlin was not. As I drove back to the hotel, I saw barbed wire entanglements and machine guns. Food shops had been raided. The poor had gone mad with hunger.

One day I visited the ward of a hospital for contagious children. It was the last word in scientific perfection. It was made of glass; in each little glass room was a bed and on each bed lay a baby. Against the glass of one room a mother pressed her face. She saw her baby was well cared for, but the baby was a skeleton. There were no milk and no cod liver oil. It was like seeing a specimen under a microscope.

I felt I could endure no more, so sought permission from the Inter Allied Commission to leave Germany, which was granted by way of Cologne and Koblentz. I visited my brother in Koblentz and saw the army of occupation was enjoying itself there. It liked the German better than the French. The people were so friendly and so grateful for every scrap of food. Indeed, many soldiers took German wives back to America.

That June President Wilson was back in Paris again. He determined to remain in Versailles until the treaty was signed and the League Covenant incorporated in the treaty. The victors were still fighting over the spoils. The Japanese, Italians, and French were all demanding gains for themselves. France was to occupy the Rhineland and the Saar Valley. In the end Wilson felt he must agree to an unfair treaty in order to preserve the League. He hoped that in the future the League might rectify things. The treaty was signed June 28, 1919 and Wilson left for the U.S. on the 29th. [Doty reached home soon thereafter.]

12
50–50 Marriage, 1919–1925

*R*OGER HAD BEEN TRANSFERRED in May 1919 from the jail in Newark to the penitentiary in Caldwell, N.J., a big farm on high hills. Here the rules were more rigid. But as a trustee he worked out-of-doors from 8:00 A.M. to 5:00 P.M., and this was good for his health. He was full of plans for his future and wrote: "I am still of a mind to go on the bum after I get out, with two or three of the radical labor boys for a two or three months' trip to get my feet solid on the ground of facts about the labor struggle. I cannot get it from books. My whole training must be overcome and my field of knowledge extended. I see no way but the laboratory."

Roger's sentence expired in August, but because of good behavior he was released early in July. He was at the dock to meet me, as were also my father and mother. It was a great homecoming. Roger thought we should be married immediately. He had written from Boston, "I feel very sure, very content, very peaceful, as you only can in a fixed, rounded, elemental relationship." He wanted me to come to Boston to meet his mother, father, two brothers, and three sisters. I met the whole crowd and was warmly received, especially by Roger's mother.

Our marriage was set for August 8. On that date Roger and I went through the civil ceremony in New York. We simply signed a marriage license for which each paid 50 cents. Marriage on a 50/50 basis had begun. We then went to the Sparta farm, where my parents were spending the summer. Roger's mother joined us. And, of course, there was Freddy.

Our real ceremony was held in Sparta. There was no dressing up, no bridal veil, not even a ring. Under a great tree, on a small island in front of our house, with the brook rushing by on each side and a small bridge to get there, Roger and I read to each other our conception of marriage. Norman Thomas as pastor presided and spoke for the community. Our parents stood gravely by. Roger's statement was:

232

To us who passionately cherish the vision of a free human society, the present institution of marriage among us is a grim mockery of essential freedom. Here we have the most intimate, the most sacred, the most creative relationship shackled in the deadening grip of private property, and essentially holding the woman subservient to the man. Its bonds are strong in ye olde customs and laws. . . . To both of us they constitute a challenge. We deny without reservation the whole conception of property in marriage. We deny without reservation the moral right of the state or church to bind by the force of law a relationship that cannot be maintained by the power of love alone. We submit to the form of law only because it seems a matter of too little importance to resist or ignore. . . . We share the view of Edward Carpenter that the highest relationship between a man and a woman is that which welcomes and understands each their other's loves. Without a sense of possession there can be no exclusions, no jealousies. The creative life demands many friendships, many loves shared together openly, honestly, and joyously. . . . For my part I pledge you to live out between us that general vision of a free creative life, adjusting, searching, understanding, loving, that we may the better understand and love all others. . . .

My primary interest and joy is the great revolutionary struggle for human freedom today, so intense, so full of promise. I regard our union only as contributing to that cause. . . . Whether my course may again lead me to prison or to distant travel and to long separation, our union will be no barrier to freedom of action, but rather a source of added strength and keener purpose. My second deep interest and joy are the processes by which we pass on to the growing generation such wisdom and vision as is ours . . . .

I come to this relationship . . . without any ambition but to live fully the truths I cherish. Success, failure, and practical achievement, as they are commonly rated, mean nothing to me. . . . As the complete expression of my way of life, let me repeat this verse from ancient Sanskrit:

Look to this Day
For this is life
The very life of life.
In its brief course lie all the Virtues and
Realities of your existence —

The Glory of Action
The Splendor of Beauty
The Bliss of Growth!

I replied:

Today we enter into partnership, the union of man and woman.
Union, passionate love, all love is the creative force of the universe. I may create not only the next generation but great deeds
and great thoughts. The true test of love is does it make those
who love bigger, finer, and more creative? Believing this, my one
desire is that our love may increase your power to live and to
love. This it cannot do unless you are absolutely free, free to love
whom you will, to go where you will, to be your own master total
and absolute. . . . I want to give and have a love that has perfect
trust and understanding. . . . The deep love that gives and does
not seek, that respects and reveres, the love that springs from
God and is for all mankind, that love I give you now and for
always until death do us part.

In so far as we work out an adjustment of personalities that will
increase the power of each, we lay the foundation for the new,
free brotherhood for which we strive, where all men shall live
together in love and harmony. . . . With gladness in my heart, an
unquestioning trust, and a deep sense of the wonder and beauty
of life, "Comrade I give you my hand, I give you my love more
precious than money, I give you myself before preaching or law,
Will you give me yourself? Will you come travel with me? Shall
we stick by each other as long as we live?

Norman Thomas' statement I no longer possess. The day after our
marriage Roger and I left for Lake Saranac for a two-week honeymoon.
To my consternation I discovered Freddy was trailing along. At this I
rebelled. Our marriage was a free union, but a Freddy on a honeymoon?
No, no matter how much he needed supervision. — I won the day.

We spent two wonderful weeks in the open. Mrs. Caroline Colgate
loaned us her camp. We had two tents, one for sleeping, the other to live
in, and the weather was fine. We cooked out-of-doors, went canoeing
and swimming, and climbed mountains. The world and its problems
were forgotten. A common love of nature bound us together.

We separated at the end of two weeks. This was a pity; I had lived
so long alone and was just getting adjusted to life with another. But
Roger was off to the Midwest to live as a manual laborer. [As he told his

biographer Lamson, he wanted "to learn by participation the facts of the labor struggle."] He made a four months' trip.[1] He worked in a coal mine and a lead smelter. He scabbed by day at a Pittsburgh steel plant, reporting secretly at night to the striking union, until the mill owners found out and fired him. He got jobs in a railway section-gang and in a brickyard. Callouses were on his hands when he returned. Roger's mother did not approve of this trip. She wrote me, "I was intensely interested in all you had to say, especially what concerned my runaway boy Roger. I wish he would come home to his wife and stay where he belongs." [On October 2 Roger had written Doty from Hull House in Chicago, after being on the picket line in Gary, Indiana: "I am now a full fledged IWW (Industrial Workers of the World) and a member of the Waiters' Union (including the Cooks', Bartenders' and Waitresses' Union!). . . . It has been joyous here with the IWW boys, Emma Goldman, ("Big Bill") Haywood, Graham Taylor, Jane Addams and the Hull House crowd. They are all intensely interested and sympathetic — and my old clothes don't seem to bother them."]

When Roger did return we settled down in my studio just off Washington Square [at 110 Waverly Place]. It was one floor in a house. There was a big front room with an open coal fire. Back of this were a bedroom, bath, and kitchen. Roger put a tent on the roof for his waifs and strays. Freddy was frequently with us. It was not easy to live with a gang, to have boys use my face powder and the bath tub and fail to wash it out. But life was gay. There was never a dull moment.

At the entrance to the house door were our two names. People came to look at them. It wasn't customary then for a wife to keep her own name. But it was Roger's desire as much as mine. He introduced me as "Miss Doty, my wife." He wrote an amusing skit entitled "Why My Wife Should Not Take My Name":

I am unalterably opposed to any woman taking my name. It's all I've got to identify me, and I am not going to give it away to a woman. Only the Lord knows what she would do with it. Like as not I'd find it on cooking recipes in the female magazines, and on checks of course, and in the society news. I can't afford any such disastrous chances. I have my own masculine reputation as a cook to protect. It's just too darn risky, this uncontrolled gift of your good male name to an irresponsible woman. Why men have stood for it down the ages can be explained only by a fear of their wives. And shall we also take from our children the ancient right to our name? Yes, certainly. Let our children take their mothers' names. Children belong to their mothers. . . .

I would leave to women only their freedom either to choose men weak enough to submit to being made female rubber stamps or to be thrown back by an indignant and revolting manhood upon their own names and deeds. Even I in my hard won freedom find myself occasionally the victim of this female mania for an alias. In *Who's Who* I find "Mrs. Roger Baldwin" and a cryptic "See Doty, Madeleine Z." Even our colored cook insists on some recognition of the marriage status and insists on referring to me as "Mr. Doty."

So I am off all this stuff of two names that look like one. I am for an absolutely unadulterated and unconditional freedom to be myself and to be myself all alone.

It was at this time, during the autumn of 1919, that Wilson set out for the West on his heartbreaking campaign for the League. My surgeon friend, who had returned from the base hospital at the front in France, wrote me in this period:

Part of my restlessness is simply groping, for I see no clear road ahead for the problems of the day and no sign of any real leadership. Everywhere is talk, most of it ill-informed, much of it purely self-seeking. Nowhere is there constructive leadership based on knowledge and wisdom and driven by unselfishness. We are literally the blind leading the blind. The spectacle of Mr. Wilson talking idealistic nonsense at one end of the country and the Senate talking narrow-minded political jargon at the other is enough to make angels weep.

Part of my restlessness, however, is less material and is due to having been an actor in a drama [medical service overseas in the War] that was capable of taking people quite out of themselves and making them for the time being superhuman. To come down to earth from such an experience is not going to be easy and will wreck many.

He never did settle down in Boston, in spite of Puritan ancestors, but went West and became the chief surgeon and director of a large hospital. I too was finding it extremely difficult not to be restless. The idealism of the pre-war days had vanished. In October 1920 the first meeting of the League of Nations was held, with representatives of 41 countries, and the only important country to remain out was the U.S.

This same year Warren G. Harding, a Republican and conservative, was elected and took as his slogan "A return to normalcy."

It grew more and more difficult to get constructive articles published. How to earn my living became a problem. I finally gave up writing and sought a job. For a while I edited a small news sheet in which Roger was interested. It was called "Friends of Freedom for India."

I was determined to make good on the 50–50 marriage. Roger wanted to keep expenses down to a working-class level. We each contributed $60 a month to cover room and food. Even in 1920 this was difficult. The rent for the studio was $50 a month. It meant buying with care. I found housekeeping for two took more time than for one. I wanted to entertain Roger's family. Moreover, we had many guests. We had a maid for three hours a day; she cleaned and she prepared one meal.

One day I announced to Roger he ought to take his share of the housekeeping, as it was a 50–50 marriage. He readily agreed. We were each to take turns of a week. Roger thought the home ought to be put on a business basis. He got down the cook book and made a list of all the recipes we liked. He numbered each one. When he left in the morning he had prepared a note for the maid, which read like this: "Soup No. 5; Entree 16; Meat 7; Dessert 21." And in addition he added: "Clean thoroughly and wipe behind all the pictures."

When I arrived home that evening, no work had been done. The maid had vanished, leaving a note which said, "I see I am not satisfactory. I am leaving." That meant I must search for another maid. I began to understand that running a house was a real job, not something done on the side. It was very difficult to concentrate on two jobs at once, though Roger in his carefree way managed it. He was an excellent cook and, provided the needed supplies were at hand, could produce a dinner in twenty minutes.

His camp, a small wooden hut on the Hackensack River in New Jersey, where we went every Sunday, was a great resource. We had many day parties there and the oddest collection of people. I remember one Sunday vividly. Roger had invited a millionaire and his chorus girl, a Communist, a social worker, a businessman, Freddy, and another ex-prisoner. Roger took the crowd walking until they were nearly starved. Then at three o'clock he produced a big dinner. Everyone declared he was the best cook in the world.

That life was all delightful and amusing, but I seemed to be getting nowhere with work of my own. My Dad, as always, offered to help me financially, but that was no solution. There was plenty of voluntary work to do. I found myself giving lectures before various organizations and joining committees engaged in welfare work. I also wrote a few articles for newspapers. And reporters constantly wanted to interview me on marriage on a 50–50 basis.

In December 1920 I was in Washington fighting for the Maternity Bill and wrote an article on it for *The Suffragist*. The bill provided for instruction on the hygiene of maternity and infancy and, where necessary, for free medical aid for mothers and infants at home or in the hospital at the time of child birth. The appropriation asked for $2,000,000. It was backed by every women's organization. The women now had the vote and the senators did not quite dare to turn it down. It was passed on January 18, but so badly cut as to nearly ruin it. It eliminated medical aid and nursing and cut the appropriation in half. Instruction was to be given but no aid.

At that time Roger wrote me an amusing letter: "Some friend of yours called tonight to say that your 'What Is Better Than Marriage' appeared in Hearst's this month. I shall not read it for fear you have reflected on my character, habits, or financial responsibility. I am thinking of changing my name if the feminists pursue the advertisement of their defenseless men. . . . Yes, I feel pretty close to you, partner, especially when I am wrestling with that goddam fire. You are a hero not to give in to a gas grate."

That spring of 1921 my father and mother decided to spend the summer in Europe. They invited me to go with them. I gladly accepted, particularly as there was to be an international congress of the Women's International League in Vienna in July.[2] We sailed in May on the French boat *La Touraine*, landing in Le Havre and going on to Paris. On the steamer were the editorial writer for the *New York Tribune* and his family. His appreciation for my work did much to restore my confidence, though it was undoubtedly bad for my ego. Then in Austria I made a new friend, Yella Hertzka. She was the chief Austrian delegate to the WILPF Congress. When the Vienna conference was over I visited her and we had a glorious three weeks together. The Austrian money was dropping in value; for a dollar a day one could live at the best hotels. Yella taught me to see Austria through her eyes. We traveled up and down the country and visited all the beauty spots. Yella's husband was a music publisher. Music became a new joy for me. I lingered until October before returning home. My father and mother had gone home ahead of me.

It wasn't easy to come back to a daily grind, but I was determined to make good. This time I got a job with the Bray Moving Picture Corp. They produced educational films, mostly pictures of animals and cartoons. My job was cutting, splicing together pictures, and writing titles. I worked from 9:00 to 6:00 at a salary of $75 a week, which was good pay in those days. This solved the financial problem but not my difficulty in adjusting to the haphazard existence: the uncertainty of dinner hour, of catching the train to Oradell [Roger's camp], of whether engagements would be kept. But Roger's ideal of freedom applied to everything. To me freedom was intellectual and spiritual; a daily routine had nothing to do with it. For me, some organization in daily life was like the red and green lights for traffic — without them there was confusion. But Roger, who had led a carefree, irresponsible life for 35 years, found it hard. He wrote me from Washington, where he had gone on business, "You are dead right about us. Much of my resistance is arguing against myself and against domination. I have an inordinate desire for a kind of personal freedom that perhaps isn't nearly as big as freedom shared."

This [total independence of each] was the ideal of that time. One was to give everything and demand nothing. But how can there be a union between independent entities? Moreover, we ignored the responsibility inevitable in marriage. From childhood I had the vision of body and spirit as one, the reverse sides of the same coin. A marriage based solely on sexual satisfaction had seemed that of the animal. A perfect union was a union of spirit as well as body. I had glimpsed what it might be when for the first time David Graham Phillips had kissed me and said, "It is at such a moment man is nearest God." Looking back on my life, I see my error. I had accepted intellectual compatibility in place of spiritual union.

But in spite of the friction there was much happiness. Roger put up over his camp these words: "Ad astera per aspera," and he sent me in a letter the following lines:

— whether dreams come true,
Whether what we will together
Ever joins the me and you,
Whether all of life's endeavor
Finds its spring of quickening here,
Whether we achieve that freedom
Of two apart yet growing near,
We have seen our Infant Dream,
Sired of stars and mothered of earth
In our first home in the forest,
Winning, joyous, through to birth.

In the spring Malini came from England to visit us and found our life delightful. Fortunately Roger and Malini were exactly suited. She wrote: "I have had a dream-happy time. I don't know when I have had such a consecutive period of absolute harmony, such delightful companionship without strain. Your flat and Sparta are both ideal homes."

All this time Roger was growing in stature. His work prospered; he began to be a public figure. His fight for freedom of speech and press was bringing him renown. It meant, of course, more and more entertaining, more and more people to see. My ideas on matrimony began to change. I came to see that running a home was a real job and a very fine one, to create a background where people could live and grow in harmony. But this needed time and thought, which an office job made impossible. Roger wrote amusingly of our situation:

> The thoughts I have of you and the state of matrimony which surrounds us are rather pleasant — amusingly reflective on the adventure of two trying to — oh, well, let's say walk a tightrope over Niagara. I am really amused most of the time, and when I am distressed or dubious it is because I don't like to see you want so much from Life, knowing that for me anyhow the road to happiness is the way of No Desire. It is Life, not wishes and dreams.

When the spring of 1922 came, my parents made another trip to Europe and again invited me. We sailed the middle of June on the *Chicago* and went to Berlin, where we rented a furnished flat. It was at the beginning of German inflation. Money dropped in value alarmingly overnight. I persuaded my German friend to buy boxes of cigarettes; she invested most of her income into tobacco, almost filling a small room. It was a wise decision, for cigarettes retained their value, enabling her to live through the crisis. From Berlin we went to Dresden.

The journey back to Berlin I will never forget. I committed what has since seemed to me the worst of sins, a sin of pride, arrogance, and self. My mother was not well. This I did not realize. It was a warm summer day; the railroad carriage was crowded. When someone opened a window, my mother objected. Against everyone's wishes she insisted it be closed. I was furious. How could she make such a scene and consider no one's comfort? I refused to speak to her. We spent the night in Hamburg. The next day I left them for Vienna to visit my Austrian friend. My father begged me to say goodbye to my mother. I refused. "At least," he said, "turn and wave to her; she will be standing in the window." But I didn't even do this. I hope God has forgiven me. It has been very hard to forgive myself. Later I joined my mother and father in London, and all was forgotten and forgiven. We sailed home September 12.

That winter had less of personal strain, but my beliefs about life were changing. I no longer thought the world was evolving and gradually growing better, that material advancement was improving mankind. Some of the people Roger worked with troubled me, particularly those of the Left. They were ready to use any means to get their end. I could see they used Roger. He was a member of at least 20 organizations. If the object of the organization was worthwhile, he didn't question the personnel. But no object, however worthy, can be achieved without people of integrity.

I remember one meeting I attended. A group of workers was striking for higher wages and better conditions. Always the appeal was to self-interest. Stand together so that you may profit, instead of stand to-gether regardless of the cost so your children may have better lives. Socialism and economic change now seemed to me useless if the people who came to the top were as greedy and ruthless as their predecessors. I felt it was changed people, not changed laws, that were essential. These thoughts led me back to religion. I was attending Dr. Harry Emerson Fosdick's Presbyterian church regularly with my father.[3] We were both inspired by his teaching. God came back into my life as a reality.

Malini had been to Dornach, near Basle, and wrote of her intense interest in the teaching of Rudolf Steiner. This led me to study anthro-posophy, an offshoot of theosophy. And when Emile Coué came to America, I went to hear him. He was having great success with his philosophy of thought control [healing through self-hypnosis or auto-suggestion].

In the winter of 1923 my mother became ill. She was 71. Slowly she went downhill. The constant use of thyroid affected her badly. She grew more and more exhausted. The last three weeks she was unconscious. I sat much of the time by her side repeating over and over Coué's famous phrase: "You are getting better and better every day in every way." That did not bring health back to my mother but it eased her last days. She died May 1st, 1923. My father was completely lost without her. I had not realized her strength and his dependence.

Life grew more and more hectic. Every day I lunched with Dad, did a daily job, at 6:00 P.M. rushed to buy supplies for the folks Roger would bring in to dinner. He and I became experts in washing the dishes; we could do it during two tunes on the victrola. That summer I went to Sparta with Dad, and, to help him overcome his loneliness, I invited in young people in whom he seemed to take an interest. When autumn came I found a young woman called Bobby to come to live with him. This freed me to return to Waverly Place.

While the United States was going through a period of reaction, England, on the contrary, had established a Labour Government [under Ramsay MacDonald from January to November 1924. He had opposed entry into the war]. Malini wrote:

> I must tell you of the thrilling events through which we are living — the joy of a Labour Government — though sobered by the thought of the immense forces of reaction which may soon assert themselves. Still the fact remains that from poor Scottish parents living in a four-room cottage a poor man has risen to the highest position in an old conservative country like ours. . . . And all without revolution or panic. . . . And among the present Parliament are 19 men and women who have suffered imprisonment for their convictions. Also there are eight women in the Parliament with all that means. . . . Once again the spirit of God moves upon the face of the waters and another page in the history of Creation is about to be written.

It was at this time that her husband, Fred Pethick-Lawrence, as a Labour candidate was elected representative for Leicester, defeating Winston Churchill.

In the spring of 1924 the Women's International League for Peace held their Congress in Washington. Money was raised to bring over European delegates who were to give lectures in many of the leading cities. On April 23 we held a great mass meeting and reception for them in the roof garden of the Hotel Pennsylvania in New York. Representatives from Belgium, Germany, France, Austria, Hungary, Ukraine, England, and Denmark spoke. When the Women's Congress opened on May 6, the press gave us good publicity. The *Washington Times* on that day said:

> Washington has a small millennium in its midst. The British lion lies down beside the German dachshund and the "Marseillaise" is symphonized with the "Blue Danube." All this is happening in the Hotel Washington, where the Congress of the WILP is meeting. An American woman through decades of her efforts in behalf of humanity is unmistakable leader of the League. This is Jane Addams. As she moulds the Congress nearer to agreement from her central chair on the platform, she looks a little weary, but her Voice and her ideas are youthful and vigorous.[4]

There were comments about other women present. Of me the paper wrote:

> Probably the most active woman in the whole Convention is Madeleine Z. Doty, the best press representative of any large meeting coming here this season. She whisks here and there through the hall, and the principal speeches come wet from the mimeograph under her direction only a few minutes after they have been delivered.

The Congress was hardly over when Dad announced he was taking Bobby to Europe. I felt I should go with them. I gave up my work with Bray Production Corp. But before leaving I had a week with Roger in camp. He had had a hard blow: Freddy had committed suicide. Freddy had not been able to live up to Roger's ideals.

Dad took a house in the suburbs of London. I left him and Bobby while I visited my friends. I had two wonderful weeks in Torquay with Malini. Rudolf Steiner was lecturing there. Like Malini, I became deeply interested in his spiritual teaching.[5] Later I joined Bobby and Dad in Paris. It was as I feared; she had wearied of Dad's attentions and decided to remain in Paris. I was thankful to be with my father and sailed for home with him.

Roger was as deeply immersed in his work as ever. In October the American Civil Liberties Union handled a case that became historic. There was an industrial strike among textile workers in the silk mill of Paterson, N.J., which began in August. On the evening of October 6 people began to gather in a public square in front of the City Hall. Among them were recognized strikers. At 7:00 a procession of 30 persons marched to the City Hall, led by two young women bearing an American flag, and directly behind them were Roger and two other men. A hall had been hired for the meeting, but the police had prevented its use. Roger then proposed an open-air meeting. When the procession reached City Hall one of the men with Roger mounted the steps and began to read the Declaration of Independence. This was done to force the issue that citizens have the right peacefully to assemble and petition for redress of grievances. Roger and four of his associates were arrested for rioting and unlawful assembly. They were held guilty and sentenced to six months in jail. There was a long legal battle over this decision before the matter finally reached the highest tribunal of the state, which overruled the lower courts. Roger did not serve his sentence but was let out on bail and after four years was completely vindicated. He had won for the citizens of New Jersey the right of peaceful assembly and free speech. Such cases were making Roger famous.

Madeleine Doty (upper right), Jane Addams, chairman, and others
at Peace Congress of the Women's International League for Peace
and Freedom, Washington, D.C., 1924

Hundreds rallied to his cause. He became a sort of Sir Galahad. Many magazine articles were written about him.

Meantime I had taken a job as the Secretary of the New York Branch of the Women's International League for Peace and Freedom. Its board included Freda Kirchwey, editor of *The Nation*, and Lillian Wald, social worker and founder of Henry Street Settlement in New York City.] My salary was half what I had earned in the Bray Studios, but I was doing work that had social significance. My work with the Bray Studios was the only time that the salary rather than the work came first. I also went on the national board of the WILPF [serving with Chairman Jane Addams, Vice Chairman Emily Greene Balch, Senator Jeanette Rankin, and others] and began to edit the Bulletin for them. This work interested me greatly. We were actively supporting the League of Nations and fighting against the growing nationalism in America.

But my personal life was growing more and more difficult. My Dad was a great anxiety; he had begun to take drugs to forget the loss of my mother. He needed constant attention. My brother Douglas had gotten a divorce, given up the publishing business, and gone out to Hollywood to write scenarios. My studio needed care; dust and dirt accumulated. Neither my income nor Roger's was sufficient for a competent maid. Hours were uncertain; I never got enough sleep. I found myself breaking under the difficulties. And even more troubling than the physical aspect was the sense that my views had changed and were often not in accord with Roger's.

Roger felt my unhappiness though I tried to hide it, and it made him unhappy. When spring came I offered to give up my job and keep house for Roger and Dad if they would support me. I would have done this gladly. But they both thought it was wrong. Roger suggested we take separate studios and I live with my Dad. But I knew that was no solution. It would again be living in two places with uncertainty plus trying to do a job. I knew I would wait and wait, and Roger would not return; after I left he would come. It was better to make a clean break temporarily.

Roger had written me from Boston in July 1925:

I cannot be content to let our present unhappy state rest without attempting to put in words what is so poorly said in the hit and miss of conversation. I only hope I can put it so you will understand. . . . For your sake and mine I am unwilling to be party any longer to the kind of strain we have both suffered under the last year particularly.

You are unhappy with me most of the time, and I am unhappy with your unhappiness. The crisis through which I have been passing this winter and spring makes me more conscious of my own shortcomings and more alive to the probability that your unhappiness is justified by my failure to meet what you have a right to expect of a husband and comrade for life. There is, however, no question of my love nor yours. I have tested mine a hundred times. I am tied to you by profounder ties than to any other human being. Even at that they may not be, by fair standards, very profound. Next to my freedom in work you come — but you come only as the largest single human tie, not as the chief nourishment of my energies. That comes from many sides. I am a crowd man. I need a variety of contacts to keep going in work and friendships. Without them I feel restless and unfulfilled. I know it is a shortcoming that I cannot also concentrate on a great personal love as do many other men who also are equally social. It is a beautiful expression of a fuller life, but it is not mine. One of the reasons it is so hard to combat your challenge of my attitude is that I think you are right, that your way is the bigger way of life, but it is not mine.

At the WILPF National Board meeting I learned that the International Office of the Women's International League for Peace and Freedom in Geneva was looking for an International Secretary. I offered my services and was immediately accepted. It was as though God had offered me a solution. He was again tapping me on the shoulder. It wasn't easy to make the break, but neither Roger nor I thought of it as permanent. I hoped that after a year's separation Roger would be willing to give up some personal freedom for the sake of a home. And he hoped I would learn to take things more easily and not get upset.

My new job had a great advantage. Dad could go with me. We packed our possessions, took Dad's rocking chair with us in our steamer cabin and sailed on October 10, 1925.

Part VI
To Promote International Cooperation

Editor's Afterword
The Geneva Years (1925–1963) and Her Enduring Legacy

*I*N OCTOBER 1925 Doty arrived in Geneva to become the third international secretary of the WILPF (1925–1927), following fellow- American Emily Greene Balch (1919–1922) and Hungarian Vilma Gluecklish (1923–1925). At the same time she served until 1931 as editor of women's first international publication for peace, *Pax International*. These jobs made her far too busy — raising thousands of dollars in several countries, managing and refurbishing their WILPF headquarters in the Maison Internationale, organizing their fifth Congress, which was held in Dublin in 1926 (Augspurg and Heyman came from Germany to help), attending international committee meetings,[1] setting up a summer school in Gland, writing editorials. In 1926 her salary was $1000 a year. In her first month on this job she was sending out 1200 copies per month of *Pax International* in three languages, often 6–8 pages in length, containing articles on issues and activities reported by various countries. By October 1927 she had increased the mailing to 1400.

In addition, she did make time for a visit from her old friends Levermore and Kirchwey, and in 1927 when Roger Baldwin came and stayed intermittently in Geneva to work on several international projects they "had a happy year as friends," as he wrote in his reminiscences. In early 1928 Doty spent three months in the United States raising $2,600 for WILPF costs by speeches and activities in Albany, Chicago, and Minneapolis, among other cities. At the 1929 WILPF Congress in Prague she gave a report and pleaded for more donations. Early in 1930 she was one of only four (one report says seven) women among some 300 reporters admitted to the London Naval Conference.

But by the end of October 1931 the doctor ordered six months of holiday. From then on the periodic attacks of ill health from gastric problems increased. Soon she was appointed by the council of the League of Nations in Geneva to serve on the Women's Consultation Committee on Nationality, which she did for several years. In 1932 she was a delegate to the WILPF Congress in Grenoble, at which the still-radical Roger Baldwin was a speaker, even urging Communism.

As always, her correspondence in the years 1925–1945 was with well-known leaders, such as, among others, Jane Addams, Eleanor Roosevelt, Secretary of Labor Frances Perkins, author Dorothy Canfield Fisher, Mrs. Leopold Stowkowski, Secretary of Agriculture Henry Wallace, and Russian activist and Soviet Ambassador to Sweden Alexandra Kollantai.[2]

In correspondence there is evidence of a lasting friendship and trust between Doty and Frances Perkins, Roosevelt's Secretary of Labor and the first woman to serve in the presidential cabinet. They had first known each other when working on similar causes in New York City. In one of Doty's letters from Geneva in 1934, seeking Perkins' advice about job openings, Doty reminded Perkins of the good time they had had when the latter was in Geneva and the fun they had trying to lose Perkins' Swiss bodyguard.

In the U.S. State Department files there is a letter from Doty to First Lady Eleanor Roosevelt dated 19 December 1939 urging that though the United States was not a member of the League of Nations a woman be sent to represent us on a newly proposed Central Com-mittee on Economic and Social Affairs at the League. Mrs. Roosevelt had Doty's letter forwarded to the State Department asking for their opinion. Then by May the next year Doty proposed to Perkins that Mrs. Roosevelt herself serve as our delegate, an idea warmly received by Perkins, who wrote Doty she thought it a "brilliant suggestion" and would follow up on it.

Indeed, from 1945 to 1953, Eleanor Roosevelt did serve as our delegate to the General Assembly of the United Nations, and from 1946 to 1953 as chairman of the UN Economic and Social Council's Commission of Human Rights. Some students in 1947–1948 Junior Year group reported that they attended some sessions of that Council and an address by Eleanor Roosevelt open to all students in Geneva.

But in 1934 Doty had had a rude shock when, on a trip to New York, she discovered that her husband was devoted to another woman. Doty returned to Geneva immediately. He remarried after a 1935 divorce from Doty. Baldwin set up a reserve fund for her, but for the rest of her life Doty had to live very frugally. Numerous letters show she had to write Roger frequently to remind him to send the quarterly checks (of $80–$200) which he had promised to send when she might be unemployed or in need.

Seeking self-support and committed to continue work to increase international cooperation and understanding, Doty developed a program for international education — starting in 1938–1939 the very first Junior Year in Geneva for American students. In youth she saw the hope for the future for world cooperation. Early in 1938 Doty had sent a brochure about the upcoming Junior Year program in Geneva to Eleanor Roosevelt at the White House, and was invited to have lunch with Mrs. Roosevelt on March 4. After their lunch Mrs. Roosevelt wrote Doty on March 22 expressing her enthusiasm for Doty's plan for the program that would prepare future workers for international affairs. Then Doty obtained sponsorship by the University of Delaware and brought to Europe three men and eleven women from ten different colleges from Massachusetts to California. She arranged group travel on the S.S. *Georgic* and summer housing for them with Parisian families while they studied at the Sorbonne until fall. From there they went on to Geneva for the academic year and studied at the University of Geneva and, by special permission, at the Graduate Institute for International Studies with its outstanding faculty. In Geneva Doty rented an entire *pension* for the group's housing and meals, a pleasant home with rooms for herself and for a French tutor from Paris, as well.

During that intense year of German expansion and takeovers just before the Second World War broke out, their memorable experiences included attending sessions at the League of Nations, hearing talks by world leaders invited to dinner at the *pension*, and travel into Mussolini's Italy and Hitler's Germany during vacations. All this was arranged by Doty as Director and house mother. Remarkably, despite the imminence of war, a black-out, and advice in October from the American consul that the students should return home, all the parents allowed their offspring to remain.

In answers to a questionnaire recently sent to all surviving members, they testified that those experiences forever changed, widened, and enriched their minds, life-long activities, and careers. Evidence of this are the following reports: Of the three men, one became an aid to Secretary of State Dulles at the Big Four Conference in Geneva in the early 1950s and by 1953 was sent to Moscow where he became First secretary in the U.S. Embassy there and *chargé d'affaires* during President Kennedy's and Johnson's terms. Another of the three became a journalist with the U.S. Information Agency and was stationed in various foreign countries, including the Congo, and in Brussels with NATO. The third became professor of Near East Studies and president of the Albany, New York, branch of the UN Association, has worked one year in Beirut, one year in Turkey, and in 1991 went to Israel as part of the Presbyterian Peace Mission led by Benjamin Weir (long-time hostage in Lebanon).

As for the women, three-fourths of them from that first Geneva group undertook careers connected with international affairs, such as in the International Labor Office in Washington during the war, another for the Air Transport Command, a third worked for a business with international affiliations. One started with the Columbia Broadcasting System for the School of the Air of the Americas, became secretary in the Embassy at Bogota, then married an American diplomat and lived with him in the foreign service in Saigon, in France, and elsewhere. Another worked in the International Student Service and then as head of the Information Section of the American Embassy in London under Ambassador John Winant. Another woman was hired by the U.S. Board of Economic Warfare and sent to Buenos Aires during the war years; then worked 24 years for *Time* magazine, primarily on Latin American affairs. And these are only selected examples.

In answering the questionnaire 52 years after the Junior Year in Geneva they wrote about the importance of those trips into Italy and Germany. About the effect of the whole year the following examples are typical: "I owe my deep concern for peace to the Junior Year," wrote the professor, or a woman answered, "I strongly feel I became a citizen of the world, thanks to Miss Doty's strongly held beliefs and to the opportunities she provided us to talk with people involved in world affairs. Amazing to know somebody with such enthusiasm and ideals, such energy and drive. The year changed me in a major way."

When the declaration of war on 3 September 1939 interrupted continuation of the program, Doty, while again managing the Maison Internationale,[3] undertook study for a Ph.D. in Political Science, awarded in January 1945 at the Graduate Institute of International Studies in Geneva.[4] At that time she was the oldest person to have received this degree. She wrote Secretary of Labor Frances Perkins that she did this "not for glory of another degree" but to make her "contribution to the world of the future — and to increase my academic standing, so it would be easier after the war to reestablish in Geneva a Junior Year for American students to study International Organization."

During these war years Doty could not get money from the United States, so Professor Rappard and other faculty of the Graduate Institute of International Studies in Geneva procured for her a Gallatin scholarshihp.

Immediately after the war the indefatigable Doty got Smith College to sponsor the Junior Year in Geneva. That program continues to this day with an average of 30 women students per year from American colleges. Doty served as Director for its first three years, together with a Smith College professor as co-director.

Through her advance planning, these three groups, like the Delaware group, had summer residence and studies in France or Switzerland prior to the academic year in Geneva. In that city she rented office space and living quarters for all on the two top floors of the Hotel de Russie on the lakefront.

Fifty participants from those first three years of the Smith program responded to our questionnaire. Their answers, like those from the Delaware group, indicate that a great number had taken up careers here and abroad in international affairs, in the diplomatic service, in the U.S. Mission to the United Nations, in UNESCO. For example, one woman wrote, "I spent from 1950–1966 in refugee settlement work with refugees from World War II — Dutch Indonesian, Cuban. Following that, I worked from 1966–1970 for the Near East Foundation as secretary to the African Projects Coordinator." Among further examples are one woman who became private secretary to John Foster Dulles, Eisenhower's Secretary of State; another worked with the Institute of International Education in New York City, then became a journalist on the foreign desk of United Press, in Washington, D.C., and was currently living in Paris working as a journalist on issues in international copyright; another had arranged a teacher exchange with Russia through the American Friends Service Committee; another took a position on a paper put out by the New York Foreign Policy Association. Others worked or studied abroad, became foreign language teachers, earned advanced degrees, married Swiss or Italian men; one of the latter lived in Rome and became director of the American Academy there. Again these are, of necessity, only selected examples.

Many recalled the impact felt upon viewing the devastation left by the war, even as late as those in the 1948–1949 group. Several even shared helpful letters from those days and one sent a fascinating scrapbook.

Doty herself was feeling demoted by the presence of powerful Smith professors as co-directors. And there was evidence in their answers that many in the Smith groups had felt considerable discomfort with and resentment of Doty's advanced age and with what they saw as her religious and idealistic impracticality. However, one of them said she used to talk with her in Doty's room and so learned more about Doty's earlier life than most. She concluded: "Miss Doty's influence on me was to give me a role model of what a woman could accomplish, coming as she did from a generation where there were few feminists. . . . I was very impressed with what she had dared to do and had accomplished. . . . Memories of the kind of imagination and courage she must have had as a younger woman still give me strength to think much is still possible in my own life."

All wrote with the same strong conviction as had the Delaware group that the Junior Year had been of paramount importance in their college education and in their lives. Typical are the following: "For me it was the first exposure to a foreign setting and culture probably changing forever how we looked at ourselves as Americans and at our country. A great year." Another wrote, "One of the most significant and fascinating experiences of my life. . . . It seemed almost a revelation — one that brought enhanced awareness, heightened intellectual curiosity, an appreciation of diversity, and an interest in world affairs that has remained with me ever since." Another: "The Junior Year Abroad was the most catalytic year of my entire formal education. It altogether changed my perception of the U.S. . . . It cast a whole new light on what the relationships of people might be. . . . After graduation in 1950, I was quite certain I wanted to find work in an international organization." [And she did, for twenty years.]

It can be assumed that the influence of Doty's program for a Junior Year in Geneva continues as strong as ever, year by year, because, as noted, approximately thirty more students from various American colleges participate in it annually under Smith College direction.

To have founded a program which continues to this day to make a difference in the thinking, voting, and, in many instances, the careers of so many able college women, directing them toward international cooperation as a means of world peace, is INDEED AN ENDURING LEGACY!

After withdrawing from the Smith Junior Year programs, Doty now needed another source of income, though Roger Baldwin was still sending small checks periodically as promised, when she was not employed. In 1950 she learned that to be eligible for U.S. Social Security benefits she must work for a time in the United States. Fortunately she found a position teaching in Miami at Miss Harris' Private School for Girls, where she taught history from 1950 through May 1953, until close to her 76th birthday.

Then it was back to her beloved Geneva, where at Professor Rappard's request she taught American history and constitutional law at the Ecole d'Interpretes for three years.

For the rest of her life she faced increasing, intermittent weakness from kidney and digestive problems and rheumatism as well as a shortage of money for expenses. During these last years she turned more and more to belief in God's direct guidance of the individual, rather than faith in man's reason and will. She became more active in the American Church in Geneva and in a prayer group. Her diaries express more and more self-condemnation for past willfulness. She was seeking to "surrender the 'I,'" as she put it.

In April 1963 she came to the United States and moved into a very inexpensive retirement home in Greenfield, Massachusetts. In her diaries she wrote of more physical pain, but of finding spiritual relief in starting a prayer group there.

During her last months she was revising her autobiography and even three days before her death was seeking a publisher for it. On 15 October 1963, at age 86, Madeleine Zabriskie Doty quietly died.

Addendum

In Hindsight on the Marriage: A Husband's Reminiscences and Editor's Commentary

*T*HE CONSENSUAL SEPARATION and continuing relationship between Baldwin and Doty are both remarkable and perplexing in some respects, in that both maintained until death their respect and love for each other. Although leaving Roger took courage, Doty was sure they had already gone through a spiritual separation. From the ship carrying her away in 1925 she wrote him:

> You have been adorable these last days. It is a big ache leaving you. But the ache of leaving is nothing in comparison to the ache of spiritual separation. That almost broke my heart.
>
> I hope our experimenting together has meant something to you. It has meant a lot to me. It has given me courage to leave you, faith to believe I can always trust you, knowledge that you and I share something that cannot be taken away. . . . I know we both love each other. You have said it to me in a thousand little ways these last days. No one could have been more helpful. . . .
>
> God bless you, my dear. My spirit is always with you, and a love that will not die.[1]

A view of the marriage from the other side is found in Roger Baldwin's 1978 "Reminiscences," deposited by him in the Smith College Sophia Smith Library on women's history, and quoted here at length by the kind permission of Carl N. Baldwin, his stepson. In this document Roger continued to show his true admiration for Doty and in hindsight indicated he had become somewhat contrite about some aspects of what he had expected of her. He wrote:

> I was attracted to her at once. . . . She was the rare type of independent woman, feminist, socialist, but not radical in a revolutionary sense. . . . She was like me essentially a social reformer.

256

. . . She was in her early thirties. . . . She seemed to know everybody in the New York crowd which dominated the social work fraternity. . . . When I moved to New York and met her again among the opponents of the war as a member of the Women's Peace Party, close friend of Crystal Eastman whom I had come on to replace as director of the American Union Against Militarism. . . . Madeleine was already involved in the Women's International League for Peace formed in 1915, and was, with me, in the Fellowship of Reconciliation. She enjoyed organization associations, and she had the tact to handle them. I do not remember hearing of any row in which she took part; she let others do that.

I met her father and mother, who lived nearby on 11th Street, and her two brothers, Douglas and Ralph, Douglas an intellectual and an editor of *Harper's*, Ralph a distinctly non-intellectual bachelor and odd-job man. . . . Madeleine was most abnormally devoted to her parents, especially her father, and he to her. He was a delightful, elderly man, courteous, soft-spoken, witty, charming. . . .

In politics I never heard her express a partisan interest. . . .Her politics like her jobs were international. She was an admirer of the Russian Revolution . . . but she never had the misplaced faith in the Communists that I had. Her socialism conformed to Norman Thomas' ideas of its relevance to America. . . . She had no vanity about her success but she took some pride in the influence she thought her books and articles had. She certainly was on the right side in all her efforts, as time showed. . . . And she was always understanding, always generous.

In these "Reminiscences" Baldwin revealed in the following excerpt two aspects of his wife's life that she completely omitted from her autobiography. The first shows her generosity and her care for the underdog. But the second is a startling piece of information about which only one letter, that from her surgeon friend, has been found. Understandably in her day she kept such a personal matter private. Baldwin wrote:

She often invited out to Sparta a ten-year-old boy she was supporting, son of a woman prisoner she had befriended. He remained in contact with her until her death. She took in another boy age eight, when his mother died and his step father refused to keep him. We found a home for him later with friends, but when they could no longer care for him I took him on as his guardian. She took to my youthful friends, some ex-prisoners, who for a time kept dropping in and must have been a nuisance to her. Madeleine was companionable with boys and girls, not motherly and I doubt she ever really wanted a family. She had one pregnancy during our early marriage but it was terminated — I never found out how. It was not her first.

Probably related to this reference to what he understood was a first abortion before he knew her, there is among the papers Doty saved but one brief letter. It was from one of her former Boston doctors dated 9 October, but no year given, though 1911 was (later?) penciled in by Doty. The letter told her "your daughter was operated on" and "survived." So, obviously, since she was told by mail, it was not an abortion, though Doty may have told Baldwin it was. Despite considerable research, no further explanation or reference to such a child could be found. Who was the father? Is the 1911 date correct and how old was the child? Did she live to adulthood? A lady did not admit to an illegitimate birth in those days. And Doty was a lady; by not telling she protected the man's reputation and her own.

In regard to an abortion early in her marriage to Baldwin, there is one clear verification of the pregnancy in the following letter from her Boston surgeon and friend, dated by him 2 February 1920:

Madeleine dear, you are a terror at proposing knotty questions. After reading your two letters carefully and thinking them over in connection with what you said over the telephone I think I have some basic opinions to express.

1. This is a very critical question and must be decided as nearly right as possible or you will never forgive yourself.

2. If you turn back now (assuming that you can properly do so) you must renounce motherhood forever. This will sterilize your life to an extent that you may not now realize. There are too few people like you in the world.

3. Roger may believe that he is justified in refusing to help but no one else will believe it and it is not so. He assumed this responsibility of his free will and accord; no other demand can displace it.

4. He must contribute to the joint undertaking to the full extent of his powers in order to enable you to do something that is greater than either of you can do alone and greater than anything else that you can do together.

5. In order to play your part you must have sound and regular advice from someone who realizes its full importance and from now on you must make everything else subordinate. This does not mean that you can not do many things but this must take precedence.

6. I do not see any legitimate ground for interrupting pregnancy and do not believe that you could persuade any good obstetrician to do it. You ought not to have it badly done.

Now, to stop being didactic and become human. Your letters, particularly the last, show a depth of human sympathy and understanding which is wonderful even in you from whom I have learned to expect it. But you can carry unselfishness too far and I think you are doing it. He can not continue to live in his own world, if only because it is too bad an example of the relations between men and women which you want so deeply and wisely to improve. He can not preach social justice unless he acts it, and that he is not doing. It will deeply hurt him in his ultimate effect on the world, to live in lack of consideration for his mate. You can not help women by exemplifying inequality of burdens in your own person.

I understand your loneliness and long to help dispel it. But your spirit is beyond all loneliness and will win through.

Yet she evidently felt she could not follow his understanding advice, probably because she knew that Roger, like David Graham Phillips, did not want the responsibility for and reduction of freedom caused by a dependent child. Or possibly it was, as Baldwin surmised, because she herself didn't want to be a mother, though no reference to such is found in her writing.

Editor's Commentary: Between the Head and the Heart

There is no doubt they loved and admired each other, but they could not accommodate to living together. As evidenced in the twenty-five letters and a dozen fragments of correspondence from him saved by Doty and in the few letters he shared with biographer Lamson, the passion cooled but the admiration and respect never did. Each held to the convictions of his/her mind, though it cost her more emotionally and perhaps professionally than it cost him.

Doty's decision to marry and the first years together demonstrate a struggle between her heart and her mind, on the one hand, between her passions, her need to be loved and close to and alone with one man, and, on the other hand, their similar intellectual concerns as reformers and their feminist, egalitarian, anti-war principles, all aggravated by the practical responsibilities of a working wife and hostess. In time she recognized this conflict between the head and the heart, for as she looked back in her autobiography and in diaries in her last years she repeatedly chastised herself for those times when she let her emotions control her judgment and described herself (rightly or wrongly) as "full of pride, arrogance, self." She even saw her donations to a poor family as penance for her emotional weaknesses. In analyzing the failure of their marriage she placed one prerequisite for compatibility above intellect; namely, she felt her mistake had been to choose "intellectual compatibility in place of spiritual union."

However, it is clear, on a less lofty level, that the problem was worsened by the mundane conflict between work and home. One of the major tenets in their rebel group in Greenwich Village was that financial independence was essential to the full freedom and fulfillment of the woman. Both she and Roger earnestly believed this. But it was exhausting her, given Roger's way of life.

But — more fundamentally — their troubles lay in a conflict between two highly idealistic, strong-willed individuals (Baldwin described her as "independent and high-powered"), both with firm, yes, harmonious convictions, but each with very different *personal needs*. Madeleine, in addition to her public role or career, needed from the marriage close companionship including alone-togetherness, which refreshed her. And she sought what she later called spiritual oneness. Roger demanded total freedom for himself and his work, on which he thrived. He even wrote her that he loved his work more than he loved a wife. Just three months before their wedding he had written her of his lifelong conviction that "our jobs are our first duty to ourselves and our time — this great generation," and a year later he signed off a letter to her with his usual frankness, "Much love, Maddy — all I've got to spare after loving myself which is my first duty."

Trips to the country camping and canoeing brought them both much satisfaction and closeness. Yet he was a "crowd man," full of sociability, a person of joy in living and doing and leading. Back in his St. Louis days he had enjoyed attending fancy balls and being sought after by the society women. She was more serious, pressured in schedule, service-oriented, and in need of one-to-one attention. Roger had recognized this personality difference between them when, a few months before their marriage he wrote that he was wondering about their compatibility in "cheer, in nonsense, in gaiety — freedom to banter. It is a department that needs careful attention for us both."

Roger told biographer Lamson that "our trouble was domination
. . . . She wasn't willing to compromise. She expected people to behave
her way. And she got so upset if you didn't. Very upset — tears and all."
Yet in his "Reminiscences, "written two years after Lamson's book appeared, he expressed more understanding:

> We had conflict from the start over our different ways of life.
> Madeleine expected me to stay home evenings, while I was al-
> ways going out to some meeting. I had friends she didn't care for,
> so I saw them outside. We tried compromises but she was still un-
> happy, mostly over the uncertainty of my comings and goings. I
> was too obstinate to yield my presumed freedom to marriage
> obligations. . . . There was no question of our love and devotion,
> but our ways could not be reconciled nor could she accept, despite
> her views on sexual freedom, my women friends, even my elderly
> aunt Ruth to whom I was devoted. I was not the good husband
> she expected. And she was right, but I could not conform. . . . We
> would spend many evenings with our books, or I with my piano,
> but we rarely went out to the theatre or movies; we did not have
> the money or a strong interest. We entertained friends at dinner.
> Among them were Henry Nevinson, the English journalist; S. K.
> Ratcliffe, English lecturer; Freda Kirchwey of *The Nation* —
> Madeleine was a close friend of the family; Upton Sinclair;
> William D. Haywood of the IWW; Elizabeth Gurley Flynn; Nor-
> man Thomas; Mary Heaton Vorse, labor reporter; "Mother" Bloor,
> later a Communist leader; and assorted subversives.
>
> I remember our times in the country as our happiest, either at
> her father's home in Sparta, N.J., or at . . . my much more
> accessible camp on the Hackensack River, where we canoed,
> swam, and hiked. . . . My best memories are of Madeleine by my
> side swinging along a country trail. (Reminiscences, 2A, 5, 6)

Letters Doty saved from Baldwin indicate that he was away
traveling a great deal even during the first years of their marriage. His
mother, sympathizing with her daughter-in-law, wrote her that she
wished Roger "would come home. . . . He's allowing you to carry all the
burden of living. . . . It seems to me Roger has reached a too visionary
state of mind."
As seen in chapter 12, Baldwin so cherished total freedom that in his
self-composed wedding vows he dwelt exclusively upon *his* wants in and
out of marriage, including even freedom to love other women, whereas
her vows speak of giving, sharing, of helping *him* to increase *his* power

to live, with less emphasis on her own needs. Admittedly, she went on to say that she too believed in absolute freedom for him "to love. . . . to go . . ., to be your own master total and absolute." But in practice, as seen in chapter 12, these intellectually held beliefs proved hard on Madeleine's expectations of marriage and on her emotional nature. Years later Roger himself, in interviews with his biographer in the early 1970s, scoffed at the idealism of their vows, calling Madeleine's "'high falutin'" and his own "'Too grandiose . . ., too . . . idealistic . . . Pretentious.'"

In an early, undated letter to his wife, as both groped to understand their differences, Roger, had poignantly recognized that the maladjustment lay in their personality differences. "It is absurd that two people who know each other as we do, who have had so much of the same experience of life, who enjoy much of the same things and people, who have the same vision of the future — should strike such snags in the adjustment of personalities — in finding a common denominator for their thinking and feeling."

Married less than a year, while in Seattle Baldwin wrote her, on 20 May 1920, of his concern over how she was being hurt. "I am pained most when I see you pained, and I'd advocate separate establishments rather than continue that condition indefinitely. I know I'm a bum husband." Yet he goes on to say her presence is always with him even when in Seattle he is seeing Anna Louise Strong,[2] to whom he had briefly been unofficially engaged before falling in love with Doty. But, he added, he could now realize marriage to A. L. would have been a disaster, — domination by the woman, loss of his freedom.

On 27 July 1921, when Doty was abroad, he wrote her that he was not expressing his desires with other women "to their natural limit" because he knew that would upset her. "I know there is a disparity between your intellectual convictions on the subject and your emotional reactions. Until you've bridged that, I'm taking no chances." On this topic Baldwin refused to let his biographer Lamson ask about his romantic affairs, what he called his "emotional excursions," and told her he had destroyed all personal letters received. Although some men who knew him have referred to him as a "rascal" and "womanizer," Doty in her autobiography and personal papers mentioned only once Baldwin's attention to another woman.

So it was that after six years of marriage Doty decided to sail off to Europe to take a two-year position in Geneva as the International Secretary of the Women's International League for Peace and Freedom with the idea that it would be a temporary separation. They did not talk of divorce. The decision was consensual. He felt the "trial separation" was "practical, even desirable." Yet it wasn't totally easy for him either at first. One month after Doty left the United States, he wrote her from his New Jersey camp on 8 November 1925, "I have had a few depressions, rather unusual for me, in which life didn't seem worth living — but I guess that's the result of being alone and trying to work out a new line of effort, and losing a wife perhaps?! My devoted love ever, Rog."

Notes

Part I: From Childhood to Law School

Introduction to Chapters 1–2

1. The land appears to have been part of or near to the original 2,000 acres purchased from the Indians by Albert Zabriskie, who came from Poland in 1662. See *National Cyclopedia of American Biography*, 18:279, under Frederick Zabriskie.

2. *Who's Who in America*, all volumes covering 1903 through 1920–1921. Also *Who Was Who in America*, 1:334. *Century* magazine was of longstanding and in the late 1800s published many great American authors, e.g., Mark Twain, Bret Harte.

3. These figures found in Nancy Cott, *Grounding of Modern Feminism* (New Haven, Conn.: Yale University Press, 1987), 40, a thoroughly documented history of the women's movement in America. Also found in Barbara Miller Solomon, *In the Company of Educated Women: A History of Women and Higher Education in America* (New Haven, Conn.: Yale University Press, 1985), 62–63, and in *Digest of Educational Statistics*, 166.

4. Solomon, 48.

5. *Outlook* 86 (Spring 1992)

6. See Cott, *Grounding of Modern Feminism*, 214; Cynthia Fuchs Epstein, *Women in Law* (New York: Basic Books, 1981), 4; June Sochen, *Movers and Shakers: American Women Thinkers and Activists 1900–1970* (New York: Quadrangle Books, 1973), 27; Solomon, *In the Company of Educated Women*, 127.

Chapter 2. College Days and an Innocent in Greenwich Village, 1896–1905

1. See references to Dr. Parkhurst in Justin Kaplan's *Lincoln Steffens*.

Part II. Introduction to Chapter 3

1. See Cott, *Modern Feminism*, 15, for strong definition. For fascinating and detailed collection of essays on the culture of Greenwich Village and on the

women's movement, see Heller and Rudnick. Other helpful resources on Greenwich Village are Alfred Kazin, "When Bohemia Was in Bloom. Greenwich Village 1830–1930" published in the *New York Times*, January 25, 1991, C:1. Also James McGovern's 1968 article "The American Woman's Pre-World War I Freedom in Manners and Morals" published in *Our American Sisters: Women in American Life and Thought* (Boston: Allyn & Bacon, 1973), ed. Jean Friedman and William G. Shade, 237–59. And see Beatrice Hinkle, "Women and the New Morality" in *Our Changing Morality: A Symposium* (New York: Albert & Charles Boni, 1924), ed. Freda Kirchwey. Also see Judith Schwarz, *Radical Feminists of Heterodoxy* (Lebanon, N.H.: New Victoria Publishers, 1982).

2. On conflicts and contradictions feminists felt between their passion for independence and their desire for love and sexuality, see Lois Rudnick (77–78) and Ellen Kay Trimberger (98–115) in Adele Heller and Lois Rudnick, *1915, The Cultural Moment: The New Politics, the New Woman, the New Psychology, the New Art & the New Theatre in America* (New Brunswick, N.J.: Rutgers University Press, 1991).

3. Cott, *Modern Feminism*, 12, 17.

4. For description of the role of emphasis on gender differences, see C. Roland Marchand, *The American Peace Movement and Social Reform 1898–1918* (Princeton, N.J.: Princeton University Press, 1972), chapter 6 "The Maternal Instinct." Also see Barbara Steinson's "The Mother Half of Humanity" in Carol R. Berkin and Clara L. Lovett, *Women, War, and Revolution* (New York: Holmes & Meier, 1980), 259–81.

5. Friedman and Shade, ed. *Our American Sisters*, 341.

6. June Sochen, *Movers and Shakers: American Women Thinkers and Activists 1900–1970* (New York: Quadrangle, 1973), 34–75.

7. For discussion of the "reproach and alarm" that these opinions raised in men and for discussion of dilemmas faced by feminists, see Christopher Lasch, *The New Radicalism in America 1889–1963* (New York: W.W. Norton, 1997).

8. Cott, *Modern Feminism*, 16, 255–61.

9. For details on Ida Rauh and her activist role, see numerous references in Heller and Rudnick, also many in Nancy Dye, *As Equals and As Sisters: Feminism, Unionism, and the Women's Trade Union League of New York* (Columbia, Mo.: University of Missouri Press, 1980). From 1911 to 1922 Rauh was the first wife of Max Eastman, brother of Crystal and author and editor of the socialist magazines *The Masses* and its successor *The Liberator*.

10. Nancy Schrom Dye, *As Equals and As Sisters: Feminism, Unionism, and the Women's Trade Union League of New York* (Columbia: University of Missouri Press, 1980), 44.

11. Cott, *Modern Feminism*, 25.

12. Indicative of the significance of Phillips are the many biographies and literary critiques of his writings, among which are those by Louis Filer, Issac F. Marcosson, Abe Ravitz, Willard Thorp (318–32), for which titles see the Bibliography herein. A summary of Phillips' work can be found in *Contemporary Authors*, 108:369–370 and in *Dictionary of American Biography*, 538–39.

13. Louis Filler, *Voice of Democracy: a Critical Biography of David Graham Phillips: Journalist, Novelist, Progressive* (University Park: Pennsylvania State University Press, 1978), 42.

14. On Phillips' lectures to Susan Lenox see Elizabeth Janeway's "Afterword" in David Graham Phillips' *Susan Lenox: Her Fall and Rise* (Carbondale: Southern Illinois University Press, 1977), xvi–xvii.

Chapter 3. The Women's Movement, Law, and Love, 1905–1911

1. The A Club in 1906 was a cooperative housing venture, "the first organized group to express the revolt of the villagers," according to Dee Garrison, *Mary Heaton Vorse: The Life of an American Insurgent* (Philadelphia: Temple University Press, 1989), 36–38, 68. The A Club was followed by the Liberal club in 1913. Garrison says "Mark Twain dropped by almost every day." In 1912 Vorse helped found the Heterodoxy Club in New York City, a discussion and activist group for liberals, some of whose most extreme members were for complete social revolution, writes Garrison (6–70). She says Doty, Ida Rauh, and Freda Kirchwey were members; the same is indicated in *Crystal Eastman on Women and Revolution* (New York: Oxford University Press, 1978), edited by Blanche Wiesen Cook. Although the latter volume (13) says Heterodoxy Club members "stood on street corners and handed out birth control literature, – helped organize strike committees and were occasionally arrested," Doty was not that extreme, apparently.

2. For helpful synopsis of the life of Gorky, Russian socialist writer, see Introduction by Ronald Wilks in Maxim Gorky's *My Childhood* (New York: Penguin Books, 1966), 5–12. Mark Twain favored the Revolution in Russia to aid the oppressed, helped raise money for it, and had publicly supported Gorky until the newspaper scandal when the latter arrived in New York on 10 April 1906 to raise money for the Russian revolutionary movement. See Justin Kaplin, *Mr. Clemens and Mark Twain* (New York: Simon & Schuster, 1968, 436–38. See also "The Gorky Incident," in Mark Twain, *Letters From the Earth* (New York: Harper and Row, 1938), 155–56.

H. G. Wells, his wife, and Doty became long-time friends and in succeeding years, as will be seen, she was invited several times for weekends at their home in England. Among her papers are six letters and three cards from H. G. Wells dated from January 1909 to October 1922, and four letters from his wife. An interesting comment is found in a 1922 letter to Doty in which he explained why he had been unable to see her in London: "I don't want any distraction from *The Outline of History* just yet, though I think anyone could do these fantastic stories." (Since that volume was published in 1920, the letter's 1922 date would cause one to think Wells may have been referring to its sequel, his *Short History of the World* published in 1922.)

3. Cook, *Crystal Eastman*, 6, wrote, "Their apartment was one of the major communication centers for labor reform and suffrage activities. The influential and often controversial leadership of Crystal Eastman is described in almost if not all histories of the women's movement in America. See Blanche Weisen Cook's writings listed in this Bibliography, which writings also contain much on

the interconnections of persons with whom Doty worked for women's rights and for peace. In Cook's Introduction to *Crystal Eastman* there are three brief references to Doty. Jean Sochen in *Movers and Shakers* says Crystal Eastman "Participated in every significant woman's rights activity during the period." And the *Continuum Dictionary of Women's Biography*, ed. Jennifer S. Aglow (New York: Continuum, 1989), describes Crystal Eastman as "one of the most charismatic and influential women of her generation." Her work in 1910 on labor conditions resulted in New York's first workers' compensation law. In 1912 she helped Alice Paul found the Congressional Union for Woman Suffrage, which became the National Woman's Peace Party, and in 1914 founded the more controversial Woman's Peace Party of New York, remaining its head until 1919. Doty is listed as its Vice-Chairman in 1918. In 1914 Crystal Eastman helped found and served as Executive Secretary of the American Union Against Militarism, and in 1917, with Roger Baldwin and Norman Thomas, Crystal Eastman founded the Civil Liberties Bureau, forerunner of the ACLU, to aid conscientious objectors, and was one of four who wrote the Equal Rights Amendment introduced in 1923.

4. Max Eastman, husband of Ida Rauh from 1911–1922, was editor of the ultra liberal magazine, *The Masses*, from 1912 until November 1917 when that publication was suppressed under the Espionage Act. In February 1918 Max and his sister Crystal together started and edited another radical journal, *The Liberator*, until in 1922 he went to Russia and became a follower of Trotsky. In 1941 Max was to become a roving editor for *Reader's Digest*. For much of his life with Ida see his two-volume autobiography *Enjoyment of Living* (New York: Harper and Brothers, 1948) and *Love and Revolution* (New York: Random House, 1964), in which one finds that his attitude toward the constraints of marriage was remarkably similar to that of Roger Baldwin (see Doty's Chapter 12).

5. Charles Edward Russell was in charge of the editorial page of Pulitzer's New York *World*, and, according to biographer Marcosson, was a socialist, muckraker, and close companion of David Graham Phillips. Barbara Gelb in *So Short a Time: A Biography of John Reed and Louise Bryant* (New York: W.W. Norton, 1973), 214, says Russell "had made a reputation as formidable as Lincoln Steffens, as a muckraking journalist". Later, in 1917, just months prior to the November Bolshevik Revolution, Russell was sent by President Wilson to serve on the Elihu Root Mission to the Provisional Government in Russia.

6. In Doty's papers at Smith College there are 55 letters from D.G. Phillips which she saved.

7. *American Magazine*, "Mormon Women and What They Think About Polygamy," (May 1908): 41–47.

8. By 1905 Dr. Richard Cabot (1868–1939) "was searching for a means to give practical expression to his conviction that social and psychic factors must be brought under systematic observation in the diagnosis of disease. . . . He launched a medical social service unit at the Massachusetts General Hospital – the prototype for this kind of medical social work" and devoted the next two decades to that unit and elsewhere in order to promote the practice of psychotherapy (*Dictionary of American Biography Supplement*. Auspices American

Council of Learned Societies, 1950, II:83–5). Also see on Richard Cabot in *Who Was Who in America With World Notables*, 1943, vol. I.

9. Jane Addams, a founder and head of Chicago's Hull House, a settlement house for poor immigrants. Later she became world leader for peace. See Robert McHenry, ed.., *Liberty's Women* (Springfield, Mass.: A. & C. Merriam, 1980), and many other sources.

10. Among Doty's papers are two letters from Judge Lindsey, noted for reforms in handling juvenile delinquents, one written 12 November 1910, saying he was coming from Denver to New York and wanted to have dinner with her and two other women he named. The second letter, dated 17 March 1914, thanked her for sending him her report on the Auburn Prison experiences.

Part III: Introduction to Chapters 4–6

1. For more on Charlotte Perkins Gilman see Robert McHenry, ed., *Liberty's Women*. Also contains accounts on Jane Addams and Emily Greene Balch. On Gilman see Carl N. Degler's article in Friedman and Shade, *Our American Sisters: Women in American Life and Thought*, 19–218. Degler calls Gillman "the major intellectual leader of the struggle for women's rights . . . during the first two decades of the twentieth century" (197).

2. One brief note on Doty's prison work appears in Estelle B. Freedman, *Their Sisters' Keepers: Women's Prison Reform in America 1830–1930* (Ann Arbor: University of Michigan Press, 1981), 222.

Chapter 4. Court Work, Three Great Men, and a Love That Should Never Have Been, 1911–1913

1. George Kirchwey's daughter Freda became the well-known editor of the liberal journal, *The Nation*, in 1919. See Sara Alpern, *Freda Kirchwey: A Woman of the Nation* (Cambridge, Mass.: Harvard University Press, 1987). Chapter 1 "The Proper Rebel" provides cultural setting and a brief reference to an interview of Doty and Crystal Eastman.

2. Gifford Pinchot, forestry conservationist head of U.S. Division of Forestry (1898–1910), a founder of Theodore Roosevelt's Progressive Party (1912), twice governor of Pennsylvania (1923–1927, 1931–1935).

Chapter 5. Maggie Martin #993, 1913

1. Elizabeth Watson served on the New York State Factory Investigation Commission and on the National Child Labor Committee.

Part IV: Introduction to Chapters 7–10

1. On Ellen Key, see Nancy Cott, *Grounding of American Feminism*, 46–49, 152; other references in Heller and Rudnick, *1915, The Cultural Moment*.
2. Copy of this report was obtained through the United States State Department and the Bureau of Diplomatic Security under the Freedom of Information Act.

Chapter 7. Women of Peace in Wartime, 1915

1. Many references to both Mr. and Mrs. Pethick-Lawrence will be found in succeeding chapters of the autobiography. See also Emmeline Pethick-Lawrence, *My Part in a Changing World* (1938; Westport, Ct.: Hyperion Press, 1976). Numerous references to her and selections by her are found in Midge Mackenzie, ed., *Shoulder to Shoulder* (New York: Alfred A. Knopf, 1975) and in Blanche Wiesen Cook, ed., *Crystal Eastman on Women and Revolution*. Marchand in his *American Peace Movement and Social Reform 1898–1918* (pp. 194–96) says Emmeline Pethick-Lawrence was "a leading lieutenant of Emmeline Pankhurst, England's most prominent suffragist" and had led stone-throwing raids on government property, was imprisoned and participated in hunger strikes. Her husband, Frederick, was an active supporter of the British women's suffrage movement, defeated Churchill for a seat in the House of Commons in 1923, served as financial secretary to the Treasury in 1929–31, and became Secretary of State for India and Burma, 1945–47. See in *Who's Who*, 133, and *The New Encyclopedia Britannica, 1994*, 9:336.
2. The *Evening Post* reported that flag was the work of Doty and Mrs. Pethick-Lawrence, the latter being in this country to stimulate Americans to push for the vote for women and to speak in Carnegie Hall on April 11. In Mrs. Pethick-Lawrence's autobiography (pp. 308–9) she attributes to Doty the success of uniting through the press the "idea of associating the women of the then neutral country of America with the endeavor to bring reconciliation and peace back to a war-riven world." Doty thus began to help organize the Hague Peace Conference. This combined the peace cause with that of suffrage. How-ever, Cott, *Grounding of American Feminism*, indicates there were disagree-ments within the women's movement about combining these two.
3. Arthur Beales, *History of Peace* (1931; reprint New York: Doubleday, 1971), 281, says President Wilson told Jane Addams, "'I consider them the best proposals that have been formulated by any association.'"

Chapter 8. "Snooping Madeleine," the *Tribune* Woman, 1916

1. "Until the summer of 1917 . . . the only opposition in the Reichstag to the war program consisted of a small group of dissident Social Democrats [of the socialist left wing] led by Karl Liebknecht and Rosa Luxembourg" (*New Funk and Wagnalls Encyclopedia*), see Liebknecht.

2. In Doty's seventh article printed in the *New York Tribune* the following 24 December 1916, after her return to the United States in October, she wrote that "women are doing heavy manual labor alongside pale, underfed-looking, unpaid Russian prisoners." She noted that the women were wearing bloomers instead of skirts, their feet swathed in rags.

3. Doty's article in the *Tribune*, 31 December, explained that Heymann, radical German feminist leader for women and pacificism, belonged neither to Liebknecht group nor the major wind of the Social Democratic party because Heymann felt the former too extreme and the latter not radical enough about demanding peace. Directly after the war their mutual friend Augspurg, like Doty, advocated reconciliation with former enemy countries and independent political action by women.

Chapter 9. Around the World to Revolutionary Russia in 1917

1. The two introductory paragraphs taken from Doty's Preface to her third book, *Behind the Battle Line: Around the World in 1918* (New York: Macmillan, 1918), vii.

2. In a letter to her parents she wrote in amusement that she had "smoked . . . to the horror of the 75 missionaries on board: and that the conductor had announced, 'There is a famous lady writer, Mary [sic] Doty, on the train.'"

3. At this time "Russian rights and privileges in the zone along the railroad were such that the Russian government virtually controlled northern Manchuria," while Japan controlled South Manchuria, according to George Kennan, *Russia and the West Under Lenin and Stalin* (Boston: Little, Brown, 1960), 91–92.

4. Kerensky, head of the Provisional Government, had fled on November 7 in an American Embassy car and gathered troops to attempt to retake Petrograd, but they were too few, and soon after November 12 he escaped in disguise to England. See John Shelton Curtiss, *The Russian Revolution of 1917* (Malabar, Fla.: Krieger Publishing, 1982, 72, 74.)

5. John Reed, author of *Ten Days That Shook the World* (New York: Random Vintage, 1960), American pro-Communist journalist on the staff of the radical American periodical, *The Masses*, in 1913, correspondent for the New York *World* and *Metropolitan Magazine*, founder of Communist Labor Party in 1919 (later known as American Communist Party) died in Russia in 1920 and was buried inside the Kremlin walls. See *Modern Encyclopedia of Russian and Soviet History*, ed. Joseph Wieczynski, 30:238–42. Also see Barbara Gelb, *So Short A Time: A Biography of John Reed and Louise Bryant* (New York: W.W. Norton, 1973) and on Reed in George Kennan, *Russia and the West Under Lenin and Stalin* (Boston: Little, Brown, 1960), 52. Walter Lippmann wrote an early article on "The Legendary John Reed" in the *New Republic*, December 26, 1914, 15ff.

6. For original writings by Kollantai, see Susan Groug Bell and Karen M. Offen, *Women, the Family, and Freedom: A Debate in Documents* (Stanford, Ca.: Stanford University Press, 1983), 2:289–91, 303– 6. For numerous references to Kollantai and Spiridonova see in W. Bruce Lincoln, *Red Victory: A History of*

the Russian Civil War and in Richard Pipes, *The Russian Revolution* (New York: Simon & Schuster, 1989).

7. For a detailed account of great dissension in Russia in the aftermath of the Brest-Litovsk Treaty see Richard Pipes, *The Russian Revolution* (New York: Alfred A. Knopf, 1990), 590–643.

Chapter 10. The Long Way Home, 1918

1. This Chapter 10 from Doty's autobiography has been slightly shortened through editing but also augmented by occasional sentences this editor has inserted word for word from Doty's more detailed, published articles about these experiences. Therefore, it is all her writing.

2. Louise Bryant told Virginia Gardner, author of *Friend and Lover: The Life of Louise Bryant* (New York: Horizon Press, 1982) it was on January 20 that she left Russia with Madeleine Doty and Bessie Beatty on the last train to get through to Finland, where civil war was raging and the Whites were massacring the Red Guard. Bryant, like Doty, described riding in an open sled under blankets from Finland into Sweden. However, Doty did not mention the date of departure nor name her companions, and, contrary to the report in Gardner, she did not go on to New York with Bryant.

3. On the severity of food shortages, which by the end of the war had reached the stage of famine throughout Central Europe and Russia, see numerous references in William K. Klingaman, *1919: The Year Our World Began*. Also in John Reed, *Ten Days That Shook the World* (New York: Random House, 1960), 12, on food and weather in Russia in 1917.

Part V. Introduction to Chapters 11–12

1. See Peggy Lamson, *Roger Baldwin: Founder of the American Civil Liberties Union* (Boston: Houghton Mifflin, 1976). Brief summaries of Baldwin's life are found in *Who's Who in America*, vol. 20 (1938–1939) through vol. 40 (1978–1979), and in *Current Biography*, vols. 1940 and 1981. Also see Oliver Jensen, "The Persuasive Mr. Baldwin" in *Harpers Magazine*, September 1951, 47–55, and long obituary of Baldwin in *New York Times*, August 27, 1981, section D, 18.

2. From dust cover of Lamson's biography of Roger Baldwin.

3. For full account of starvation in Europe, see Klingaman's *1919: The Year Our World Began* (New York: Harper & Row, 1989).

4. For full reproduction of the Spider-Web Chart and discussion, see Nancy Cott, *Grounding of American Feminism* (New Haven, Ct.: Yale University Press, 1987), 242, 249–50, 259. That volume also contains details on conflict over feminist organizations for peace, Chapter 8, "In Voluntary Conflict."

5. From records of the American Fund for Public Service, reel 13.

6. Liberal club, successor to the A Club by 1913. See Steven Watson, *Strange Bedfellows: The First American Avant-Garde* (New York: Abbeville

Press, 1991), 154–55. Also in Dee Garrison, *Mary Heaton Vorse: The Life of an American Insurgent* (Philadelphia: Temple University Press, 1989), 36–38.

7. Excerpts from Peggy Lamson, *Roger Baldwin*, 43, 88–89.

8. For further helpful discussion of the strain and toll on the personal lives of male and female proponents of total individual freedom, see Adele Heller and Lois Rudnick, ed., *1919: The Cultural Moment* (New Brunswick, N.J.: Rutgers University Press, 1991).

Chapter 11. Love and Post-war Europe, 1918–1919

1. In a letter from Doty in New York to Jane Addams on December 1, 1918, Doty expressed her hesitancy to marry Baldwin more from concern for *his* well-being than her own. "I did not feel he ought to belong exclusively to any one. But perhaps I will tie him down less than almost any one else he knows, and we certainly are very happy together. . . . There is much I should have liked to talk over with you, about Russia and the wonderful new spirit developing in England [less vindictiveness toward the Central Powers by leaders she knew]. In spite of all restrictions I managed to see the radicals everywhere, from Bertrand Russell to Trotsky."

In the same letter she urged that the upcoming Congress of the WIL should meet at the same time as the Versailles conference and in some neutral nation so that women of Central Powers could attend. With foresight she wrote, "I feel we are going to be greatly disappointed in many things that happen at Versailles, and if the women . . . put forth a better and wiser program, it might do something toward shaming the diplomats and forcing them into more liberal terms." (Swarthmore Peace Collection on WILPF.)

2. The Irish Free State was not set up until January 1922, by a treaty with England, with Sinn Fein members heading its provisional government. DeValera for several decades was to lead the program for gradual elimination of British influence in Irish affairs, serving as president of Eire in 1937 and 1951–1954. In 1933 and again from 1938–1939 he became president of the League of Nations Assembly in Geneva. He approved Chamberlain's appeasement of Hitler by the Munich Pact of 1938 and maintained the neutrality of Ireland throughout World War II.

3. Bonar Law, ultraconservative statesman, Chancellor of the Exchequer 1916–1918, British plenipotentiary to Paris Peace Conference in 1919. He signed the Versailles Treaty.

4. William K. Klingaman, in his informative book *1919: The Year Our World Began* (New York: Harper & Row, 1989), wrote: "A gradually spreading sense of dissatisfaction with the postwar world kept England in a constant state of agitation in the summer and autumn of 1919. Doubtless much of this was inevitable – promises had been made during the war and then broken with the coming of peace, hopes had been raised that could never be fulfilled in such a short time." His book documents the ominous disillusion in most of Europe over terms of the Versailles Treaty.

5. From the United States 27 delegates, Great Britain 26, Germany and Switzerland 25 each, among others, according to the Official News Sheet of their meetings.

6. The WILPF Congress at Zurich sent telegrams to the leaders at Versailles stating their criticisms and urging the diplomats to accept amendments to correct these unworkable policies and return to Wilson's principles. For further reading on disillusionment over Versailles, see Klingaman's *1919* and Wallace Ferguson and Geoffrey Bruun, *A Survey of European Civilization* (Boston: Houghton Mifflin, 1936), 954–60.

7. Bela Kun in late March 1919, as founder and leader of the Hungarian Communists, organized a successful revolution against the Hungarian People's Republic and established the Hungarian Soviet Republic, in which he served as Premier. By June, when Czech forces were threatening his borders, Kun launched an offensive and set up a short-lived Soviet Republic in Slovakia. His radical communization of the economy precipitated a counterrevolution that same year, collapsing his Hungarian Soviet. On 1 August he fled to Vienna and in 1920 to the Soviet Union, where he was given an important position in the administration, until in 1937 he was charged with conspiracy against Stalin and executed. See Klingaman (5, 189–93, 328–30, 465–66).

Chapter 12. 50–50 Marriage, 1919–1925

1. Perhaps to make himself look less culpable for his absences or perhaps from an error of recollection, by the mid 1970s Baldwin told his biographer Lamson that it was a month after the wedding before he left and that he was away only two months. However, back in 1951 he had told Oliver Jensen of *Harpers Magazine* he was away four months, as Doty said.

2. Because her request for passport renewal in 1921 was by then under suspicion, she was required to have a special interview with a New York City agent. A copy of his three-page report to the New York Special Agent of the State Department was recently obtained through a Freedom of Information Review and the Diplomatic Security Service. It shows that he summarized not only her travels and activities but also her publications, and specifically listed the titles of her post-war articles as well as of each chapter of her book *Behind the Battle Line: Around the World in 1918* (New York: Macmillan, 1918).

3. The life of the renowned preacher Harry Emerson Fosdick is summarized in *Encyclopedia of World Biography*, 1973, 4:164.

4. The *Washington Times* articles by Jim Ring appeared in the 6 May 1924, issue along with a large cartoon caricature of the heads of seven of the women leaders, among them a profile sketch of "Madeline Doty, the Publicity Representative."

5. Roger Baldwin in his "Reminiscences" (1978, Sophia Smith Collection, Doty papers) wrote of Doty, "I think she was basically a happy person. She had her fears which prompted her to take on such queer cults, a bit other-worldly they seemed to me. I could not follow her into Krishnamurty or Rudolf Steiner. . . . Madeleine was not a mystic nor did she ever accept sectarian religion, save as she and her father attended Harry Emerson Fosdick's church and later in

Geneva the American Church, where she became quite active. She was essentially a humanist with concern for mankind, not the hereafter."

Editor's Afterword. The Geneva Years (1925–1963) and Her Enduring Legacy

1. The 1926 committee meeting in Paris added discouragement and strain, as seen in a letter to Jane Addams. "It was a heart breaking affair," she wrote. "There was so much bitter feeling exhibited, — so little understanding that I often wondered how it was possible for the WIL to continue. . . . The English were contemptuous and superior. The Germans indignant, self-righteous and obdurate. There was no attempt to work out a common denominator, some kind of common policy and understanding." (Swarthmore Peace Collection)

2. Letters to United States officials located in State Department files.

3. An interesting report from a Red Cross resident in the Maison at that time indicates there was some criticism of Doty for renting a room to Noel Field, a mysterious and suspect pro-Communist spy. The *New York Times* on 14 November 1970, ran a long obituary on his life of intrigue, explaining that "he was pictured as a Communist while working for the United States State Department, then branded by Stalinist Communists as an American agent." Numerous articles on Field appeared in leading American journals from 1949 until his death, e.g., *New Statesman, Nation, Time, Newsweek, Saturday Evening Post.* See also Flora Lewis's two volumes *Red Pawn* (New York: Doubleday, 1965) and *The Man Who Disappeared* (London: Barker, 1966).

4. Doty's dissertation is described as "an excellent study" by historian Blanche Wiesen Cook, *Bibliography on Peace Research in History* (Santa Barbara, Calif.: Clio Press, 1969), 41, entry 691.

Addendum. In Hindsight on the Marriage

1. Roger N. Baldwin papers, Princeton Archives, Seeley G. Mudd Manuscript Library.

2. For a biography of pro-labor activist, radical journalist, and pro-Bolshevist Anna Louise Strong see Tracy Strong and Helen Keyssar, *Right in Her Soul: The Life of Anna Louise Strong* (New York: Random House, 1983).

Bibliography

Addams, Jane, Emily Greene Balch, and Alice Hamilton. *Women at the Hague: The International Congress of Women and Its Results*. New York: Macmillan, 1916.

Alonso, Harriet. *Peace as a Women's Issue: A History of the United States Movement for World Peace and Women's Rights*. Syracuse, N.Y.: Syracuse University Press, 1993.

Alpern, Sara. *Freda Kirchwey: A Woman of the Nation*. Cambridge, Mass.: Harvard University Press, 1987.

American Fund for Public Service microfilm records, Rare Books and Manuscript Division. New York Pubic Library. Astor, Lenox and Tilden Foundations.

Anderson, Bonnie and Judith P. Zinsser. *A History of Their Own*. New York: Harper and Row, 1988, vol. 2.

Bacon, Margaret Hope. *Mothers of Feminism*. San Francisco: Harper and Row, 1986.

Baldwin, Roger Nash, ed. *Kropotkin's Revolutionary Pamphlets*. New York: Vanguard, 1927.

_____. *A New Slavery. Forced Labor: The Communist Betrayal of Human Rights*. New York: Oceana Publications, 1953.

_____. "A Note on Madeleine Zabriskie Doty for the files of Smith College." Reminiscences, 1978. Doty papers, Sophia Smith Collection, Smith College.

_____. Roger Baldwin papers. Seelye G. Mudd Manuscript Library, Department of Rare Books and Special Collections, Princeton University Libraries.

Banner, Lois W. *Women in Modern America: A Brief History*. New York: Harcourt Brace Jovanovich, 1974.

Beales, Arthur. *History of Peace*. New York: L. MacVeagh, Dial Press, [1931]. Reprint: New York: Doubleday, 1971.

Bell, Susan Groug and Karen M. Offen, eds. *Women, The Family, and Freedom: A Debate in Documents*. Stanford, Calif.: Stanford University Press, 1983, vol. 2.

Berkin, Carol R. and Clara M. Lovett. *Women, War, and Revolution*. New York: Holmes and Meier Publishers, 1980.

Bibliography Index: A Cumulative Index to Biographical Material in Books and Magazines. Bronx, N.Y.: H. W. Wilson. See Noel Field, vol. 2.

Blair, Karen J. "Women's Voluntary Associations" in Eric Foner and John A. Garraty, eds. *The Reader's Companion to American History*. Boston: Houghton Mifflin, 1991.

Bussey, Gertrude and Margaret Tims. *Prisoners for Peace: WILPF 1915–1965*. London, 1980.

Cantor, Milton. *Max Eastman*. New York: Twayne Publishers, 1970.

Century Magazine. October 1914 and April 1915.

"Civil Liberties News Letter." Spring 1995.

Contemporary Authors. Detroit: Yale Research. See David Graham Phillips, 1983, vol. 108.

Continuum Dictionary of Women's Biography, ed. Jennifer S. Uglow. New York: The Continuum Publishing Company, 1989.

Conway, Jill K., Susan C. Bourque, and Joan W. Scott, eds. *Learning About Women: Gender, Politics, and Power*. Ann Arbor: University of Michigan Press, 1989.

Cook, Blanche Wiesen. *Bibliography on Peace Research in History*. Santa Barbara, Calif.: Clio Press, American Bibliographical Center, 1969

_____, ed. *Crystal Eastman on Women and Revolution*. New York: Oxford University Press, 1978.

_____. "Crystal Eastman" in Foner and Garraty, 1991, 307.

_____. "Max and Crystal Eastman on Peace, Revolution and War" in *The Garland Library of War and Peace*, ed. by Blanche Weisen Cook, Charles Chatfield, and Sydney Cooper. New York: Garland Publishers, 1971, vol. 30.

Cott, Nancy. *Grounding of American Feminism*. New Haven, Conn.: Yale University Press, 1987.

Cowen, Richard W. "Fruit-Picker to Liberty's Vanguard." *The Morning Call*, Allentown, Pa., Oct. 11, 1981.

Current Biography. New York: H. W. Wilson. See Roger Nash Baldwin, vol. 1940 and 1981.

Curtiss, John Shelton. *The Russian Revolution of 1917*. Malabar, Fla.: Krieger Publishing, 1982.

Dictionary of American Biography. Auspices of American Council of Learned Societies. New York: Charles Scribner's Sons, 1934, xiv. See David Graham Phillips.

Dictionary of American Biography Supplement. American Council of Learned Societies. New York: Charles Scribner's Sons, 1950, vol. XXII, suppl. II. See Richard Cabot.

Digest of Educational Statistics. Washington, D.C.: U.S. Bureau of the Census, 1991.

Doty, Madeleine Z. *Behind the Battle Line. Around the World in 1918*. New York: Macmillan, 1918.

_____. *Short Rations: An American Woman in Germany 1915–1916*. New York: Century, 1917.

_____. *Society's Misfits*. New York: Century, 1914, 1915, 1916.

_____. "What a Woman's College Means to a Girl." *Delineator*, March, 1910.

_____. See under *Delineator*, as well as numerous articles cited.

Dye, Nancy Schrom. *As Equals and As Sisters: Feminism, Unionism, and the Women's Trade Union League of New York*. Columbia: University of Missouri Press, 1980.

Eastman, Max. *Enjoyment of Living*. New York: Harper and Brothers, 1948.

_____. *Love and Revolution. My Journey Through an Epoch*. New York: Random House, 1964.

Encyclopedia of World Biography. New York: McGraw Hill, 1973. See Harry Emerson Fosdick, vol. 4. See Alexsandra Kollantai, vol. 6.

Epstein, Cynthia Fuchs. *Women in Law*. New York: Basic Books, 1981.

Faderman, Lillian. *Odd Girls and Twilight Lovers: A History of Lesbian Life in Twentieth Century America*. New York: Columbia University Press. 1991.

Federal Bureau of Investigation (FBI) through Freedom of Information Act. Washington, D.C. Files on Madeleine Z. Doty and on Roger Nash Baldwin.

Ferguson, Wallace and Geoffrey Bruun. *A Survey of European Civilization*. Boston: Houghton Mifflin, 1936.

Filler, Louis. *Voice of Democracy: A Critical Biography of David Graham Phillips: Journalist, Novelist, Progressive*. University Park: Pennsylvania State University Press, 1978.

Foner, Eric and John A. Garraty, eds. *The Reader's Companion to American History*. See "Feminist Movement." Also individuals by name. Boston: Houghton Mifflin, 1991.

Foster, Carrie. *The Women and the Warriors: The U.S. Section of the WILPF 1915–1946*. Stanford, Calif.: Stanford University Press, 1995.

Freedman, Estelle B. *Their Sisters' Keepers: Women's Prison Reform in America 1830–1930*. Ann Arbor: University of Michigan Press, 1981.

Friedan, Betty. *The Feminine Mystique*. New York: W. W. Norton, 1963.

Friedman, Jean and William G. Shade, eds. *Our American Sisters. Women in American Life and Thought*. Boston: Allyn and Bacon, 1973.

Galsworthy, John. Letter to Doty, June 17, 1915, in Sophia Smith Collection, Smith College, Doty papers.

Gardner, Virginia. *Friend and Lover: The Life of Louise Bryant*. New York: Horizon Press, 1982.

Garrison, Dee. *Mary Heaton Vorse: The Life of an American Insurgent*. Philadelphia: Temple University Press, 1989.

Gatty, Charles Neilson. *The Bloomer Girls*. New York: Coward-McCann, 1968.

Gelb, Barbara. *So Short a Time: A Biography of John Reed and Louise Bryant*. New York: W. W. Norton, 1973.

Gilman, Charlotte Perkins. "Comment and Review," *Forerunner* magazine, vol. 5, Nov. 1914. For Gilman's reviews of articles by Doty see references in Scharnhorst.

Goodwin, Doris Kearns. *No Ordinary Time*. New York: Simon and Schuster, 1994.

Gorky, Maxim. *My Childhood*. New York: Penguin Books, 1966 edition.

Good Housekeeping magazine, 26 September and October, 1917.

Haines, C. Groves and Ross Hoffman. *The Origins and Background of the Second World War*. London and New York: Oxford University Press, 1943.

Heller, Adele and Lois Rudnick, eds. *1915, The Cultural Moment: The New Politics, the New Woman, the New Psychology, the New Art & the New Theatre in America*. New Brunswick, N.J.: Rutgers University Press, 1991.

Hicks, Granville. "David Graham Phillips: Journalist." *The Bookman*, May 1931: 257–266.

Hinkle, Beatrice. "Women and the New Morality" in *Our Changing Morality: A Symposium*, edited by Freda Kirchwey. New York: Albert and Charles Boni, 1924.

Janeway, Elizabeth. "Afterword" in David Graham Phillips' *Susan Lenox: Her Fall and Rise*. Southern Illinois Press, 1977 edition, xvi–xvii.

Jensen, Oliver. "The Persuasive Mr. Baldwin," *Harper's Magazine*, Sept. 1951, 47–55.

Kaplan, Justin. *Mr. Clemens and Mark Twain*. New York: Simon and Schuster, Pocket Book Division, 1968.

_____. *Lincoln Steffens*. New York: Simon & Schuster, 1974.

Kazin, Alfred. "When Bohemia Was in Bloom, Greenwich Village 1830–1930." *New York Times*, Jan. 25, 1991, C1.

Kennan, George F. *Russia and the West Under Lenin and Stalin*. Boston: Little Brown and Co., 1960.

Kirchwey, Freda, ed. *Our Changing Morality. A Symposium*. New York: Albert and Charles Boni, 1924.

Klingaman, William K. *1919 The Year Our World Began*. New York: St. Martin's Press, 1987 and Harper and Row, 1989.

Kohn, Hans. *Living in a World Revolution*. New York: Trident Press, 1964.

_____. *Nationalism: Its Meaning and History*. Princeton, N.J.: D. Van Nostrand, [1955] 1965.

Lamson, Peggy. *Roger Baldwin: Founder of the American Civil Liberties Union*. Boston: Houghton Mifflin Company, 1976.

Lasch, Christopher. *The New Radicalism in America: 1889–1963*. New York: Alfred A. Knopf, 1965.

Lash, Joseph P. *Eleanor and Franklin*. New York: W. W. Norton, 1971.

Leeming, Winifred Claxton. "Senior Class History." Smith College Class of 1900 Classbook, Smith College Archives.

Lewis, Flora. *Red Pawn*. New York: Doubleday, 1965.

_____. *The Man Who Disappeared: The Strange History of Noel Field*. London: Barker, [1965], 1966.

_____. *Few Are Chosen: American Women in Political Life Today*. Boston: Houghton Mifflin, 1968.

Lincoln, W. Bruce. *Red Victory*. New York: Simon and Schuster, 1989.

Lippman, Walter. "The Legendary John Reed." *New Republic*, Dec. 26, 1914, 15–16.

Lunardini, Christine. *What Every Woman Should Know About Women's History*. Holbrook, Mass.: Bob Adams Inc., 1994.

Luxemburg, Rosa. *The Russian Revolution and Leninism or Marxism*. Ann Arbor: University of Michigan Press, 1961.

Mackenzie, Midge, ed. *Shoulder to Shoulder*. New York: Alfred A. Knopf, 1975.

Mainiero, Lina, ed. *American Women Writers*. New York: Frederick Unger, 1979. See article on Crystal Eastman.

Marchand, C. Roland. *American Peace Movement and Social Reform 1898–1918*. Princeton, N.J.: Princeton University Press, 1972.

Marcosson, Isaac Frederick. *David Graham Phillips and His Times*. New York: Dodd, Mead and Co., 1932.

McGlen, Nancy E. and Karen O'Connor. *Women's Rights*. New York: Praeger Publishers, 1983.

McGovern, James R. "The American Woman's Pre-World War I Freedom in Manners and Morals" in *Our American Sisters: Women in American Life and Thought,* edited by Jean Friedman and William G. Shade. Boston: Allyn and Bacon, 1973.

McHenry, Robert, ed. *Liberty's Women.* Springfield, Mass.: A. & C. Merriam Company, 1980.

Modern Encyclopedia of Russian and Soviet History, ed. Joseph L. Wieczynski. Gulf Breeze, Fla.: Academic International Press, 1982, vol. 30.

Morgan, Angela. "The Women's Congress at the Hague." *Christian Work,* May 22, 1915.

National Archives, State Department, Washington, D.C. on Madeleine Doty.

National Cyclopedia of American Biography. New York: James T. White, 1922, vol 18. See under Frederick Zabriskie for ancestor Albert Zabriskie.

New Encyclopaedia Britannica Micropaedia. Chicago: Encyclopaedia Britannica, 15ᵗʰ edition, vol. 9. See Frederick Pethick-Lawrence.

New Funk and Wagnalls Encyclopedia. Mahwah, N.J.: Field Corp. See Karl Liebknecht.

New Republic, April 17, 1915. Editorial Note.

Osborne, Thomas Mott. "Introduction" to *Society's Misfits* by Madeleine Z. Doty. New York: Century, 1916.

"Outline History of the Women's International League 1915–1929." Washington, D.C.: U.S. Section, National Headquarters of WILPF. No date. Located in and permission obtained from Sophia Smith Collection, Peace Subject Collection, WILPF section.

Outlook. Washington, D.C.: American Association of University Women, Spring 1992, vol. 86, no. 1.

Pares, Bernard. *Russia.* New York: Penguin Books, 1941.

Perkins, Dexter. *America's Quest for Peace.* Bloomington: Indiana University Press, 1962.

Pethick-Lawrence, Emmeline. *My Part in a Changing World.* London: Victor Gollancz Ltd., 1938, and Westport, Conn.: Hyperion Press, 1976,

Phillips, David Graham. *Susan Lenox, Her Rise and Fall.* Carbondale: Southern Illinois Press, republished 1977.

Pipes, Richard. *The Russian Revolution.* New York: Alfred A. Knopf, 1990.

Post, Alice Thatcher documents in WILPF Collection, Swarthmore College, Swarthmore, Pa.

Post, Charles Johnson. New York *Evening Post,* May 13, 1915.

Rappard, William E. *The Quest for Peace Since the World War.* Cambridge: Harvard University Press, 1940.

Ravitz, Abe. *David Graham Phillips.* New York: Twayne Publishers, 1966.

Readers' Companion to American History. Edited by Eric Foner and John A Garraty. Boston: Houghton Mifflin, 1991. See especially "Feminist Movement," "Women's Voluntary Associations," and leaders by names.

Reader's Guide to Periodical Literature. New York: H. W. Wilson Company.

Reed, John. *Ten Days That Shook the World.* (Orig. New York: Boni and Liveright, 1919.) New York: Random House, Vintage Book, 1960.

"Report of the First International Congress of Women." Amsterdam, Netherlands: N. V. Concordia, n.d. Quoted with permission of the Archives, University of Colorado at Boulder Libraries.

Robertson, "Pat." 1992 fund-raising letter.

Roosevelt, Eleanor. *This I Remember*. New York: Harper Brothers, 1949.

Rupp, Leila J. *Worlds of Women: The Making of an International Women's Movement*. Princeton, N.J.: Princeton University Press, 1997

Scharnhorst, Gary. *Charlotte Perkins Gilman: A Bibliography*. Metuchen, N.J.: The Scarecrow Press, 1985.

Schott, Linda. *Restructuring Women's Thoughts: The WILPF Before World War II*. Stanford, Calif.: Stanford University Press, 1997.

Schwarz, Judith. *Radical Feminists of Heterodoxy. Greenwich Village 1912–1940*. Norwich, Vt.: New Victoria Publishers, revised edition, 1986.

Sicherman, Barbara, and Carol Hurd Green, with llene Cantrov and Harriet Walker, eds. *Notable American Women: The Modern Period*. Cambridge, Mass.: Belnap Press, 1980, vol. 4.

Smith College *Alumnae Quarterly*, 1900 Class Notes, 1916; Nov. 1963; and see "Fortieth Anniversary for the Junior Year in Geneva," Fall 1987.

————. *Class Book, 1900*. "Senior Class History." Sophia Smith Collection.

————. Doty papers. Sophia Smith Collection, Smith College, Northampton, Mass.

Sochen, June. *Movers and Shakers: American Women Thinkers and Activists 1900–1970*. New York: Quadrangle Books, 1973.

Solomon, Barbara Miller. *In the Company of Educated Women: A History of Women and Higher Education in America*. New Haven: Yale University Press, 1985.

Sophia Smith Collection, Smith College, Northampton, Mass. Madeleine Z. Doty papers and Peace Collection on WILPF.

Steinson, Barbara. See in Berkin and Lovett. *Women, War, and Revolution*. New York: Holmes and Meier Publishers, 1980.

Strong, Tracy and Helene Keyssar. *Right in Her Soul: The Life of Anna Louise Strong*. New York: Random House, 1983.

Swanberg, W. A. *Norman Thomas: The Last Idealist*. New York: Charles Scribner's Sons, 1976.

Swarthmore College Peace Collection, Women's International League for Peace and Freedom Records, Swarthmore, Pa.

Thorp, Willard, ed. *The Lives of Eighteen from Princeton*. Princeton, N.J.: Princeton University Press, 1946.

Trimberger, Ellen Kay. "The New Woman and the New Sexuality: Conflict and Contradiction in the Writings and Lives of Mabel Dodge and Neith Boyce." *1915, The Cultural Moment*, edited by Adele Heller and Lois Rudnick. New Brunswick, N.J.: Rutgers University Press, 1991.

Twain, Mark. *Letters From the Earth*. New York: Harper and Row, 1938.

Watson, Steven. *Strange Bedfellows: The First American Avant-Garde*. New York: Abbeville Press, 1991.

Webster's American Biography. Springfield, Mass.: G. & C. Merriam, 1974.

West, Rebecca. "Eroto-Priggery." *New Republic* (March 13, 1915), 150–52.

Who's Who. London: A. and C. Black, and New York: Macmillan, 1933. See Pethick-Lawrence.

Who's Who in America. Chicago: A. N. Marquis. See Douglas Doty in volume dated 1903 through volumes dated 1920–1921. On Madeleine Z. Doty see vol. 10 (1918–1019) through vol. 18 (1934–1935).

Who Was Who Among North American Authors. Detroit: Gale Research, 1976. See Madeleine Z. Doty.

Who Was Who in America with World Notables. Chicago: A. N. Marquis, 1943. See Madeleine Z. Doty.

Wolfe, Bertram D. "Introduction" and "Notes" to republication of *Ten Days That Shook the World* by John Reed. New York: Random House, 1960.

————. "Introduction" to republication of Rosa Luxemburg, *The Russian Revolution and Feminism or Marxism?* Ann Arbor: University of Michigan Press, 1961.

Woman's Who's Who in America, 1914–1915. [1914]. 1976 reprint Detroit: Gale Research, 1976. See Madeleine Z. Doty.

Women's International League for Peace and Freedom, Swarthmore College Peace Collection, Swarthmore, Pa.

Index

"A Club," 59, 60, 265n.1

Adams, Maude, 41

Addams, Jane, 74, 128, 132, 162, 209, 211, 223, 224, 235, 242, 245, 250

"A. E." *See* Russell, George

American Academy in Rome, 253

American Church of Geneva, 273n.5

American Civil Liberties Union, 209, 243

American Embassy in London, 252

American Friends Service Committee, 253

American Fund for Public Service. *See* Garland Fund

American Union Against Militarism, 132, 213, 257

Anthony, Susan B., 54

Ashley, Clarence D., 43, 62

Ashley, Jessie, 43, 45, 50, 56, 62

Ashley, Pope and Doty, law firm, 58, 62

Auburn State Prison, confinement in, 79–80. *See also* Chapter 5; for attempt at reform from within, *see* Chapter 6

Augspurg, Anita, 133, 211, 249

Austria in 1919, effects of war and blockade, 225–26

Baker, Newton D., 164

Balche, Emily Green, 132, 224, 245, 249

Baldwin, Roger, 75, 205, 209, 210, 211–12, 243, 245, 246, 249, 250, 273n. *See also* chapters 11, 12, and Addendum. Mother of, 218, 232, 235, 261. Stepson Carl N., 13, 256

Behind the Battle Line, 129, 130, 165, 192, 205

Belloc, Hilaire, 135

Bergen Point, N.J., Zabriskie home, 25, 30, 31, 34

Bernstorff, Johann, 229–30

Birth Control League, 209

Bismarck Denkmal, 139

Blatch, Harriet Stanton, 56

Blockade of central Europe, postwar British opposition to, 221

Bloor, "Mother," 261

"Bobby," 242, 243

Bogota Embassy, 252

Bray Moving Picture Corp., 238, 243, 245

Brearley School, 36, 58

Brest-Litovsk Treaty, 190, 191, 192; negative results, 224–25

Brubaker, Howard, 59

Bryant, Louise, 270n.2 (under Chapter 10)

Cabot, Richard, 74, 85, 88, 267n.8

Chernov, Victor, 181, 183, 184

Child Welfare Exhibit, 74–75

Children's Court Committee, 79, 80, 82–83, 84, 87, 91

China in 1917, 167–68

Christian Work Fund for Starving Children, 137, 143–44, 152

Churchill, Winston, 242

Civil Liberties Bureau, 213

282

Clemenceau, Georges, 224
Colgate, Carolyn, 234
College education for women, 25–27
Coué, Emile, 241

Darrow, Clarence, 209
Denmark in 1916, 137
De Valera, Eamon, 219, 272n.2.
Dewey, John, 209
Doten, Edward, 29
Doty, Charlotte ("Lottie") Zabriskie,, 26, 29, 35–36, 38, 50,161, 237, 240–41, 257
Doty, Douglas, 25, 50
Doty family lineage, 29
Doty, Ralph, 32, 35, 222, 230
Doty, Samuel and wife "Lottie," 25, 29-31, 35, 41, 43, 50, 69, 161, 204, 237, 240, 241, 244, 257
Dreiser, Theodore, 61–62
Dulles, John Foster, 251, 253

Eastman, Crystal, 62, 81, 132, 211, 266n.3
Eastman, Max, 62, 205, 265n.7, 267n.4
Ecole d'Interpretes, 254
England in early 1918, 196–98; in 1919, 218–22
Equality League for Self-Supporting Women, 56
Europe, post-war conditions in, 218–30

Feminist movement, 53–56
Field, Noel, 273n.3
Finland, early 1918, 191, 193–95
Fisher, Dorothy Canfield, 250
Flynn, Elizabeth Gurley, 261
Fosdick, Harry Emerson, 241
Fourteen Points, 133, 205
France, in March 1918, 198–202; in 1919, 222
France, Anatole, 201
Frankfurter, Felix, 209

Freddy, 217, 218, 232, 234, 235, 237, 243
Friends Service Committee, 253

Galsworthy, John, 80, 83–84
Garland Fund, 14, 209
Gates, Eleanor, 161
German Press Bureau tour, 145–51
Germany in 1915, 133; in 1916 see chapter 8; in 1919, 227–30; in 1922, 240
"Germans in Petrograd," 190–92
Gilman, Charlotte Perkins, 54, 80
Gluecklish, Vilma, 249
Goldman, Emma, 235
Gorbachev, Mikhail, 210
Gorki, Maxim, 59–60, 61, 72, 130, 178, 188, 195, 266n.2
Graduate Institute of International Studies, 251, 252
Greenwich Village, see chapter 2, and 17–18, 53, 264n.1 under Part II

Hague Congress of Women in 1915, 127, 132–33
"Happy Jack," the trial of, 88–91
Harding, Florence, 165
Harding, Warren G., 237
Hatch and Wicks, law firm, 49–50
Haywood, "Big Bill," 235, 261
Hazen, Charles D., 41, 128
Hertzka, Yella, 238
Heymann, Lida, 133, 153, 154, 210, 211, 224, 249
Hindenburg Denkmal, 140
Hitler, Adolf, 251
Hoover, J. Edgar, 211
Hoyt, Franklin C., 82, 83
Hungary in 1919, 226–27

Institute for International Studies, University of Geneva, Graduate School, 251
Institute of International Education, 253

International Labor Office, 252
International Student Service, 252
Ireland in 1919, 219–20
IWW, 235

Japan in 1917, 166–67
Junior Year in Geneva, 250, 251–54
Juvenile courts. See Children's Court Committee
Juvenile reformatories, 122–23

Keller, Helen, 209
Kerensky, Alexander, 172, 173, 175, 179, 189, 270n.4
Key, Ellen, 130–31
Kirchwey, Freda, 245, 261
Kirchwey, George, and family, 37, 75, 82, 91, 249
Kollantai, Aleksandra, 189, 190, 250
Korea in 1917, 167
Kun, Bela, 226–27, 272n.7
Kyi, Aung San Suu, 19–20

Landsbury, George, 225
Law, Bonar, 221
League of Nations, 162, 218, 235, 244
League of Women Voters, 211
Lenin, Nikolai (Vladimir), 129, 175, 179, 182, 183–84, 190
Levermore, Charles, and wife, 36–38, 249
Liberal Club, 211–12
Liebknecht, Karl, 141, 145, 151–52, 154, 155, 228
Lindsey, Benjamin, 75
Lloyd George, David, 224
London Naval Conference (1930), 249
Longuet, Jean, 162
Luxemburg, Rosa, 191, 228

MacDonald, Ramsay, 242
Maison Internationale, 249, 252,

273n.3
Martin, Maggie. See chapter 5
Mary Haskell's School, 50
Marx, Karl, 190
Maternity Bill, 55, 237
Melan, Mlle., 224
Miss Harris' Private School for Girls, 254
Moral Rearmament. See Oxford Group
Mormon women, 68
Mott, Lucretia, 54
Muckraking, 56, 62
Mussolini, Benito, 251

National Association Opposed to Woman Suffrage, 55
NATO, 251
Near East Foundation, 253
Nevinson, Henry, 219, 220, 261
New York Foreign Policy Association, 253
New York State Prison Reform Commission, 91–92
New York University Law School, 27, 42–49
Nicholas II and Czarina Alexandra, 172, 185
Non-Governmental organizations 1995 Beijing conference, 19
Norway in 1916, 136; in early 1918, 195–96
"Notman, Otis," 61–62

Osborne, Thomas Mott, 80, 91–92, 93, 94, 122
Oxford Group, 20

Pankhurst, Cristabel and Emmeline, 133
Parkhurst, Rev. Charles H., 43, 47, 73
Paterson, N.J. silk mill strike, 243
Pax International, 249
Perkins, Frances, 59, 250, 252
Peshkoff, Marie, 60, 72

Peshkoff, Zeni, 72
Pethick-Lawrence, Emmeline
("Malini"), 132, 133, 160, 196,
197, 218, 220, 223, 240, 241,
242, 268n.1 and 269n.2 under
chapter 7
Pethick-Lawrence, Frederick, 198,
242, 268n.1 under chapter
7
Phillips, David Graham, 18, 56–
57, 62–75, 239, 259, 265n.8, 9
Pinchot, Mrs. Amos, 161
Pinchot, Gifford, 85
Poole, Ernest, 59
Post, Charles Johnson, 133
Pourishevitch, General, 187
Press tour in 1916 Germany, 145–
51
Prison reform, 79–80. *See also*
chapter 6

Rankin, Jeanette, 55, 129, 162,
163, 210, 245
Rappard, William, 252, 254
Rasputin, Grigori, 187
Ratcliffe, S.K., 261
Rauh, Ida, 43, 45, 50, 55–56, 58,
59, 62, 71–72, 132, 265n.7
Reed, John and Louise Bryant
Reed, 54, 176, 177, 178, 179,
270n.5
Robertson, Pat, 55
Roland, Romain, 159
Roosevelt Campaign Committee,
84
Roosevelt, Eleanor, 250, 251
Roosevelt, Theodore, 56, 62, 84–
85, 129
Russell, Bertrand, 198
Russell, Charles Edward, 62, 70,
267n.5
Russell, George, ("A. E."), 220
Russell Sage Foundation, 82, 83
Russian League for Women's
Enfranchisement, 189
Russian Revolution, 130, 162,
170–92, 257

Sanger, Margaret, 130, 209
Saratoga Springs, N.Y., 33
School of the Air with Columbia
Broadcasting System, 252
Sedgewick, Ellery, 204
Seelye, Harriet, 41, 49
Seelye, L. Clark, 40
Shaw George Bernard, 221–22
Short Rations, 128, 132, 136, 162,
163, 204
Siberia in 1917, 173
Sinclair, Upton, 261
Sing Sing, 88, 122
Sinn Fein, 219
Slackers' Oath, 211
Sloan's School for Young Ladies,
34
Smith College, 25–26, 40–42, 49,
213, 252. *See also* Junior Year
in Geneva
Snowden, Mrs. Philip, 223
Social Democrats in Germany. *See*
in chapter 8
Social Reform Club, 36
Social Security, 254
Society's Misfits, 80, 161
Sparta, N.J. home, 69, 71, 123,
204, 232, 241
Spider-Web Chart, 211
Spiridonova, Maria, 183, 189, 190
Stalin, Joseph, 175
Stanton, Elizabeth Cady, 54
Steel, Walter, 209
Steffens, Lincoln, 54
Steiner, Rudolf, 241, 243
Sterling, George, 68
Stokes, J. G. Phelps, 59
Stowkowski, Mrs. Leopold, 250
Strong, Anna Louise, 262
Suffrage, 55, 81, 84, 127, 129, 189,
197, 198
Surgeon, relationship with, 87–
88, 202, 236, 258–59
Sweden in 1916, 136; in early
1918, 194–95
Switzerland in May 1919, 222–25

Taylor, Graham, 235
Textile workers' strike in
    Patterson, N.J., 242
Thomas, Norman, 209, 232, 257,
    261
Thomson, Valentine, 201
Trotsky, Leon, 175, 179, 182–83,
    184, 190, 191, 192

Ukraine, 191
UNESCO, 253
United Nations, 21
United Nations Association,
    Albany N.Y. branch, 251
United Press, 253
United States Board of Economic
    Warfare, 252
United States Information
    Agency, 251
United States Mission to the
    United Nations, 253
University of Delaware, 251
University of Geneva, 251

Versailles Treaty, 223–25, 230,
    271n.1, 272n.4
Villard, Oswald Garrison, 132
Vorse, Mary Heaton, 132, 261

Wald, Lillian, 132, 245
Wallace, Henry, 250
Walling, English, 59
Watson, Elizabeth. See chapter 5
Weir, Benjamin, 252
Wells, H. G., 198, 221, 222, 266n.2
William II, Kaiser, 228
Wilson, Paul, 59
Wilson, Woodrow, 124, 133, 161,
    162, 163, 205, 218, 220, 223,
    230, 236

Winant, John, 252
Wise, Rabbi Stephen, 132
Woman's Peace Party of N.Y., 81,
    132, 161, 210, 266n.3
Women: employment of, 28; in
    higher education, 25–26; in law
    practice, 27–28; in Russia, 188–
    89
Women's Consultation Committee
    on Nationality, 249
Women's International League for
    Peace and Freedom (WILPF),
    132, 197, 209–10, 211, 222–25,
    237, 242–46, 249–50, 262;
    national Board, 244, 245
Women's International Peace
    Party: German branch, 153;
    New York branch, 244
Women's Joint Congressional
    Committee, 211
Women's Lawyers Association,
    132
Women's movement, 18–19, 53–
    56
Women's Trade Union League, 55
World Conference of Women
    (Beijing, 1995), 19
World War I, declaration of, 123.
    For impact on Doty see
    chapters 7–10
Wyle, Walter, 59

Yeats, William Butler, 219

Zabriskie: family lineage and
    home at Bergen Point, N.J., 30
Zeretelli, 181
Zetkin, Clara, 154–55